Linux Clustering:
Building and Maintaining
Linux Clusters

Charles Bookman

New Riders

www.newriders.com

800 East 96th Street, Indianapolis, Indiana 46240
An Imprint of Pearson Education
Boston • Indianapolis • London • Munich • New York • San Francisco

Linux Clustering
Building and Maintaining Linux Clusters

International Standard Book Number: 1-57870-274-7

Library of Congress Catalog Card Number: 2001092460

Interpretation of the printing code: The rightmost double-digit number is the year of the book's printing; the right-most single-digit number is the number of the book's printing. For example, the printing code 03-1 shows that the first printing of the book occurred in 2003.

Printed in the United States of America

Trademarks

All terms mentioned in this book that are known to be trademarks or service marks have been appropriately capitalized. New Riders Publishing cannot attest to the accuracy of this information. Use of a term in this book should not be regarded as affecting the validity of any trademark or service mark.

Warning and Disclaimer

This book is designed to provide information about Linux. Every effort has been made to make this book as complete and as accurate as possible, but no warranty of fitness is implied.

The information is provided on an as-is basis. The authors and New Riders Publishing shall have neither liability nor responsibility to any person or entity with respect to any loss or damages arising from the information contained in this book or from the use of the discs or programs that may accompany it.

Publisher
David Dwyer

Associate Publisher
Stephanie Wall

Production Manager
Gina Kanouse

Managing Editor
Kristy Knoop

Acquisitions Editor
Deborah Hittel-Shoaf

Development Editor
Nancy Sixsmith

Product Marketing Manager
Kathy Malmloff

Publicity Manager
Susan Nixon

Senior Editor
Sheri Cain

Copy Editor
Cris Mattison

Indexer
Ginny Bess Munroe

Manufacturing Coordinator
Jim Conway

Book Designer
Louisa Klucznik

Cover Designer
Brainstorm Design, Inc.

Cover Production
Aren Howell

Composition
Jeff Bredensteiner

Linux Clustering: Building and Maintaining Linux Clusters

Contents At a Glance

❖

*This book is dedicated to Ethan. May he grow up
normally and without too many issues.*

❖

Table of Contents

About the Author

Charles Bookman fell in love with the personal computer when he was 12. He would stay after school to teach himself programming on the Commodore Pet. His experiences with Linux started during the 2.0.30 days, when he took the work computer at his counseling job and converted it into something that nobody there had ever seen. After they fired him, he knew that he was on to something, and has been a Linux evangelist ever since.

Charles' hobbies include being up to no good, using sarcasm, listening to music, being snobbish about art, playing bass and guitar, and painting and drawing when he finds the time. He'll kick your butt at table tennis, and is learning a great game of pool as well.

Charles currently works at the University of the Pacific as a UNIX systems administrator, maintaining its high-performance cluster. He runs a design company, and consults in his spare time.

About the Technical Reviewers

These reviewers contributed their considerable hands-on expertise to the entire development process for *Linux Clustering: Building and Maintaining Linux Clusters*. As the book was being written, these dedicated professionals reviewed all the material for technical content, organization, and flow. Their feedback was critical to ensuring that this book fits our readers' need for the highest quality technical information.

Joe "Zonker" Brockmeier has been using Linux since 1996, and writing about it for nearly as long. A refugee from the world of dot-coms, Zonker regularly writes for *Linux Magazine*, *UnixReview.com*, and other online and print publications. You can contact Zonker through his web site at www.dissociatedpress.net/.

John Marquart has seven years of computer industry experience. His focus has been UNIX system administration, with an emphasis on Linux. John worked for Indiana University, managing the Digital Library Program's server infrastructure and digital assets. He now works for Planalytics, where he is responsible for the standardization, integration, and automation of the company's UNIX platforms. John received a degree from Indiana University in Cognitive Science, with a focus on AI systems.

Acknowledgments

Kids, don't try this at home. Writing a book takes personal sacrifice, including many hours staring at your monitor while just knowing that nobody will actually read this, except your relatives. And even then it becomes obvious that they'll nod their heads with a vacuous look on their faces and say, "Clustering what? Does that include Nougat in some fashion?"

With that off my chest, many people stood beside me and helped me a great deal while I wrote this book.

I must thank Brad Stone for tricking me into calling my bluff about writing a book. I also want to thank Ed Winters, one of those guys who gives endlessly; Ben Cottrell, for introducing me to the joys of UNIX; and Dave Prado, for believing in me enough to give me my first chance. I'd also like to thank Joel Baker of Mnemosyne Consulting for his invaluable advice regarding high-availability clustering.

To my wife, Chriss, for being there for me through thick and thin, and for being my best friend for 11 years.

Finally, I would like to thank my friends who have stood by me and knew I could do this, even when I didn't.

Tell Us What You Think

As the reader of this book, you are the most important critic and commentator. We value your opinion and want to know what we're doing right, what we could do better, what areas you'd like to see us publish in, and any other words of wisdom you're willing to pass our way.

As the Associate Publisher for New Riders Publishing, I welcome your comments. You can email, or write me directly to let me know what you did or didn't like about this book—as well as what we can do to make our books stronger.

Please note that I cannot help you with technical problems related to the topic of this book, and that due to the high volume of mail I receive, I might not be able to reply to every message. When you write, please be sure to include this book's title and author as well as your name and phone or fax number. I will carefully review your comments and share them with the author and editors who worked on the book.

Email: stephanie.wall@newriders.com
Mail: Stephanie Wall
            Associate Publisher
            New Riders Publishing
            800 East 96th Street
            Indianapolis, IN 46240 USA

Introduction

Linux has been increasing in popularity ever since its inception. With the explosive growth of the open-source movement and the viability of what it can do with an alternative operating system, Linux has grown into a mature, stable environment in which to host mission-critical applications and research.

It's this very nature of Linux and its open-source code that makes it attractive for hobbyists, educators, and research environments. Thousands of programs are available to enhance the user experience and allow the serious administrator to enhance or create his environment with Linux. It's this flexibility and maturity of the operating system that allows people to easily cluster their Linux machines.

Having two or more machines act in concert with one another isn't rocket science; in fact, anyone with any motivation and a skill for reading a book can make computers do wondrous things. From load balancing to developing a thousand node parallel computer, Linux is more than able to handle the task.

This book takes you through the construction of several types of clustering by using Linux, and explains step by step how to get there. We'll cover handy tips on the way, as well as explain why things work the way they do. In no time, you'll be able to create high availability and Beowulf type clusters with the best of them.

Who Should Read This Book

This book is for Linux enthusiasts and users who want to get a Linux cluster up and running with the least amount of fuss. Administrators will find this book particularly helpful in learning the why's and how's of getting Linux to do amazing things with more than one computer at your disposal.

This book will help if you need to introduce a large parallel or distributed computing cluster to your environment, and the ways that one can solve large computational problems using Linux. Methods to install, maintain, and back up large cluster farms are discussed. We'll also cover the software and hardware needed to create such a solution.

If you're looking for an enterprise-level load balancing or high-availability solution to your environment, Chapters 5 and 6 cover installation and configuration of Linux solutions to these issues. Not only does this book cover the basics behind these, but it also tells the best practices and methods to get a solution up in the quickest amount of time. Software installation and configuration examples are given to bring readers up to speed.

Who This Book Is Not For

This book assumes that the reader is comfortable with Linux. It does not lead the user though basic tasks, such as installation of the operating system, adding users, or window manager configuration. More knowledge might need to be garnered to bring the user up to speed.

This book is also not for seasoned professionals who have a deep understanding of clustering. This book does not cover performance tuning or deep cluster theory. This book is specifically designed for those who need a cluster up, now. This book is not designed for those who already have a cluster planned or running in their environment.

Overview

This book is divided into four parts that describe the planning and configuration of Linux clusters. Part I is designed as an introduction to planning and configuring the environment that is needed to bring a cluster up to speed in the shortest possible time. Part II is devoted to the installation and support of the various types of Linux clusters. Part III introduces programming libraries and what to do when a cluster fails.

Part I is separated into four chapters. Chapter 1, "Clustering Fundamentals," briefly introduces Linux clustering in general, and why it might be applicable to you or your environment. Chapter 2, "Preparing your Linux Cluster," discusses how best to select the parts that are needed to install your cluster and the environment in which it's housed. Chapter 3, "Installing and Streamlining the Cluster," discusses best practice methods on how to install large numbers of machines in the shortest and easiest amount of time. Chapter 4, "Alternative File Systems," discusses the limitations of the current standard file system, ext2, and discusses other methods to improve on it, and file system tricks.

Part II includes four chapters that deal with the clustering technologies themselves. Chapter 5, "High Availability and Fault-Tolerant Clusters," introduces high-availability systems, how they work, and how best to implement the hardware and software. Chapter 6, "Load Balancing," talks about the best ways that Linux can direct traffic to multiple machines. Chapter 7, "Distributed Computing," introduces the distributed model as a means to solve large computational problems. Chapter 8, "Parallel Computing," also expands on this model in a slightly different approach. This chapter is skewed to parallel and commodity computers.

Part III deals with the care and feeding of a cluster. Chapter 9, "Programming a Parallel Cluster," references programming libraries and programs that illustrate these libraries. Chapter 10, "Cluster Management," discusses best practices to keep your cluster in check and monitored for problems. The final chapter, Chapter 11, "Recovering When Disaster Strikes," deals primarily with disaster recovery.

Part IV contains reference material for the cluster designer. Appendix A includes cluster resources on the web and where to find more information. Appendix B is a reference for Kickstart options for Red Hat Linux. Using these options, one can populate a cluster in no time with an unattended install. Appendix C details DHCP options in greater depth for the cluster, so that one can maintain large clusters in a central location with ease. Finally, Appendix D details class attributes for Condor, which is a distributed environment cluster.

If you're familiar with clusters in general, it might behoove you to peruse Part I and move right on to Part II where the cluster you're interested in is discussed. You'll want to hit Part III right after because of the information that discusses keeping your applications and servers up.

Conventions

This book follows a few typographical conventions:

- *Italics* indicate new terms the first time they're introduced, and are used for emphasis.

- A special monospace font indicates code, a filename or pathname, or an Internet address.

I

An Overview of Clustering for Linux, Preparing Your Network, and Linux Servers

1

Clustering Fundamentals

ASK ANYONE ON THE STREET, AND THEY'LL tend to agree with you. Bigger is better. Get more bang for the buck. He who dies with the most toys wins. It stands to reason that, in most cases, more is better than only one. If one is good, two must be great.

It comes as no surprise, then, that computing has followed this trend from its infancy. Why even the ENIAC, widely regarded as the world's first computer, didn't have just a few parts. It had 19,000 vacuum tubes, 1,500 relays, and hundreds of thousands of resistors, capacitors, and inductors (http://ftp.arl.army.mil/~mike/comphist/eniac-story.html). Why did the founders use so many parts? If you had a device that could add two numbers together, that would be one thing. But given the budget, why not add three or even four together? More must be better.

As time went on and computing started to mature, the "more is better" approach seemed to function quite well. Where one processor worked well, two processors could at least double the processing power. When computer manufacturers started making larger and more efficient servers, companies could use the increased horsepower to process more data. It became evident early on that more processors equaled more computing power. Even with the advent of Intel's 386 processor, magazines reported that a single computer could handle the workload of 15 employees!

The descendants of ENIAC were monster computers in their own right, although as we know, with the advent of the transistor, the parts inside got smaller and smaller. More parts were added to machines the size of refrigerators to make them faster, yet these supercomputers were out of the financial reach of most corporations. It didn't take long to realize (okay, it happened in the 1990s) that supercomputer-like performance also could be achieved through a number of low-cost personal computers. More computers were better indeed—or simply cost much less.

Clustering for the Enterprise

Today's computing environments require the needs of many computers to solve the tasks that only one wouldn't be able to handle. Today's large-scale computing environments involve the use of large server farms, with each node connected to each other in a clustered environment. The ASCI Project (Accelerated Strategic Computing Initiative), for instance, consists of several different clustered environments in a bid to provide "tera-scale" computing. ASCI White, capable of 12 trillion calculations per second, runs on IBM's RS/6000 hardware and is becoming increasingly typical of solutions to large-scale computing problems. The ASCI plant at Sandia National Laboratories is comprised of Linux machines that run on Intel hardware and are part of the growing trend to emulate supercomputer performance.

Clustered computing, at its most basic level, involves two or more computers serving a single resource. Applications have become clustered as a way of handling increased data load. The practice of spreading attributes from a single application onto many computers not only improves performance, but also creates redundancy in case of failure. A prime example of a basic cluster is the Domain Name Service (DNS), with its built in primary, secondary, and cache servers. Other protocols have also built in clustered/redundancy characteristics, such as NIS and SMTP.

How Clustering Can Help

Although clustering might not be a panacea for today's ills, it might help the organization that is trying to maximize some of its existing resources. Although not every program can benefit from clustering, organizations that serve applications, such as web servers, databases, and ftp servers, could benefit from the technology as loads on the systems increased. Clusters can easily be designed with scalability in mind; more systems can be added as the requirements increase, which spreads the load across multiple subsystems or machines.

Entities that require a great deal of data crunching can benefit from high-performance computing, which greatly reduces the amount of time needed to crunch numbers. Organizations such as the National Oceanic and Atmospheric Administration are able to use clusters to forecast trends in potentially deadly weather conditions. The staff at Lawrence Livermore Lab use clustered computers to simulate an entire nuclear explosion without harm to anyone (except the backup operators who have to maintain all that data).

Companies serving a great deal of bandwidth can benefit from load-balanced clusters. This type of cluster takes information from a centralized server and spreads it across multiple computers. Although this might seem trivial at first, load balancing can take place in a local server room or across wide-area networks (WANs) spanning the globe. Larger web portals use load balancing to serve data from multiple access points worldwide to serve local customers. Not only does this cut down on bandwidth costs, but visitors are served that much more quickly.

These load-balanced servers also will benefit from the High Availability (HA) model. This model can include redundancy at all levels. Servers in a HA cluster benefit from having two power supplies, two network cards, two RAID controllers, and so on. It's unlikely that all the duplicate devices of a HA cluster will fail at once, barring some major catastrophe. With the addition of an extra component to the primary subsystem or the addition of an extra server, an extra component can be put in place to help in case of failover. This is known as *N+1 redundancy* and is found in clusters, RAID configurations, power arrays, or wherever another component can take over in case of failure.

Using Linux for Clustering

With all the possible platforms from which you could choose, one might wonder why you would choose Linux as an operating system (OS) in which to house your critical applications. After all, with clustering being such a hot topic, each vendor has its own implementation of clustering software, often more mature than the homegrown efforts of dozens of programmers. All major OS vendors support clustering. Microsoft includes its clustering application directly into its Windows 2000 Advanced Server OS. Sun Microsystems offers its High Performance Cluster technology for parallel computing, as well as Sun Cluster for high availability. Even Compaq, Hewlett Packard, IBM, and SGI support clustered solutions.

So why are these companies starting to embrace Linux when they have their own product lines? With the exception of Microsoft, these vendors are starting to recognize the value of open source software. They realize that, by incorporating Linux into their business strategies, they'll utilize the benefits of hundreds, if not thousands, of programmers scrutinizing their code and making helpful suggestions. Although open source methodology remains to be seen as a viable business model, large companies reap the socialistic benefits of having such a philosophy.

Linux runs on just about any hardware platform imaginable. Just as it's proven to be more than capable of powering large mainframes and server farms as well as desktop machines, the versatile OS has been ported to hand-held devices, television recorders, game consoles, Amiga, Atari, and even Apple 040 computers. Linux is well known for being an easy-to-use commodity, off the shelf parts. Although the availability for Linux drivers might not be as prevalent as other operating systems, there is still plenty of hardware that works without a hitch. Linux also supports a great deal of legacy hardware, enabling older computers to be brought back into service. The creators of Linux even envision it as the premiere OS of embedded devices because the kernel can be modified in any shape or form. (Although Linus Torvalds invented Linux and holds the copyright, he didn't write the entire thing himself.)

No other OS allows for this level of versatility. It's this approach to modular computing that makes Linux perfect for clusters.

Disadvantages of Using Linux

Although Linux has many advantages for clustering, it also has faults that might make it an unattractive solution for certain types of clusters. The bottom line is that Linux is a relatively new OS (albeit based on tried-and-true technologies). For the most part, you've got an OS written by volunteers in their spare time. Though the code is readily available for scrutiny by anyone, the thought does exist that top-notch programmers might be whisked away by companies that can afford to pay top salaries. (Of course, that does happen, and for some reason, programmers even manage to work on Linux with something called spare time.)

The level of support is not as robust as you can get with other operating systems. That isn't to say that you can't get good vendor support; on the contrary, the quality of support for Linux is top notch. There just isn't as much support out there for the product as there is for other operating systems.

A few bugs are still inherent with the OS and kernel. The native file system, ext2, doesn't support journaling. USB support has typically been spotty. There tends to be a smaller amount of drivers for Linux than there are for other operating systems, even though the most common solutions are addressed.

However, most, if not all, of these issues are being addressed. Robust file systems are available for Linux other than ext2, and support for USB is improving with each release (as of 2.2.18, anyway). Typically, most of these issues don't come into play when you're deploying large cluster farms. Most of these limitations will only be applicable when you use Linux on the desktop. But the development of the Linux kernel is rapidly outpacing the development of other operating systems as the developers strive to fix issues such as USB support.

The system administrator has to keep a sense of perspective when rolling out any OS. Linux is primarily a server class OS. It's designed to handle large tasks supporting many users and processors, and it does that well. With the support of projects such as Gnome and KDE (not to mention every other window manager out there), Linux can be used primarily as a workstation in addition to a server. The development for Linux-based workstation class computers is more advanced than most other UNIX systems. However, both Macintosh and Microsoft tend to own more market share and usability than the rapidly advancing Linux desktop.

Clusters Aren't Just for High Performance Anymore

The loud hum of the air conditioning breathes through the massive data center as thousands of computers lie still in the darkness. The single green eye from the power switch illuminates racks upon racks of servers as far as the eye can see. Evocations of the giant machine are immediately brought to attention as the almost haunting image of a single entity bears down upon the onlooker.

Okay, so even though it's not really such an ominous entity, the high performance cluster is arguably the most popular type known to the masses. Vector computing, a type of high-performance machine, tends to be cost prohibitive for commodity use due to the specialized hardware that it requires. Parallel computers, on the other hand, have become immensely popular due to the fact that almost anyone can build one with spare parts. The name Beowulf is almost as synonymous with parallel clustering as Jello is with flavored gelatin. Parallel computers have grown tremendously in popularity as researchers and hobbyists alike are able to mirror supercomputer performance. Of course, clustering doesn't begin and end with the parallel or Vector computer.

So now that you have a basic understanding of the different types of clusters that we discuss in this book, I'm sure you're asking, "Yes, that's all well and good, but what does it all mean?" For that, you should consult your favorite religious text. For the person who is comfortable with his or her beliefs and wants to get in to the business of setting up Linux clusters, Chapter 2, "Preparing your Linux Cluster," would be perfect. For the curious individual who wants to understand the theories behind clustering technologies, the rest of this chapter is for you.

Making two or more Linux machines interact with each other is quite easy. The simplest way is to assign each machine an IP address and a subnet mask, attach a crossover cable between them, and voila—instant network. Things start to get more complicated when there's a few more machines involved, although it's still not rocket science. Add another computer, and you have to add a switch or hub. Connect your computer to another network, and you have to add a router of some kind. Getting clustered computers to talk to each other at the most basic level is as simple as setting up a network. However, getting them to *interact* in different ways is another story.

High Availability and Fault-Tolerant Clusters

Computers have an annoying tendency to break down when you least expect. It's a rare find to come across a system administrator that hasn't received a phone call in the middle of the night with the dreaded news that a critical system is down, and would you please attend to this situation at your own convenience (right now!).

The concept of highly available and fault-tolerant clusters tend to go hand in hand. If a system is going to achieve high uptimes, the more redundant subsystems it needs to remain operating—such as the addition of servers in a clustered configuration. The bottom line for high availability clusters is that the application is of such high importance that you take extra steps to make sure it's available.

Single Point of Failure

The single point of failure (SPOF) is a common theme in HA clusters. Having a single component is just asking for trouble, and the SPOF is a paradigm to be avoided at all costs. In a perfect world, each server would have a redundant subsystem for each component in case the primary died or stopped responding. Critical subsystems that usually fail include hard drives, power supplies, and network cards. It's a sad fact of life, but user error tends to account for most downtime. Operators have been known to unmount volumes of critical live data, and contractors reorganize cables that are poorly labeled.

Such redundancy planning might include adding a RAID controller in case of hard drive failure, but what if the controller died? A whole different set of controllers and RAID devices could be implemented to reduce the risk of the SPOF. An architecture would have to be considered that would allow for hot-swappable CPUs. Two network cards could be implemented in case connectivity problems become an issue. A network card could be tied to a different switch or router for backup. What then for the network itself? What if a switch went bad? A second switch then could be set in place in case the first one died, and then a redundant router, redundant network provider might all be considered. It's a fine line between handling an SPOF and total redundancy of all systems, where budget is usually the deciding factor.

Achieving 100 percent uptime is near impossible, although with the right technologies, you can come quite close to that. A more realistic goal to set when planning a HA solution is providing for an uptime of 99 percent or higher. In doing so, you can plan scheduled downtime for maintenance, backups, and patches requiring reboots. Having an uptime requirement of greater than 99 percent requires different models, such as redundant systems.

Server Redundancy

Although there are servers designed with redundancy in mind, their prices tend to be much larger than SPOF servers. There are companies that develop servers with no SPOF, including two motherboards, two CPUs, two power supplies, and so on. These are even more expensive, but for the organization that can't afford downtime, the cost to data integrity ratio evens out.

Fortunately, there is another way to achieve such redundancy without the high cost of redesigning single server architecture. Incorporating two or more computers achieves a second layer of redundancy for each component. There are just about as many ways to achieve this redundancy as there are people implementing servers. A backup server that can be put into production is among the most common methods that are currently implemented. Although this works in most environments, offline redundant servers take time to prepare and bring online. Having an online failover server, although more difficult to implement, can be brought up almost immediately to replace the initial application.

In Figure 1.1, two computers are connected to the same network. A heartbeat application that runs between them assures each computer that the other is up and running in good health. If the secondary computer cannot determine the health of the primary computer, that computer takes over the services of the primary. This is typically done with IP aliasing and a floating address that's assigned with DNS. This floating address will fail over to the secondary computer as soon as the heartbeat detects an event such as the primary server or application failing. This method works well if all the served data is static. If the data is dynamic, a method to keep the data synched needs to be implemented.

Shared storage is the method where two or more computers have access to the same data from one or more file systems. Typically, this could be done through a means of shared SCSI device, storage area network, or a network file system. This would enable two or more computers to access the data from the same device, although having the data on only one device or file system could be considered an SPOF.

Managing Shared Storage and Dynamic Data

It's no surprise to any of us that today's mission-critical servers need access to data that's only milliseconds old. This isn't a problem when you have one server and one storage medium. Databases and web servers can easily gain access to their own file systems and make changes as necessary. When data doesn't change, it's not a problem to have two distinct servers with their own file systems. But how often do you have a database of nothing but static data? Enter shared storage and another server to avoid the SPOF. Yet that scenario opens up a new can of worms. How do two servers access the same data without the fear of destroying the data?

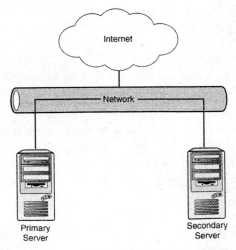

Figure 1.1   Load balancing explained.

Let's examine this scenario more closely. Imagine if you will, employees at XYZ Corporation who install a database server in a highly available environment. They do this by connecting two servers to an external file storage device. Server A is the primary, while server B stands by idle in case of failover.

Server A is happily chugging away when Joe Operator just so happens to stumble clumsily through the heartbeat cables that keep the servers synched. Server B detects that server A is down and tries to gain control of the data while the primary continues to write. In "high availability speech," this is known as a split-brain situation. Voila—an instant recipe for destroyed data.

Fencing is the technology used to avoid split-brain scenarios and aids in the segregation of resources. The HA software will attempt to fence off the downed server from accessing the data until it is restored again, typically by using SCSI reservations. However, the technology has not been foolproof. With advances in the Linux kernel (specifically 2.2.16 and above), servers can now effectively enact fencing and, therefore, share file systems without too many hassles.

Although shared storage is a feasible solution to many dynamic data requirements, there are different approaches to handling the same data. If you can afford the network delay, a solution that relies on NFS, or perhaps rsync, could be a much cleaner solution. Shared storage, although it has come a long way, adds another layer of complexity and another component that could potentially go wrong.

Load Balancing

Load balancing refers to the method in which data is distributed across more than one server. Almost any parallel or distributed application can benefit from load balancing. Web servers are typically the most profitable, and therefore, the most used application of load balancing. Typically in the Linux environment, as in most heterogeneous environments, this is handled by one master node. Data is managed by the master node and is served onto two or more machines depending on traffic (see Figure 1.2). The data does not have to be distributed equally, of course. If you have one server on gigabit ethernet, that server can obviously absorb more traffic than a simple, fast ethernet node can.

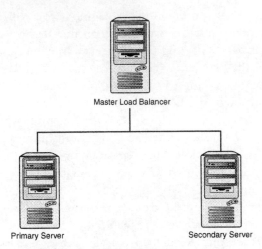

Figure 1.2   Load balancing 101.

One advantage of load balancing is that the servers don't have to be local. Quite often, web requests from one part of the country are routed to a more convenient location rather than a centralized repository. Requests made from a user are generally encapsulated into a *user session*, meaning that all data will be redirected to the same server and not redirected to others depending on the load. Load balancers also typically handle failover by redirecting the traffic from the downed node and spreading the data across the remaining nodes.

The major disadvantage of load balancing is that the data has to remain consistent and available across all the servers, though one could use a method such as rsync to keep the integrity of data.

Although load balancing is typically done in larger ISPs by hardware devices, the versatility of Linux also shines here.

Programs such as Balance and the global load balancing Eddie Mission are discussed in Chapter 6, "Load Balancing."

Distributed Computing

Take over three million users, tell them that they too can join in the search for extraterrestrial life, and what do you get? You get the world's largest distributed application, the SETI@home project (http://setiathome.ssl.berkeley.edu/). Over 630,000 years of computational time has been accumulated by the project. This is a great reflection on the power of distributed computing and the Internet.

Distributed computing, in a nutshell, takes a program and assigns computational cycles to one or more computers and then reassembles the result after a certain period of time. Although close in scope to parallel computers, a true distributed environment differs in how processes and memory are distributed. Typically, a distributed cluster is comprised of heterogeneous computers, which can be dedicated servers but are typically end-user workstations. These workstations can be called on to provide computational functionality using spare CPU cycles. A distributed application will normally suspend itself or run in the background while a user is actively working at his computer and pick up again after a certain timeout value. Distributed computing resources can easily be applied over a large geographical area, constrained only by the network itself.

Just about any computationally expensive application can benefit from distributed computing. SETI@home, Render Farms (a cluster specifically set up to harness processing power to do large scale animations), take over three million users, tell them that they too can join in the search for extraterrestrial life, and what do you get? And different types of simulations can all benefit.

Parallel Computing

Parallel computing refers to the submission of jobs or processes over more than one processor. Parallel clusters are typically groups of machines that are dedicated to sharing resources. The cluster can be built with as little as two computers; however, with the price of commodity hardware these days, it's not hard to find clusters with as little as 16 nodes or perhaps several thousand. Google has been reported to have over 8,000 nodes within its Linux cluster.

Parallel clusters have also been referred to as Beowulf clusters. Although not technically accurate for all types of HPCs, a Beowulf type cluster refers to "computer clusters built using primarily commodity components and running an Open Source operating system."

Parallel computers work by splitting up jobs and doling them out to different nodes within the cluster. Having several computers working on a single task tends to be more efficient than one computer churning away on the same task, but having a 16-node cluster won't necessarily speed up your application 16 times. Parallel clusters aren't typically "set up and forget about them" machines; they need a great amount of performance tuning to make them work well. Once you've tuned your system, it's time to tune it again. And then after you've finished that, it might benefit from some more performance tuning.

Not every program benefits from a parallel configuration. Several factors must be considered to judge accurately. For example, is the code written to work under several processors? Most applications aren't designed to take advantage of multiple processors, so doling out pieces of your program would just be futile. Is the code optimized? The code might work faster on one node instead of splitting up each part and transferring it to each CPU. Parallel computing is really designed to handle math-intensive projects, such as plotting the expansion of the universe, render CPU-intensive animations, or decide exactly how many licks it actually takes to get to the center.

The parallel cluster can be set up with a master node that passes jobs to slave nodes. A master node will generally be the only machine that most users see; it shields the rest of the network behind it. The master node can be used to schedule jobs and monitor processes, while the slave nodes remain untouched (except for maintenance or repair). In a high production environment with several thousand systems, it might be cheaper to totally replace a downed node than to diagnose the error and replace faulty parts within the node.

Although several methods have been designed for building parallel clusters, Parallel Virtual Machine (PVM) was among the first programs to allow code to run across several nodes. PVM allows a heterogeneous group of machines to run C, C++, and Fortran across the cluster. Message Passing Interface (MPI), a relative newcomer to the scene, is shaping up to be the standard in message passing. Each is available for almost every system imaginable, including Linux.

How Now, Brown Cow

Included within the Parallel Processing model exist cluster configurations called NOWs and COWs—or even POPs. Generally, the concept of a NOW and a COW can be synonymous with any parallel computer; however, there tends to be some disagreement among the hardcore ranks. A NOW is a network of operating systems, the COW is a cluster of operating systems, and a POP is a Pile of PCs (*Engineering a Beowulf Style Computer Cluster*, http://www.phy.duke.edu/brahma/beowulf_book.pdf). If one takes the approach that a parallel cluster is comprised of machines dedicated to the task of parallel computing, then neither a NOW nor a COW fit the bill. These typically are representative of distributed computing because they can be comprised of heterogeneous operating systems and workstations.

Amdahl's Law

From the earliest days of computing, people would stare at their monitors with utter impatience as their systems attempted to solve problems at mind-bogglingly slow speeds (okay, even with modern technology, we still haven't solved this problem). In 1967, Gene Amdahl, who was working for IBM at the time, theorized that there was a limit to the effectiveness of parallel processing for any particular task. (One could assume that this theory was written while waiting for his computer to boot.) More specifically, "every algorithm has a sequential part that ultimately limits the speedup that can be achieved by a multiprocessor implementation" (*Reevaluating Amdahl's Law* by John L. Gustafson; `www.scl.ameslab.gov/Publications/AmdahlsLaw/Amdahls.html`). In other words, there lies certain parts to each computation, such as the time it takes to write results to disk, I/O limitations, and so on.

Amdahl's Law is important in that it displays how unreasonable it is to expect certain gains above a typical threshold. Even though Amdahl's Law remains the standard in demonstrating the effectiveness of parallel applications, the law remains in dispute and even begins to fall apart as larger clusters are becoming commonplace. According to John L. Gustafson in *Reevaluating Amdahl's Law*:

> "Our work to date shows that it is *not* an insurmount-
> able task to extract very high efficiency from a
> massively-parallel ensemble. We feel that it is important
> for the computing research community to overcome
> the 'mental block' against massive parallelism imposed by
> a misuse of Amdahl's speedup formula; speedup should
> be measured by scaling the problem to the number
> of processors, not fixing problem size." (See *On
> Microprocessors, Memory Hierarchies, and Amdahl's Law*;
> `www.hpcmo.hpc.mil/Htdocs/UGC/UGC99/papers/alg1/`)."

Although certain people dispute the validity of Amdahl's Law, it remains an easy way to think about those limitations.

SMP and the Primary Processor Paradigm

Symmetric multiprocessing (SMP) includes any SMP architecture. In layman's terms, it's a computer with more than one processor. SMP architectures differ from asymmetrical processing architectures primarily in the way that they can truly be considered multitasking rather than time-sharing devices. Any idle processor can be delegated to take on additional tasks or handle increased loads.

Generally, a well-written and optimized application performs much better on an SMP machine than on two or more computers with a single processor. Several factors determine the speed at which the application runs, including the speed of the motherboard bus, the memory, the speed of the drives, as well

as the I/O throughput. Like the addition of more nodes for parallel computing, the programs have to be rewritten or optimized to enable multiple
threads. Processes and kernel space threads are naturally distributed among
SMP machines. User processes generally aren't; however, the kernel does a sort
of natural load balancing across each of the CPUs. Applications that can make
use of fork() can benefit from an SMP architecture. fork() allows a process to
split itself into two identical copies, which, depending on the OS, will share
the same memory, yet will run on a different CPU. If the application is primarily CPU driven, that application will see benefits from the SMP architecture. However, the price for computers with more than one processor might
outweigh the benefits of an SMP processor machine.

Linux added support for SMP with the addition of the 2.0 kernel, which
included support for Intel 486 and higher (and clones), as well as hypersparc
machines. With the addition of the 2.2 kernel, Linux added support for
UltraSparc, SparcServer, Alpha, and PowerPC machines.

Although the 2.2.x and 2.4.x kernels' SMP support is added by default, it
can be added in with the following settings (the latest kernel can always be
found at www.kernel.org, or at ftp://ftp.kernel.org/pub/linux/kernel):

- Configure the kernel and answer "yes" to the question, "Symmetric
  Multi-Processing Support."
- Enable "Memory Type Range Register (MTRR) Support" (both under
  Processor Type and Features).
- Enable real-time clock support by configuring the "RTC Support" item
  (under Character Devices).
- On the x86 kernel, do *not* enable Advanced Power Management (APM).
  APM and SMP are not compatible, and your system will almost certainly
  crash while booting if APM is enabled.

You must rebuild all of your kernel and kernel modules when changing to and
from SMP mode. Remember to make modules and make modules install. You
can display the result with cat /proc/cpuinfo.

Quick and Dirty Clustering

As previously mentioned, clusters are made up of two or more different
machines (or processors) that serve the same application. Even though it takes
a little more to make a full-fledged clustered solution for most applications, it's
easy to bring basic services to most networks.

All Linux actually needs to be involved in a cluster is to talk to other machines in a network, which includes most of the machines out there. Put two boxes together that talk to each other, and you have a cluster—not a very effective cluster, mind you, but one that works. It's a simple matter, really, to enable basic clustering features to existing servers.

Dial Ping for Service

A basic HA cluster can be achieved with nothing more than straight ping. If you were to set up a script that would enable a failover server to ping a primary application server every minute or so, the failover server could determine when the primary failed. As soon as the secondary couldn't find the other server, it would assume that it was down and launch scripts to enable its own services. After all, if the failover server can't reach the primary, neither can any other service or user.

You need to consider some options before you start planning for your basic HA cluster. Are you going to have the failover server in standby mode with an application already running, ready to go? Is the standby server already in production with other elements running? Here's what you need to set up a basic HA cluster:

- Script that will ping the other server.
- Crontab entry to call the script.
- If the other server responds, then sleep.
- If the other server doesn't respond, ping again.
- If the other server still doesn't respond, assume failover sequence.
- Take over IP address of failed server.

The first step when implementing such a cluster is to assign a virtual IP to the servers. This serves as the floating address that resolves to a DNS entry. Initially, the primary server owns the IP and then the secondary assumes it after failover.

IP aliasing has to either have been compiled in the kernel or have been loaded as a module. The kernel configuration for 2.2.x kernels is under Networking Options, IP: Aliasing Support, and is unchecked by default. Module support is only available in 2.0.x kernels. 2.2.x kernels either have support compiled in or not.

The module that you'll be looking for is `ip_alias`. To insert it into the 2.0.x kernel, use the `insmod` command.

RedHat 7.1 default install allows for an IP alias right out of the box. A stock 6.2 does as well, yet Debian 2.2 doesn't, so check your distribution.

After IP aliasing is available, an extra alias (or several) can be added with the same ease as a regular IP. The format is

```
/sbin/ifconfig <interface>:<virtual number> <ip> netmask <netmask> up
```

For example,

```
/sbin/ifconfig eth0:1 172.16.0.1 netmask 255.255.0.0 up
```

brings up virtual interface one and attaches it to adapter eth0 with an IP of 172.16.0.1 and a class B /16 netmask. Assign the virtual interface to the interface of the primary server and make sure that this entry is resolved by DNS.

The next step includes setting up the failover script. This script, placed on the failover server, initially pings the primary server and exits if a response is given. If a response is not given, the program waits for 20 seconds and pings again. If the failover server doesn't receive a ping response from the primary a second time, the server then sets the virtual IP on itself and optionally sends out a notification. Don't forget to set the script executable.

```bash
#!/bin/bash
# Poor Man's Cluster
# Script to Test for Failover
#
host="172.16.0.2"
netmask="255.255.0.0"
while true; do
/bin/ping -c 5 -i 3 $host > /dev/null 2>&1
if [ $? -ge 1 ]; then
        #This doesn't look good, let's test again.
        /bin/ping -c 5 -i 3 $host > /dev/null 2>$1
                if [ $? -ge 1 ]; then
                # We need to assume host is really down. Assume
                # failover sequence
                /sbin/ifconfig eth0:1 $host netmask $netmask up
                echo "$host is down. Please check immediately." > /bin/mail -
s "$host is down!" user@host.com
                else
                #second ping returned a value. Whew.
                :
else
:
fi
done
```

The script should be able to run in the background and mail the designated user if a connectivity problem occurs. The script can easily be adapted to ping more than one host, if you're creative enough.

Load Balancing Using DNS Records

A quick and dirty way to enable load balancing can be achieved with simple A records in DNS. Although it presents itself as a dirty hack, enabling the same name with two or more different IP addresses does offer a measure of load balancing, albeit limited in scope. The same effect does not work, however, when enabling different IP addresses in /etc/hosts.

To illustrate, we have the following zone enabled:

```
[root@matrix named]# cat zone.dns
;
; Zone file for zone.com
;
@       IN      SOA     zone.com. postmaster.zone.com. (
                        19990913        ; serial
                        10800           ; refresh
                        3600            ; retry
                        604800          ; expire, seconds
                        86400 )         ; minimum, seconds
IN NS      ns1.zone.com.
IN NS      ns2.zone.com.
host1           IN A    10.2.2.10
host1           IN A    10.2.2.11
host1           IN A    10.2.2.12
```

In this example, each host carries the same domain name, yet the A record points to a different address. Pings of the machine show the following:

```
    [root@matrix named]# ping host1

PING host1.zone.com (10.2.2.10) from 10.2.2.100 : 56(84) bytes of data.
    [root@matrix named]$ ping host1

PING host1.zone.com (10.2.2.11) from 10.2.2.100 : 56(84) bytes of data.
    [root@matrix named]$ ping host1

PING host1.zone.com (10.2.2.10) from 10.2.2.100 : 56(84) bytes of data.
    [root@matrix named]$ ping host1

PING host1.zone.com (10.2.2.12) from 10.2.2.100 : 56(84) bytes of data
```

As you can see, it's not a foolproof situation, but it does offer some method of load balancing between hosts.

Alternate File Systems

The second extended file system, ext2, was developed by René Card as an alternative to the first file system derived from Minix. Although Linux supports many different file systems, ext2 remains the default for most distributions. Many vendors have improved on the default file system to offer features such as journaling, volume management, network block file systems, and shared disk file systems. Ext2 does not have these features built in.

Journaling File Systems

Enter the journal, the most popular alternative method to keep track of the file system. Depending on the implementation, journaling file systems use different methods based on a database to keep track of file system data. What's so attractive about journaling file systems is that fsck isn't needed. In the event of a system crash, the logs from the database can be replayed to represent the data at the time of a crash. This method tends to bring the system up to a consistent state much faster than a file system run with fsck; however, it doesn't do anything special for data reliability. A large RAID device that's using ext2 might take several hours to go through fsck checks, although with the addition of a journaling file system, no checks are made. All writes are made and played back from the journal, which results in a boot time of only minutes.

Different journaling file systems also have support for synchronous I/O, increased block size support, integration with NFS, quota support, and support for access control lists (ACLs).

Network File Systems

Network file systems manage to take one or more devices and appear to the server as one logical volume. The trick here is to fool the OS into thinking that the volume is a locally attached RAID or clustered device. The network file system naturally shows some performance loss due to the network overhead.

Networking 101 for Clusters

Networking is an essential part of clustering. Computers just can't talk to each other on their own; that would be creepy. Parallel networks need a dedicated networking environment, where in comparison, quite a few load balanced, distributed, and even some HA solutions are designed over a WAN environment. To better understand the relationship between the network and the cluster, we need to understand network issues and how they affect cluster communications. Although we won't get into a detailed explanation of TCP/IP and networking, a cursory examination is provided here.

The OSI Networking Model

The International Organization for Standardization (ISO), an international body comprised of national standards bodies from more than 75 countries, created the *Open Standards Interconnection (OSI) model* in order for different vendors to design networks that would be able to talk to each other. The OSI model, finally standardized in 1977, is basically a reference that serves as a general framework for networking.

It wasn't uncommon to find vendors about 30 years ago who produced computers that didn't have the ability to talk to other vendors. Along with creating operating systems and mainframes that were rather proprietary, the communications of the time were mostly proprietary as well. In 1977, the British Standards Organization proposed to the ISO that an international standard for distributed processing be created. The American National Standards Institute (ANSI) was charged with presenting a framework for networking, and they came up with a Seven Layer model (*The Origins of OSI*; http://williamstallings.com/Extras/OSI.html). This model is shown in Figure 1.3.

The top layer, Layer Seven, is the Application Layer and is where the end user actually interfaces with the computer itself. Layer Seven encompasses such applications as the web, telnet, SSH, and email.

Layer Six, the Presentation Layer, presents data to the Application Layer. Computers take generic data and turn it into formats such as text, images, sound, and video at this layer. Data translation, compression, and encryption are handled here.

Layer Five, the Session Layer, handles data by providing a means of transport for the Presentation Layer. Examples of applications that utilize the Session Layer include X Window, NFS, AppleTalk, and RPC.

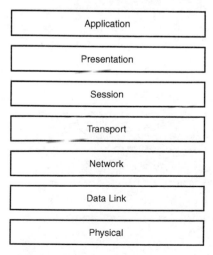

Figure 1.3 OSI Network Layer diagram.

The Transport Layer, Layer Four, provides error detection and control, multiplexing transport connections onto data connections (multiplexing allows the data from different applications to share one data stream), flow control, and transport to the Network Layer.

Layer Three, the Network Layer, is responsible for transmitting data across networks. Two types of packets are used at this level, including data packets and route updates. Routers that work on this level keep data about network addresses, routing tables, and the distance for remote networks.

Layer Two, the Data Link Layer, translates messages from the Network Layer into the Physical Layer. This layer handles error control, reliability, and integrity issues. The Network Layer adds frames to the data and adds a customized header containing the source and destination address. The layer identifies each device on the network as well.

The bottom layer, Layer One, or the Physical Layer, sends and receives information in the form of ones and zeros. The characteristics of this layer include specifications for signal voltages, wire width and length, and signaling.

Many devices operate at different levels. The hub, when cabled, only amplifies or retransmits data through all its ports. In this way, it operates only on Layer One. However, a switch operates on Layers One and Two, and a router operates on Layers One, Two, and Three. The end user's workstation would typically handle Layers Five, Six, and Seven (although the versatility of Linux could allow it to handle much more).

The point of having such a layered approach is so that the different aspects of networking can work with each other—yet remain independent. This allows application developers the freedom to work on one aspect of a layer while expecting the other layers to work as planned. Without these layers, the developer would have to make sure that every aspect of the application included support for each layer. In other words, instead of just coding a simple game, the development team would not only have to code the game itself, but also the picture formats, the TCP/IP stack, and have to develop the router to transmit the information.

Why is learning this so important for clustering? First of all, it aids in troubleshooting. Knowing where the problem lies is the most important step to solving the problem. Every troubleshooting method needs to start somewhere, and by going over the OSI model, you can easily diagnose where the problem lies. By isolating each layer, you can track down problems and resolve them.

Network Topology

Different types of clusters need different types of network topologies depending on the framework involved. A HA network might need more attention to detail regarding security to maintain uptime than a distributed computing environment or a parallel clustering scenario.

Picture the following HA scenario, if you will, as shown in Figure 1.4. A nationwide bank has Points of Presence (POP) in three cities across the United States. Each city has its own cluster with its own database and each is connected directly to the Internet from its own city, but yet each city has to have access to the other's data. How is this best achieved? Topologies have to be clearly thought about in advance. Consider the topology of clusters spread across a WAN, for instance.

In this scenario, three sites are connected over the public Internet, with a firewall for security. This isn't the most effective method of achieving high availability, but it's a common scenario.

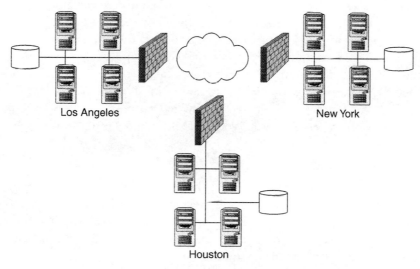

Figure 1.4   High availability across the WAN.

One way to go about redesigning this scenario is to remove two satellite cities from the Internet and connect each of these cities through direct frame relay to the internal network, thereby dropping the firewall from two of the satellite offices. Another approach would be to implement a load balanced network. POPs could easily be placed in key locations across the country so that customers could have relatively local access to the financial data. But because the data has to be synchronized between three cities in real time, the bandwidth involved would be tremendous.

A parallel cluster still needs a network design, although one that is much simpler in scope. Before fast ethernet to the desktop and gigabit ethernet for servers was the common standard, *hypercubes* were the primary means for designing high-performance clusters. A hypercube is a specific method to layout a parallel cluster, usually using regular ethernet. The trick to designing a hypercube was that each computer would have to have a direct network connection to each other node in the cube. This worked well with smaller cubes, although the size of the cube was somewhat limited due to the amount of network cards that could fit in any one computer. Larger clusters required meshed designs with hubs to support each node and the requisite multiple connections. Needless to say, they're quite messy because of all the inter-meshed cabling. With the advent of fast ethernet and gigabit ethernet, a simple managed or unmanaged switch will take care of most of the bandwidth problems. Of course, "the faster, the better" is the general motto, so be sure to consider the network when budgeting your cluster.

Services to Consider

Along with the physical development of the cluster and the network topology, deciding which services to enable is the next step toward a finished clustering solution. Although most Linux distributions offer access to all the standard services listed in /etc/services, the system administrator has to determine if those services are applicable to their environment.

In a high-security environment, the system administrator might have no choice but to tighten down these resources. The most common ways of disabling services include restricting access to them through the firewall, by setting up an internal network, or by utilizing hosts:deny and hosts:allow. Those services that are accessible though inet can be commented out in /etc/inetd.conf.

It's no surprise that, to enable web services, you have to keep access to port 80—and 443 if you're going to enable web support over Secure Sockets Layer (SSL). In addition, what you also have to keep in mind when designing your cluster is access to the backup devices, whether or not to allow SSH, telnet, or ftp, and so on. In fact, it's a good idea to totally disallow telnet across the environment and replace it with secure shell. Not only does this allow secure logins, but also secure ftp transfers for internal office use. FTP servers should still use regular ftp, of course, but only for dedicated servers.

Keeping Your Services Off the Public Network

After you decide which services to keep on the public network, it's a wise idea to make a nonroutable network strictly for management purposes. This management network serves two purposes: One, it enables redundancy. The administrator has the ability to gain access to the box if the public network goes down or is totally saturated from public use. Secondly, it gives the opportunity for a dedicated backup network. The bandwidth from nightly backups each night has the potential to saturate a public network.

Realistically, you don't want to keep your parallel cluster on a public network. A private network lessens the chance of compromised data and machines. Unless you keep your cluster so that anyone can run jobs on it, the added benefit of a nonroutable network greatly outweighs the potential risks.

Summary

Just as the state of computing has come a long way, so has clustering in general. As Linux matures, so does its ability to handle larger clusters using commodity hardware, as well as mission-critical data across HA clusters.

Clustering under Linux is similar to clusters under other operating systems, although it excels in its ability to run under many different commodity hardware configurations. With the right configuration, however, it can provide supercomputer-like performance at a fraction of the cost. The right configuration, of course, changes upon the needs of the organization and the cluster that is implemented.

2

Preparing Your Linux Cluster

BUILDING A CLUSTER TAKES A GREAT deal of preparation and forethought. Depending on the solution involved, clusters can run from a few hundred dollars in spare parts to several hundred thousand for the larger, more intricate clusters. To create the right solution for your cluster, all design aspects need to be thought out properly in advance.

If the budget doesn't involve throwing money at a vendor to come up with an instant solution, planning rests on your shoulders. Once the go ahead has been given, it's time to create an installation checkist.

You need to keep several things in mind when you start your checklist. What equipment best suits your needs? Do you have a preexisting service contract with a particular vendor? Does this vendor offer systems prebuilt with your needed specs, or are you going to have add extra parts? What sort of network will you build? What sort of network cards will work best with your environment? The entire topology must be mapped out before you begin.

You also have to ask yourself what kind of cluster will best suit your needs. If your company's goal is to build a web server, does that solution include high availability (HA) and load balancing? Do you really need an SMP processor for your parallel application, or will single processors work? This chapter examines different ways to design your environment to bring your various cluster configurations up to speed quickly and easily.

Planning the Topology

Designing your cluster doesn't stop at the hardware level. If you don't take into account and plan for every little thing, you'll find yourself quickly running over budget. You have to plan for network cabling, power and cooling requirements, and replacement costs should anything fail. The physical placement of the computer is important, so you need to decide if the corner table is appropriate, if a dedicated rack should be designed for the environment, or even if a new datacenter would work best.

One of the things most overlooked in the budget is the maintenance. Clusters take time and overhead to run, not to mention a qualified administrator. If something goes wrong, it's nice to have someone who knows what the problem is right away or have a maintenance contract to bring in someone to solve the problem for you.

One Format Yields One Solution

Although it isn't absolutely necessary, providing a standard for your equipment helps reduce overhead and maintenance costs. Having disparate systems means keeping track of all the separate items, which increases administrative overhead. Most system administrators already have heterogeneous networks that they have to deal with on a daily basis. Unless you're fortunate enough to administrate one operating system and one computer vendor, planning for one solution alleviates headaches down the road.

One of the benefits of using (staying with) GNU applications for clustering is the availability of support. Although the documentation for software can be sparse, help is usually an email or newsgroup away, with responses often coming from the writer of the application itself. When selecting software for your cluster, look and see what support options are available. A great deal of software written for Linux under the Gateway Naming Utility (GNU) license is written by people in their spare time, so answers to questions are usually found in the same manner.

Keeping the same set of hardware in your cluster allows for decreased administration time. Having all nodes built exactly the same decreases the amount of guessing during maintenance checks or replacement time when devices fail. Having the same hardware solution across all the nodes lets you maintain a smaller pool of replacement parts rather than having to stock replacement parts for multiple systems. Having the same ethernet card on all nodes allows you to keep one set of drivers on hand, maintain one set of patches, and look in one place for updates. Maintaining a heterogeneous environment just adds to the complexity of the solution when you have to look in several places to find the proper drivers and patches.

Spending a little extra in maintenance can be a double-edged sword. On one hand, support contracts can usually be purchased where hardware support is never more than four hours away. In case of a downed node, parts can be replaced quickly by a trained technician to bring the system up cleanly and easily. Sometimes, that limits an organization due to the trained technician being the only one allowed to fix the server by contract. Nowadays, some companies are replacing their Linux servers and workstations every two years or so rather than paying high maintenance costs.

The whole idea behind HA clustering allows for failover so that downtime becomes a non-issue. Failover happens when a secondary system detects that the primary has stopped proving services. The secondary system in an HA configuration then moves itself into the foreground, allowing the primary to be worked on and brought back to service. Knowing that there's a secondary server that can be switched over allows an organization a certain amount of breathing room, so a maintenance contract might not even be needed. A downed node in a parallel cluster will not adversely affect the system. Processes could be easily migrated or started on other nodes.

Get the Best Components for the Price

Although this sounds like a no-brainer, getting the best components for the price is extremely important for designing a cluster. A penny saved here and there on parts that aren't top of the line will come back to haunt you when you least expect it.

The greatest bottleneck in any cluster configuration is the network. Faster processors and bigger hard drives don't mean anything if the network isn't there to be able to drive it. You can find cheap fast ethernet cards that are designed to work under Linux, although they're not compatible with each distribution. Gigabit ethernet cards are becoming reasonable, and Myrinet seems to be the cluster hardware of choice now. If you can afford it, spend a little more and check out the hardware-compatibility list that's associated with your distribution. Even though a card says that it works with Linux, find out if it works with your distribution before you purchase it. Some cards are designed only to work with RPM distributions right off the bat. Although you can tweak the drivers to your own distribution, finding out ahead of time saves lots of potential hassles down the road. You'll be thankful you checked ahead of time.

Replacement Considerations

One thing to keep in mind is that the cost of the hardware is negotiable compared to the data kept within. Hardware is easily replaced and generally cheap compared to the time it took to create that data. It's vital that you keep good backups. With a parallel or distributed cluster, the relevant data resides mainly on the master nodes. This makes it easy to replace nodes that have failed. With today's cheap commodity computers, it might be easier to replace the entire node in the cluster than take the time needed to work on the unit. This makes sense with diskless clusters, as the only parts involved typically are the motherboard, CPU, RAM, and network interface.

Avoid the Single Point of Failure

When designing HA or load balanced networks, keep in mind where the single points of failure (SPOF) typically lie. Often, the items that have the most moving parts are affected the most, but these incidents of failure can be reduced. Hard drives can be hooked together in a RAID type configuration to lessen the chance of a single disk bringing down the entire machine. Dual network cards attached to the same network offer a good level of redundancy should a card fail. A better solution is to attach each network interface card (NIC) to a different switch, then to a different network, and then ultimately to a different ISP. Remember that only one method of calling the administrator on duty results in an SPOF; at times, cellular service is spotty. The admin needs to carry a pager as well.

Plan for Administrative Overhead

One of the most overlooked aspects of any budget is administration. Sure, hardware is included, perhaps maintenance, but what about the Linux administrator to handle the cluster itself? Yes, you might be the person to set up the system, but are you available to maintain and monitor it constantly? Do you have the proper training to set up this network? If not, the budget might be amended to include for training or time set aside to study the applications included within the cluster. You also might include overtime pay, budget for consultants, training new employees, and budget for employee turnover.

Select the Right Distribution

When experienced users talk about Linux, they're talking about the kernel itself. The rest of the operating system happens to be optional depending on the distribution. This leaves each individual or company to add whatever software they see fit. If parts of the software don't fit your needs, feel free to either add your own, take away the things that don't fit, or modify the kernel in such a way that that it fits your needs. As of this writing, Linux isn't at version 8.0 and won't be for some time. That's a common misconception that people who are unfamiliar with Linux tend to have.

Keeping this in mind, you have to select the right distribution that best suits the needs of the cluster and those who administer it. Are the administrators familiar with Linux in the first place? How about the users? Will they be able to handle any distribution that you throw at them, or will they have to have an installation that guides them through the process?

There are more Linux distributions now that you can shake a stick at, and more are growing daily. There are distributions for almost every purpose imaginable—from embedded devices, security focused distributions, distributions that start from within Windows, to even distributions that run on game consoles. Some distributions cater to new Linux users more than other distributions. Most distributions let you configure most of the operating system in the installation dialogues; however, there are certain distributions whose installers are more advanced than others. For example, Mandrake Linux appears to have a full-featured graphical install that adjusts to the correct video resolution, whereas Debian leaves more of the configuration to the more experienced user in the XF86config file.

Differences in Distributions

The first thing to keep in mind is the layout of the system files. Remember, there's nothing that says any Linux distribution has to have things in common with any other. This leads to fragmentation and lack of standards within the Linux community. Distributions, such as Red Hat, tend to place their system files in non-traditional places. Of course, it works for them, but these discrepancies must be kept in mind when moving from one install to the other.

Different distributions support their own implementation of init scripts. Red Hat and similar distributions tend to be more Sys V compliant, while images like Slackware have no distinct directories for their run levels. Which version you choose is a personal preference, but keep in mind that what works on one system might not work on all Linux implementations. For example, Slackware starts NFS in the rc.inet2 file, which initializes at boot time. Red Hat and like distributions start those services individually in /etc/rc.d/init.d.

Distributions to Avoid

When building a cluster, avoid distributions that don't run natively with ext2 or a journaling file system such as ext3. Some distributions can run under DOS, FAT, or even use NTFS file systems. These Linux installs mimic the native ext2 file structure, although the underlying file structure is still DOS or FAT. This creates an abstraction layer between the Linux file system and native formatted file system that results in a lack of performance. For optimal performance, stick with a system that stays away from these abstraction layers. Common sense also warns against using any Linux distribution with "Phat" in the name for production use.

UMSDOS and loopback file systems run in mostly the same manner. Essentially, Linux creates a file system in an individual file that can be accessed by the local hard drive. Although these distributions are fine for a person starting out with Linux, they're not recommended for production use (though they could be used in a test environment or an encrypted loopback file). If your company is short on lab equipment, a good solution is VMware (www.vmware.com), which allows for multiple virtual Linux installs on a single box.

Planning the Environment

After you decide on the distribution and type of cluster you're going to implement, the next step is to plan the surrounding environment to house the cluster. If the cluster you're implementing contains an excessive amount of components, you need to think about additional power, cooling, and UPS requirements to maintain them. In addition, special types of clusters need enhanced security requirements. If you're just putting up a small load balanced solution, chances are you're not going to need extra power requirements. If you already have a datacenter or Network Operations Center (NOC), chances are that you've already got the infrastructure in place to support a few extra computers. Of course, large parallel clusters of a few thousand nodes are going to need special design and consideration.

Consider Power and Cooling Requirements

Planning the power requirements of a large cluster requires forethought and careful layout. After the selection of the servers, monitors, UPS systems, and network equipment, an inventory is required to plan for the power infrastructure. The trick here is to plan for everything that is going to need power, not just the servers. Your existing NOC might have these components accounted for, but if you're a home user or building an NOC from the ground up, you're going to have to provide for the power somehow.

When planning for the infrastructure to house your cluster, remember that there is no magic solution. Many factors play a part in the design, such as the amount of space you have to work with, the outside average temperature, and the ambient room temperature. If the floor on which the cluster sits is raised, the cooling requirements will obviously be different.

Electricity Requirements

A small cluster setup can generally get away with being placed on a 20-amp circuit. If the goal is high availability, you would ideally place each server on its own circuit attached to its own UPS. A home-built cluster can fit nicely plugged into normal outlets rated for their region. Excessive cooling isn't required, although remember that any network equipment tends to be more sensitive to temperature changes than your servers. Remember to exercise caution; you'll notice any overdraw in power if the lights or monitors start dimming and your equipment starts smoking.

On the other hand, planning for a large cluster of powerful servers requires space in a datacenter or reserved room. If you haven't decided to colocate your equipment, you need to either add on to your existing NOC or build one from scratch. The first step in determining the power requirements is to catalog all the devices and add up their power requirements. When calculating for your requirements, remember to calculate with the total power draw possible, rather than the average. Your server should have the total output labeled on the power supply itself or supplied in the documentation. If you're not sure, call the manufacturer.

During the inventory, don't forget to include anything that might have a power draw or that could generate heat. This might include special cards inside the server, the monitors, powered racks themselves, the lights, tape drives, and even the power strips themselves. Keep in mind extra cards and peripherals that you've added to the system that might cause an extra power draw, such as tape drives. If the cluster in question is a large parallel cluster, this is made easier by simply adding up the power in a rack and multiplying by the number of racks.

A cluster needs (proper or adequate) power requirements and circuit breakers. All outlets need to have three wire-grounded plugs, for it's only a matter of time before you start putting in power strips and extending the power draw on the existing infrastructure. For this reason, you need to estimate for future growth and the cost of replacement after the lifetime of your equipment. What seems appropriate today will probably be outgrown sooner than later.

Provisioning for Cooling

After you generate all kinds of heat with the electricity you're consuming, you must decide how to get rid of it. Thankfully, you've considered the requirements and you've come up with proper air conditioning to alleviate the heated air. Before preparing your datacenter architecture, here's some handy terms that you'll want to arm yourself with:

- **HVAC**—Heating, Ventilation, and Air Conditioning.
- **BTU**—British Thermal Unit. A standard of measuring how much heat it takes to raise or lower one pound of water by one degree Fahrenheit. Heat generated in BTUs equals the total power in watts multiplied by 3.41.
- **Ton**—12,000 BTUs per hour, or 3,510 watts. (Ton refers to an old ice-cooling term, back when ice was used for air conditioning.)

A one-ton air conditioning unit can remove 288,000 BTUs of heat in 24 hours, while a two-ton air conditioner can remove twice this amount. To keep this in perspective, a typical 1,350 square foot house will require a four-ton air conditioner. When planning for an HVAC system, make sure that the air is circulating several times an hour. The more times you're able to circulate the air through the room, the faster you'll recover from a power outage. The amount of times you'll be able to clear the air from a room depends on the layout of the items in the room, the external environment, and the extraneous space.

A rough guideline to plan for the air conditioning required is to take the total power in watts and multiply that by 3.41. A datacenter that puts out 20,000 watts would then put out 68,200 BTUs per hour that have to be dissipated.

Cooling the cluster from a raised floor can be achieved more effectively than by using ambient room air conditioners. The holes in the floor can move air directly into the racks enabling the air to circulate within the racks themselves. Cooling the servers in this way is more effective than trying to cool the servers by lowering the room temperature. A raised floor in a datacenter offers the ability to run cables and piping underneath the server racks. Not only does this allow for greater safety, it keeps unsightly cables and piping out of the way. Keep in mind that normal floors can't handle the stress that a large cluster places on it.

Space: The Final Frontier

When planning for the layout of your equipment, keep in mind that you'll actually have to reach the back of your servers once in a while. Putting your servers against the back wall assures that you'll have to get at those more often than not. There's nothing like twisting your body around in positions that aren't humanly possible. Then again, if you're into yoga, misplacement of servers might be a blessing. For the rest of us, sane placement of the equipment is a must.

Adequate space is needed for air to circulate through the racks. A basic rule of thumb: Keep the servers at least 1 1/2 inches from the sides of the cabinets. This allows for proper airflow and cooling of the equipment.

Racks for Servers and Desktops

The design of the server storage will most likely depend on the choice of servers themselves. If you're able to build your parallel cluster from scratch, consider spending a little extra money on 1U servers. The space saved with a racked system such as this will result in lower cooling costs and higher cooling efficiency. The rack will also provide housing for keyboard, video, mouse (KVM) switches, network gear, and the UPS. Racks can easily be found in configurations of over 72"-80," housing over 50 servers in each rack.

If you're not considering server racks for your cluster, your local home improvement store should sell tool racks that function fine for the placement of desktop or tower servers. Be sure that if you use this type of storage solution, that the rack lends itself well to cooling and has plenty of airflow around the system.

You can find specialized computer companies that fit multiple servers in a small amount of space. For example, eAppliance Corporation sells a 1U server with four hot-swappable servers, each with three fast ethernet jacks for redundancy. You can find them at www.eappliancecorp.com/. RLX Technologies has a device with 24 servers on blades, which fits nicely in a standard 19" 3U cabinet (www.rlxtechnologies.com).

Switches and Connectivity

With the speeds of today's computers, the biggest bottleneck is the network. You can alleviate some of your bandwidth problems with a simple fast ethernet solution. Fast ethernet today is acceptable for most implementations, but for the cluster that needs the most out of its performance, gigabit ethernet is becoming the standard.

When choosing connectivity for your professional cluster solution, try not to skimp on any of the network components. The cluster is essentially a communication medium between nodes. When you drop the medium, you don't have a cluster.

Connectivity with a straight hub allows for traffic between the nodes, although it transmits the traffic across the entire hub. This not only slows down the network traffic by exposing the packet to each interface, but is also inherently insecure. Anyone with knowledge of network snooping gear can sniff out passwords or other sensitive data. A switch is sufficient for most cluster implementations. This allows for direct data transfer between hosts, and the chance of snooping is greatly minimized. Managed switches, in turn, allow for greater granularity at the port level. Some allow for the implementation of virtual networks.

A second interface is a good idea when implementing heartbeat connectivity between two machines. These can be of any standard; however, consider using crossover cables rather than hooking the interfaces up to the network. In this case, the network just adds another point of failure in case something goes wrong.

Regular 10bt ethernet cards will be more than fine for any home network solution that's dependent on an ISP. The speed of the cable or DSL link will not be able to saturate the ethernet card, and response times are not as critical from internal servers. Because people are practically giving their 10bt cards away in favor of fast ethernet, any real home solution using Linux can easily be implemented on the fly. If you're contemplating a parallel cluster, you can use the leftover 10bt cards, but you'll notice a large performance hit.

Donald Becker, CTO and founder of Scyld Computing Corporation, wrote a great deal of the ethernet drivers for Linux. You can find drivers for most supported cards at www.scyld.com/network/.

A Few Words About Security

We would be doing a great disservice to the computing community as a whole if we didn't share a few words about security. Almost every day a new exploit is found, a new virus hits the net, or a denial of service attack is launched. The majority of these attacks cost companies thousands of dollars in lost manpower recovering from downed or defaced servers.

Where do these attacks come from? A great majority of the attacks come within the company itself. A disgruntled employee in a low-security environment can destroy years of work in a matter of minutes. Crackers (and thieves) are opportunists. By minimizing the opportunities that exist, you minimize the chance that your cluster will be compromised.

Many books have been written on the concept of security, and it's a full-time job for many administrators. A full examination of security is beyond the scope of this book, so we cannot hope to engage a full discussion, although we can go over some important security highlights.

Security in Layers

Security at the system level is only one part of the equation. Just like the OSI networking model, the security model encompasses the entire organization. To fully secure your environment, you need to restrict access to the server on the Network Layer, the OS level, at the physical machine, and the datacenter area. After a hacker gets physical access to the server, that's it. Game over.

There lies a ratio between usability and security. There is no way to make your system totally secure; however, you can take steps to reduce the chance of a compromise. Take a proactive approach in security prevention. Subscribe to security newsletters and newsgroups. Have a well-defined security policy at your site. Hacking at the OS level is only one way to get in. As others might tell you, social engineering (basically, the art of getting people to tell you password or security information) is easy to pull off if you're knowledgeable enough. Take the time to educate your users; tell them who has access to what areas and which passwords. Encourage your users to use passwords that are hard to guess. Basically, the more parts of the keyboard that you can use, the harder it will be to guess and/or crack the password. You might suggest acronyms for phrases, rather than words or dates.

It's possible to have too many security measures in place. You want to make sure to have the most restrictive security policy in place without restricting access to your needed services, and that's a fine line. If everyone in your environment is using ftp to access services, implementing secure ftp as a replacement can be an uphill battle. Be ready to strike some compromise. Try to get upper management involved in the decisions and get them to support whatever security policies you have in place. Otherwise, the buck will stop with you.

Security at the System Level

Use /etc/hosts.allow and /etc/hosts.deny liberally to secure who gains access to which services.

Check your password and group files at regular intervals. A sure sign of a compromise is to find extra users on your system that nobody recognizes. Utilize shadow passwords and change them on a regular basis. Use only secure transmission of passwords. Telnet should never be used in most circumstances. SSH is a fine replacement and is found in both an open sourced and closed source version. You can find the commercial version of SSH at ftp.ssh.com, and the open-sourced version at www.openssh.com.

Close down unnecessary ports in /etc/inetd.conf or edit the file so that it passes through TCP Wrappers. Keep a watch for programs that are set SUID.

Install traps to detect intrusion, such as Tripwire (`www.tripwire.com`). Be sure to monitor the reports.

Patch your system. Although patching can be a full-time job in the enterprise, try to keep an eye out at least once a week to download and install fixes for services you're running.

It's also a good idea to have an image of your more important servers off-hand in case your server is compromised. Newer technologies make bare metal recovery much easier; at the least, a decent system imager and a restore option can bring your system up in hours rather than days.

Security at the Network Level

Examine the services listed in `/etc/services` and only allow access through the firewall to the ports you absolutely need. Remember that this method doesn't work if you're on the same subnet. Consider blocking insecure services, such as telnet and ftp from the firewall as well.

Monitoring tools, such as Big Brother (`http://bb4.com`) and NetSaint (`www.netsaint.org`), can be set up to notify a responsible person on certain events.

Physical Level Security

Keep your cluster behind locked doors, inaccessible from the general public. A knowledgeable cracker can easily gain root access at the boot prompt if not properly secured, or with a CD-ROM in hand. If that weren't enough, a simple disconnected power cord would wreak havoc on the live data and potentially cause a great deal of lost revenue.

For increased security at the local level, one might consider even implementing passwords at both the `bios` and the `lilo` level, which helps prevent local access. You also might consider removing the CD-ROM and floppy drives, which helps prevent someone from booting the system by using alternate methods.

Many datacenters have some sort of keycard access to restrict access to the servers in addition to regular surveillance methods. More advanced colocation centers have a scale that weighs everyone so that security personnel can be assured that customers don't leave with more than they take in.

Don't Let Your Security Turn Against You

Keep the firewall access down to a minimum; only a select few should be able to modify the rules. A misconfigured firewall can be set to deny needed ports, or worse, all access from the internal network.

Honest, I was Only Trying to Help!

One of the dangers of working at a university where information is supposed to be freely accessible is that the users leave the decision to themselves to determine what should be freely accessible and what shouldn't. Not only does the university offer services on a public subnet, but you've also got several thousand students who are absorbing all they can about computers. Imagine my surprise when during one of my daily checks, I found a compromised system with a nifty cluster tool, Parallel Virtual Machine (PVM), already compiled for me! Something told me that the hacker wasn't trying to be nice in compiling a cluster solution for me to help with my work but was in fact probably using the distributed tool to set up for a nice denial of service attack. I took no chances and wiped the machine and had it back in service in no time—on a private subnet.

Keep tabs on your clusters. A malevolent user can easily hijack a process on a parallel cluster to run a crack program, enabling your high performance solution to compromise security or worse yet, another's security on your equipment. Just imagine what could happen if your distributed cluster were somehow pointed against a popular site in a denial of service attack.

TCP Wrappers

TCP Wrappers was written by Wietse Venema to log incoming connections. Like the name says, TCP Wrappers provides tiny daemon wrappers to log incoming hostnames and the services that they request. TCP Wrappers can be downloaded at `ftp://ftp.porcupine.org/pub/security/` and comes preinstalled on many distributions.

TCP Wrappers can monitor and secure incoming connections to popular services, such as telnet, ssh, rsh, and so on. In essence, it becomes like a front end, or "wrapper," for these services and logs the connection information, allowing or denying resources based on the finding from these wrappers.

To install, first grab the latest release and uncompress to your local machine. The installation isn't that hard, although some edits are necessary. After uncompressing the image, chmod the Makefile to 644.

Edit Makefile for the correct choice of REAL_DAEMON_DIR. Set FACILITY to log to LOG_AUTH.

Edit percent_m.c file to comment off sys_errlist[] declaration:

```
/*  extern char *sys_errlist[]; */
```

Compile.

```
make linux
```

TCP Wrappers does not come with make install functionality. Here's a simple script that does just that.

```
#!/bin/sh
for file in safe_finger tcpd tcpdchk tcpdmatch try-from
do
/usr/bin/install -m 0555 -o root -g daemon $file /usr/sbin
done
/usr/bin/install -m 0444 -o root -g daemon tcpd.h /usr/include
/usr/bin/install -m 0555 -o root -g daemon libwrap.a /usr/lib
```

Set up syslogd to log by AUTH. Add the following line in /etc/syslog.conf. Don't forget to use a tab to separate fields.

```
auth.info     /var/log/authlog
```

Create the logging file:

```
touch /var/log/authlog
chmod 600 /var/log/authlog
chown root /var/log/authlog
```

Send HUP signal to syslogd and test with logger program:

```
logger -p auth.info Test
```

If everything goes right, you'll see the "Test" message that you just sent in /var/log/authlog.

Edit /etc/inetd.conf to use TCP Wrappers for services. For example, change

```
ftp stream     tcp     nowait   root     /usr/sbin/tcpd   in.ftpd
```

to read:

```
ftp  stream  tcp     nowait  root     /usr/local/sbin/tcpd
/usr/sbin/in.ftpd
```

Send HUP signal to syslogd. Congratulations, you now have a working TCP Wrappers.

If you're curious to know how Wietse Venema pronounces his name, download the .wav file at www.porcupine.org/wietse/wietse.wav.

Secure Shell

Secure Shell (SSH) was developed as an alternative to insecure login methods. It is a replacement for rsh, rcp, and rlogin, as well as telnet and ftp. SSH also allows for secure X connections, as it never sends a clear text password. SSH, when used effectively, can easily replace these programs without the end user being the wiser. SSH provides the same functionality as telnet; however, SFTP includes more features, such as a percent transferred monitor. Scp can securely copy files across the wire without clear text. Two different implementations of the SSH protocol exist: One is a commercial version that you can buy with support—the other, a non–commercial, open sourced version. OpenSSH is becoming the standard in the Linux/BSD community.

SSH uses different ciphers for encryption, such as 3DES, IDEA, Blowfish, Twofish, ArcFour, and Cast128-cbc. SSH also uses DSA and RSA for authentication. You can authenticate using a public key, password, kerberos, or .rhosts login. SSH protects against IP and DNS spoofing, attacks based on X authentication data, as well as attacks from snooping.

SSH comes in two versions, appropriately named 1 and 2. 1 has largely been superceded by 2, although it remains in wide use. 2 is by far the most common. Version 3 is available, but it doesn't refer to protocol; it still installs only Versions 1 and 2 by default.

Be sure that, when using SSH, your passwords are more than two characters. A bug in the commercial release, 3.0.0, enabled users to bypass authentication if the password contained two characters or less. In general, it's good practice to have as many varied characters in your passwords as possible.

The non-commercial versions can be downloaded anonymously from ftp.openssh.com, in the /pub/ssh directory. Commercial versions allow for support, whereas non-commercial versions are restricted to submitting bug reports.

Installing SSH in your environment is easy. If at all possible, install SSH using TCP Wrappers so that all incoming connections are logged. In the most simple installation, you can install SSH by using configure, make, make install. Due to the nature of this program, be sure that you get it from a reliable source. Just like whenever you download a program, it's got the potential to be compromised to enable security loopholes and backdoors. In some countries (notably Russia, Iraq, Pakistan, and France), it might be illegal to use encryption without a special permit.

By default, SSH 2 isn't compatible with SSH 1. You can make them compatible by doing a few manual edits. It's a good idea to read the README file before starting; there might be other options that you want to have in your environment. First of all, install SSH 1 with TCP Wrappers and disable the SUID bit:

```
tar xzvf ssh-<version number>
cd ssh-<version number>
./configure —with-libwrap="<path to libwrap>" —disable-suid-ssh
make
su
make install
```

SSH 2 can be installed using the same method. After installing SSH 1, alter SSH 2 configuration so that it can call SSH 1 when needed.

Insert/edit the lines in /etc/ssh2/ssh2_config so that the following are in the file in this form:

```
Ssh1Compatibility          yes
Ssh1Path                   /usr/local/bin/ssh1
```

Insert/edit the lines in /etc/ssh2/sshd2_config so that the following are in the file in this form:

```
Ssh1Compatibility              yes
Ssh1Path                       /usr/local/sbin/sshd1
```

Starting with 3.0.0, the SSH distribution comes with startup scripts in ssh-<version>/startup/linux/redhat. This sshd2 script can easily be modified to support any version of Linux you happen to be running. With Red Hat, this is designed to go in the /etc/rc.d/init.d/ directory, with appropriate links in rc3.d and rc0.d. Other distributions can easily start this daemon up at boot with an entry in rc.local.

SSH can usually be invoked with the following syntax:

```
/usr/local/bin/ssh user@remote_host.
```

Sftp is handled in much the same way:

```
/usr/local/bin/sftp user@remote_host.
```

When copying a file with Secure Copy, the syntax is as follows:

```
/usr/local/bin/scp user@local_host:/path_to_file/file
user@remote_host:/pathtofile/file
```

For more information, check out the SSH guide for UNIX administrators at www.ssh.com/support/ssh/ssh2-adminguide.pdf.

SSH Tips and Tricks

SSH is a great tool for remote connections, although documentation is hard to come by at times. Here are some little known tips and tricks that every user should have at his or her disposal.

SSH supports the tilde character (~) for escape sequences. Pressing ~? presents you with a list:

```
Supported escape sequences:
~.  - terminate connection
~^Z - suspend ssh
~#  - list forwarded connections
~&  - background ssh (when waiting for connections to terminate)
~?  - this message
~~  - send the escape character by typing it twice
(Note that escapes are only recognized immediately after newline.)
```

You can restrict your users from logging in remotely as root by changing the /etc/ssh2/sshd2_config file. Change the following line:

```
PermitRootLogin    yes
```

to

```
PermitRootLogin    no
```

Using X11 forwarding, you can export the display of your favorite X application, even behind a firewall. Forwarding only works if you didn't expressly disable it during configuration. To enable X11 forwarding, edit or add the following in your /etc/ssh2/sshd2 configuration file:

```
ForwardX11 yes
```

At the remote server, simply type the name of the X program you'd like to forward. Do not set the DISPLAY variable to the local machine; SSH takes care of that for you.

Distributing Patches, Updates, and Software Securely

SSH distributes software to remote machines through scripts and without user intervention. One way to distribute code is to set up a script with a dummy account using SSH and without having to type passwords in every time. Here's a method to enable SSH 1 to accept logins without a password:
Log on to the client and generate a new passkey:

```
ssh-keygen1 -b 1024 -C ssh-key
```

When the script asks for a passphrase, hit Enter twice for no passphrase. Next, copy the passphrase over to the remote machine in which you want to authenticate to:

```
scp localhost:~/.ssh/identity.pub user@remotemachine.fqdn:
```

Log on to the remote machine with SSH:

```
mkdir .ssh

chmod 700 .ssh

cp identity.pub .ssh/authorized_keys
```

Exit the shell. When you log back in with SSH 1, you are not prompted for a password. This enables you to use scp to securely copy scripts and files within scripts.

Developing a Backup Policy

It's been said that your data are only as good as your last backup. With that in mind, it's absolutely essential that you keep current backups of your data. Often, the data on the computer is worth more than the computer. Although clusters are expensive, replacing them is a much easier task than replacing all the data on them. It might be okay to lose the data on your home workstation, but when your HA cluster goes down at the multinational bank, it's time to break out the resume.

Only the master server from a cluster should be backed up. There's no sense in backing up repetitive data from slave nodes. HA clusters should back up the master node at least once a day (more if the data is sensitive). On parallel and distributed clusters, all the data is stored on the master node with jobs being farmed out to slave nodes. Backups of these slave nodes would just result in copies of the operating system.

Develop a Comprehensive Backup Plan

The first part of any backup plan has to include the retention policy. All further choices should revolve around how long you're going to keep your tapes around before being reused.

Depending on the data being backed up, you're going to have to keep some tapes around for quite some time. Financial institutions and records departments need data around for a minimum of seven years. If this is included in your backup strategy, be sure to keep it in mind when choosing your backup media (tapes don't come cheap).

Who is going to pay for the tapes? If your environment has different cost centers, a good strategy is to develop a service-level agreement (SLA) between the backup operator and the department whose data is being backed up. Depending on the urgency of the data and the cost center, a department might not need to have its server included in a backup scheme.

When reusing tapes, decide on a lifecycle complementary to your budget and your environment. Although some tapes are rated at millions of reuses, do you really trust your company's data to a worn tape?

Decide how often you're going to do full backups. A fine line exists between backup and restore functionality. On one hand, a full backup once a day might be a bit excessive if the data is relatively static; however, if you can afford the media and time, this is among the best strategies out there. More common is the full backup once a week. In that scenario, if you lose data midweek you've either lost that amount of data or have to restore not only the full backup, but also the incremental data since the last full backup. This can take some time, so decide which is more important: budget and backups or data and restores.

Make sure that the network backbone is capable of supporting backups if you're doing it over the network. A nightly backup can totally saturate a regular ethernet network and render communication (even backups) useless due to the amount of time involved. Consider a separate backup network if your regular network can't handle the traffic or your backup data needs to be secure.

Backups aren't inherently secure. Anyone with access to a tape drive can pull off sensitive data. Several popular programs, including Veritas Netbackup and Legato Networker, are installed with root permissions. Therefore, a malicious user can pull whatever he wants from disk and dump it wherever he wants. A backup tape can also be read back into almost any file system. Secure your media as closely as you would your most sensitive data.

Select the Best Backup Strategy Available

Budget is often the deciding factor when selecting the proper backup program for any particular environment. You can find several open source programs that can back up data well, although the closed source programs support tape robots and autochangers.

Linux support from the closed source vendors has typically been spotty in the past, with the operating system being more of an afterthought than a supported OS.

dump

dump is the good ol' reliable standard for UNIX backups and provides the back end for a good many programs.

dump scans the inodes of a particular file system to decide whether or not to backup a file that resides in a single partition. dump stores its information about backups in text format in /etc/dumpdates. This file keeps track of dates so that incremental backups can be performed.

dump can span more than one tape, although it takes user intervention to do so. Adding the -F flag tells dump to run a script at the end of each tape. This can flag a backup operator and let him know that a tape must be changed. The -n flag, when used, also sends a "wall" type request to all users in the operator group when dump needs attention.

A Note About dump Levels

Level 0 is always a full backup. Levels 1 through 9 are incremental, with no specific meaning to the number. With the exception of 0, a backup taken at a certain level will always back up data that has changed from the last previous number less than that number. For example, on Monday, you do a full level 0 dump. This backs up all your data. On Wednesday, you do a level 5 dump (the number here doesn't matter, just pick one relative to the other numbers in your backup schedule). This backs up all data that changed since Monday. On Friday, you choose to do a level 3 dump; this takes all the information that had changed since Monday, given that this is a lower number than your Wednesday dump of 5. A higher dump level on Friday would ensure that you would get everything that had changed since Wednesday.

The format of dump (from the man page) is

```
/sbin/dump [dumplevel] [-B records] [-b blocksize] [-d density] [-e inode
number] [-f file] [-h level] [-L label] [-s feet] [-T date] file_to_dump
```

In other words, it's something similar to

```
/sbin/dump -0u -f /dev/st0 /usr/src
```

This invokes dump with a full backup, adds the information to /etc/dumpdates, and writes the data from /usr/src to the first SCSI tape device. If you specify dump without the -u flag, it automatically assumes a full dump because of the fact that it doesn't consult the /etc/dumpdates—and, therefore, doesn't know that there was ever a previous dump.

You also can use the -f flag to send the dump to a remote device. Using /sbin/dump -0u -f remote:/dev/st1 /dev/hdc1 sends the contents to the machine called "remote."

restore

Now that you've got all your data backed up, the way to restore it is by simply using the restore command. restore works either by restoring the entire file system that you initially backed up using dump or by an interactive file mode.

To restore a file system interactively, use the i switch. This allows you to browse the dump with ls, cd, and pwd. To mark the directories and files that you want to restore, use the add command. After you're done selecting the files to restore, the extract command restores the files to the directory (recursively, if needed) in which you started the restore. Entering help gets you a list of available commands.

When finished, an interactive restore gives you an option to set owner/mode for '.'? [y/n]. Answering y changes all permissions to root or whomever did the restore. It's almost always a good idea to answer n to keep the permissions intact.

Restoring an entire file system takes a different approach but isn't much harder. Hopefully, you'll never have to do this, but sometimes the situation presents itself during the most inopportune moments. The file system in question must first be prepared with mkfs. After that, you have to restore from the last full dump, then each incremental on top of that.

First, prepare the file system with mkfs:

```
mkfs /dev/hdc1
mount /dev/hdc1 /mnt
cd /mnt
restore rf /dev/st0
```

This initial `restore` restores from the first file dumped onto tape. If you're restoring more than one file from the same tape, be sure to use the `no rewind` device and use the `mt` command to move backward and forward around the tape.

g4u

Ghost for UNIX (`g4u`) is a simple program that takes a snapshot of an operating system, passes it through `gzip`, and sends the image over the network to a preconfigured ftp account. `g4u` works on Intel-based hardware only, yet it will make an image of virtually any OS, including Linux, BSD, and Microsoft Windows.

Although not a backup program per se, its use is most invaluable for providing quick and inexpensive images. `g4u` is basically a great little hack. It entails a preconfigured NetBSD distribution on a floppy that supports most ethernet cards. It will back up an entire drive, including boot sector information, `lilo`, and the partition tables. It supports IDE and SCSI drives.

To setup `g4u`, download the image at www.feyrer.de/g4u/ and copy it to a floppy with either

```
dd if=/g4u-1.5.fs of=/dev/fd0
```

or

```
cat g4u-1.5.fs > /dev/fd0
```

`g4u` needs an ftp server that contains an "install" username and a working DHCP server. (See Chapter 3 for information on configuring the DHCP server.)

Boot the server with the floppy installed. The NetBSD kernel will boot, detect the ethernet card if it supports it, and then offer a prompt. The format for the upload is easy:

```
uploaddisk ftp.server.com <filename>
```

The program then prompts for the install account's password. Enter the password and wait for the image to be uploaded.

Restoring the image is done in much the same way. Boot from the floppy and enter `slurpdisk` instead of `uploaddisk` at the prompt.

If you'd like to use an SCSI disk instead of an IDE disk, append `sd0` at the end of the command line.

Veritas Netbackup

Netbackup is really two programs marketed as one backup solution. Veritas uses its Media Manager to control the tape robot and the inventory of the tapes or other media. The other program is GNU Tar.

Netbackup is an enterprise-level backup scheme, as its price range tends to be outside the budget of most home users. Netbackup also doesn't support Linux as a server, but it will back up a Linux client.

The java interface is kludgy and tends not to work at times, and the wizards that are included tend to configure the program incorrectly. The tools included in the command line follow the UNIX standard of sharp, distinct tools. All the configuration files are stored in text format, making editing easy, although Veritas provides tools to manipulate the data. A motif-based interface is also available, which works well, but isn't as feature-rich. When used properly, you don't need Netbackup to restore the tapes; you can simply use tar to read back the information—provided you know which image is on which tape.

Technical support for Netbackup tends to follow the typical Veritas approach of "ask no questions." Support tends to be outstanding, and the tech support engineers freely offer their direct lines.

Legato Networker

Legato's Networker product offers a relatively easy GUI to navigate, and the setup is straightforward. Networker has a great data transfer rate monitor on the display, which makes tuning easy. Networker also includes a separate command-line program that makes controlling remote backups easy without having to memorize all the command-line tools and options.

Networker stores its data and logs in a proprietary format, making parsing by hand impossible, although there are command-line programs that you can run. Networker also grooms the logs at random times, which can cause data corruption should you attempt a backup at the same time. Data corruption in the logs usually means that you have to start from scratch with an individual client—meaning that you've lost all previous backups.

Legato bundles Networker for sale by other vendors, so you might be able to get more attractive pricing under a different name.

Backup Tips

Hopefully, the first thing you learned in system administrator school was how to make decent backups and that they need to be taken at reasonable periods of time, like every day, for example. With all the emphasis on backups, it's a good chance that you've got some method already in place, although you might not have considered all aspects of backup management. Here are a few tips to help the beginning cluster administrator along.

Do You Really Need All that Data?

There's nothing wrong with full backups. In fact, there's no such a thing as too many backups. The more sensitive and volatile the data is, the more frequent the backups occur. Some companies do backups every half hour of important data.

It doesn't hurt, however, to be selective about the type of data you back up. All the dynamic data directories should be backed up, of course—the log files and the user files. But how often do you need to back up the root partition? On many systems, this partition should not change often, if at all. The same goes for `/usr/local/bin`. It's not a bad idea to back these up constantly, but you just don't need to. These generally won't change, and you should be able to replace most of the data with a master image.

Keep your Backups Offsite

There's nothing like a good disaster to rid your datacenter of equipment. A small planet falling on your organization can really ruin your day, especially if it also destroys your disaster-recovery plan.

Make sure that you've got an offsite strategy for your media. This can include your backup operator taking the tapes home with him or finding a service that will do this for you. Services like these often have reasonable rates and secure, temperature-controlled storage. Be sure your SLA with your tape company (or your backup operator) includes a short retrieval time.

Yes, But Can You Recover the Data?

You can run backups all night long, day after day, but the data is only as good as the restore. I can't stress this enough. Do test restores often. Don't wait until you've lost critical data to find out that all the data you've been backing up isn't valid. Optimally, set aside time to do test restores on a backup server that mirrors your primary server. It's also a good idea to be able to read tapes from drives that aren't your own. It would be of no value if you couldn't read from a brand new drive after your entire datacenter burned down.

Secure Backups

Running remote backups over SSH is easy. Just do

```
tar cvf - | ssh user@host "dd of=/dev/tape"
```

Summary

Proper planning of a Linux cluster doesn't only start with the choice and purchasing of computer equipment, but also with the designing the environment to go with it. Special considerations include the air conditioning requirements, security, and a decent backup strategy.

It's important to weigh these decisions and plan them out with management approval as a concise strategy that you stick with. It'll save you many headaches down the road.

3

Installing and Streamlining the Cluster

THERE ARE ALMOST AS MANY WAYS TO deploy a Linux install as there are distributions themselves. Installing Linux in a clustered environment requires a different approach than installing for a standalone workstation or server. The trick is to find an install method that you're comfortable with and that works for you.

The installation method will vary with the distribution that you have selected. Some distributions have stringent requirements on how they're to be set up. Most distributions can be installed from just about any source imaginable—from a CD-ROM, NFS, FTP, floppy, Kickstart, or hard drive. Scyld Linux for parallel clusters has a distinct install procedure for the master and slave nodes. Linux router type distributions (single floppy) are among the easiest to set up due to the fact that they're self-contained, although they are dependent on a predefined type of ethernet card.

Installation from a CD-ROM is the preferred method due to security requirements. If your server is not on the network, it's much harder for hackers to break in. (Okay, if you're in a movie, it could probably be done. Make sure you've read the script before proceeding.) A number of distributions allow for remote login before the system is fully up and patched. For a cluster roll out, it's not too feasible to install every node from a CD-ROM, so take as many precautions as possible. You might consider taking the switch off the main network until your servers are patched.

When installing for a large clustered environment, it's best to find an install method that will be able to hit the most boxes in the shortest amount of time. Install methods such as Kickstart, SystemImager, Ghost, or g4u are preferred because they can handle several installs at once. This is particularly important to free the system administrator for more important tasks, such as playing ping-pong.

This chapter covers the various methods of autoinstalling Linux and ways to push patches and software. Feel free to browse the method that works best for you and implement it as you see fit.

Setting Up the DHCP Server

When installing clusters in an enterprise environment, the system administrator has to decide between static and dynamic addressing.

Choosing a static addressing scheme gives the end user more control over the individual system. When setting up a cluster with static addressing, the administrator knows that that server will get that same address after each reboot and not have to worry if the DHCP server is able to respond or not. Static IP addresses have to be entered in by hand, as well as all the networking information. When installing from an image type install, the servers must have dedicated floppies or images associated with them to maintain the different IP/networking schemas.

This method is preferred in HA environments because of situations when network connectivity could be an issue. If the network goes down, so does access to the DHCP server. If the server can't access DCHP, there's no network connectivity and, therefore, no network services—simple as that. Small, cluster configuration can benefit from this model, seeing as how setting up a DHCP server is just a tad bit overkill for just a few servers.

DHCP is required for SystemImager, Ghost For UNIX, and others. The reason why it's so popular is that you just have to set up an initial scope, and your configuration remains the same each time. Static reservations can be given so that a server can get the same IP address each time the lease is up. All you have to do is record the MAC address of the ethernet card. Any configuration can easily be changed just by making a few modifications to /etc/dhcpd.conf, rather than by locating the individual server and making all the changes there.

Setting up a DHCP server in Linux can be done in just a few minutes, and there are many benefits. Just the simple fact that you can also use it to force a configuration that actually works onto the end user is reason enough.

Installing from Source

If your distribution doesn't come with a DHCP daemon installed, it stands to reason that you're going to have to install one. One of the more popular daemons is distributed from the Internet Software Consortium and is fully capable of handling the DHCP requirements of your entire organization, as well as an image server and large cluster.

Before installing, you need to make sure that you have a CONFIG_PACKET and CONFIG_FILTER enabled in your kernel. This enables packet and socket filtering. Most distributions have these enabled, but it doesn't hurt to check, just in case, so it does not present an issue in later 2.2 or 2.4 kernels. You can check to see if you have these enabled by getting the source for your distribution and taking a look at it through the config. The kernel also has to support multicast. You can determine if your kernel has multicast enabled by running /sbin/ifconfig -a.

Versions of the Linux Kernel before 2.2 have a tendency to change the broadcast 255.255.255.255 address to that of the local broadcast address. This can play havoc with buggy clients such as Microsoft. According to the ISC's DHCP How-To, there's a workaround. Two methods that have worked are shown here:

```
route add -host 255.255.255.255 dev eth0
route add -host <host> dev eth0
```

or

```
route add -net 255.255.255.0 dev eth0
```

where eth0 is the primary interface. Choose the primary interface that's right for your system.

Download the source at a mirror closest to you. You can find a list of mirrors at www.isc.org/ISC/MIRRORS.html. Unpack the distribution, change into the source directory and ./configure, make, and make install as root.

Setting DHCP Options

Options that you pass to your clients are located in /etc/dhcpd.conf. The minimum options that you need to send to the clients are the initial IP address, a subnet mask, a gateway, default-lease-time, and max-lease-time. Comments are prefaced with a hash mark(#), and all options must be appended with a semicolon. For more information, check out man dhcp-options.

Here's a sample configuration that shows a basic DHCP setup:

```
#/etc/dhcpd.conf
default-lease-time 259200;
max-lease-time 604800;
ddns-update-style ad-hoc; #backwards compatibility for older versions
option routers 192.168.1.1;
```

```
option domain-name "domain.com";
option domain-name-servers 192.168.1.250, 192.168.1.251;
option subnet-mask 255.255.255.0;
option broadcast-address 192.168.1.255;
subnet 192.168.1.0 netmask 255.255.255.0 {
        range 192.168.1.2 192.168.1.15;
        range 192.168.1.100 192.168.1.150;
}
```

This configuration assigns these DHCP options in the ranges of 192.168.1.2–192.168.1.15 and 192.168.1.100-192.168.1.150. Static reservations are based on MAC addresses and are done as follows:

```
host hostname {
        hardware ethernet 0:3:ba:8:53:e6;
        fixed-address 192.168.1.16;
}
```

More popular options taken from the man pages are listed as follows:

```
option subnet-mask ip-address;
```

This option assigns a subnet mask to the client. If this option isn't defined, dhcpd assigns the subnet based on which the master server lies.

```
option routers ip-address [, ip-address...  ];
```

This option specifies a list of IP addresses for routers on the client's subnet. Routers should be listed in order of preference.

```
option domain-name-servers ip-address [, ip-address...  ];
```

The domain-name-servers option assigns domain name servers to the client. Servers should be listed in order of preference. Be sure to put the IP addresses rather than the fully qualified names.

```
option domain-name string;
```

This option assigns the client its domain name for use with DNS.

```
option broadcast-address ip-address;
```

This option assigns the client's broadcast address for use on the client's subnet.

```
option static-routes ip-address ip-address  [,  ip-address
  ip-address...  ];
```

This option specifies a list of static routes that the client should install in its routing cache. If multiple routes to the same destination are specified, they are listed in descending order of priority.

The routes consist of a list of IP address pairs. The first address is the destination address, and the second address is the router for the destination.

A complete list of DHCP options is given in Appendix C, "DHCP Options."

Starting the DHCPD Server

After you configure the /etc/dhcpd.conf file, you need to give dhcpd a place to store its lease information. This is done by touching the file /var/state/dhcp/dhcpd.leases:

```
touch /var/state/dhcp/dhcpd.leases
```

This is a flat text file that serves as a database for all the lease information. All times in there are given in GMT format and not in the local time zone for standardization. For more information on this file, you can check the man page on dhcpd.leases.

To start the server itself, you simply enter

```
/usr/sbin/dhcpd
```

If your DHCP server is listening on multiple subnets with multiple interfaces, simply add the interface on the end of the command line:

```
/usr/sbin/dhcpd eth1
```

That's it. To test if your server is assigning IP addresses, you might first run the server in the foreground with the -d and -f switches. Try to boot up a client on your local subnet and watch as it gets an address.

Unattended Red Hat Install with Kickstart

To solve the problem of installing Linux on a large number of servers, Red Hat incorporates a program called *Kickstart* with their distributions. Kickstart is an unattended install over CD-ROM, NFS, or FTP. The trick to Kickstart is that it places a configuration file (ks.cfg) on a network boot floppy, which has all the installation information you've already written on it. The ks.cfg file is a straight text file in a particular format, so it can easily be created by hand.

A decent strategy is to copy the entire contents of the CD-ROM(s) onto a hard drive that's shared over NFS. After creating the Kickstart disk, use that to install Red Hat wherever you go. Need another node to the cluster? Install the boot disk, turn the computer on, and walk away. Come back in a half hour, and you've got another node. Got a problem user that erased his kernel? Not a problem. Slip in the floppy, reboot, and in no time, you've got a fresh install.

The advantage of a Kickstart install over a normal image is that Kickstart actually creates a new install every time. The install is fresh and not copied over from any other install, such as what you'd get from a ghosted image. If you set the server up to boot from DHCP in your configuration file, that's all you need to do for each server. For static addresses, a Kickstart disk for each server is necessary.

Although this is a great method for unattended install, there's a catch. As of this book's publication, Kickstart only works on i386 machines. So those of you who dream of installing Red Hat on your Sparc IPX or Sega Dreamcast will have to wait a little while.

Creating the Configuration File

Starting with release 7.1, Red Hat shipped with a program called Kickstart Configurator, as shown in Figure 3.1. This program is quite the helpful GUI because it exports some of the requisite `ks.cfg` options in a format that Red Hat can read. If the file is incomplete or if Kickstart encounters invalid options, the install turns interactive and prompts you to insert the correct options so that it can continue.

The Configurator program is rather self explanatory. However, remember that the program is designed to serve as a basic template; you'll have to edit the resulting configuration file itself if you want a more detailed installation.

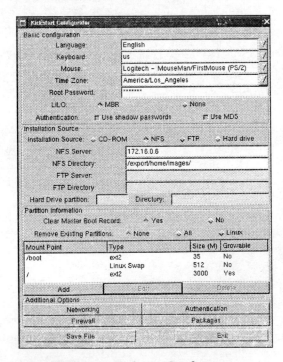

Figure 3.1   Kickstart Configurator.

In the GUI, the options in the Basic Configuration are mandatory, so you'll have to choose the Language, Keyboard, Mouse, Time Zone, Root Password, LILO, and Authentication.

Keep in mind that, although the program doesn't display the root password, the resulting file will—and in straight text no less. Be sure to either encrypt the password or keep the Kickstart disk secure. You can encrypt the password easily by editing the file, copying over the password from /etc/passwd, and by appending the —iscrypted parameter to the rootpw option by editing the configuration file. See the Kickstart example that follows for configuration examples.

The next section, Installation Source, enables you to specify which install method you'd like to pursue. NFS or FTP is the preferred method, simply because that frees you from either carrying around a CD-ROM or pre-installing the distribution from a hard drive. You could easily install Kickstart from a locally attached CD-ROM, but that's the whole point of Kickstart— you don't have to. The program grays out the other options you don't select so that you can't accidentally set up an FTP install when you're actually looking for an NFS install.

Under partition information, you have the option to select to clear out the Master Boot Record when installing lilo. The Configurator doesn't allow you to pass kernel options during boot, nor does it let you specify more than one drive for install. The installer picks and chooses for you if you're not careful. Be sure to edit the configuration file by hand if you're concerned about this functionality.

The Networking option at the bottom of the screen lets you configure the primary interface. Neither the GUI nor the command line option lets you configure a secondary card. The installation program assumes that you're instal-ling off a network on eth0 and will not enable networking if Kickstart is not taking place over a network.

The Additional options given with Kickstart Configurator include NIS, LDAP, Kerberos, and Hesiod. The GUI launches a different screen that includes all the command-line options.

The firewall settings can be applied to different ethernet devices if you choose the Customize option. The command-line option can be used to include different ports and protocols using the format port:protocol. For exam-ple, to include SSH in your configuration, you'd use 22:tcp, 22:udp. Separate all settings with commas.

Packages, the last selection, are a set of predefined options that mirror the default install. For a list of packages and what they contain, see the RedHat/base/comps file. It's a good idea not to install packages that you know you're not going to need; they might pose a security risk later.

Booting with Kickstart

Red Hat can start a Kickstart installation from the configuration file on a floppy, CD-ROM, network, or the hard drive.

To install from a floppy, use the `bootnet.img` from the `/images` directory on the installation media and copy the Kickstart file over. The simplest method of doing this is to use `dd`:

```
dd if=/images/bootnet.img of=/dev/fd0
mount /dev/fd0 /mnt/floppy
cp ks.cfg /mnt/floppy
```

After the initial install, boot off the floppy drive and enter at the boot prompt:

```
linux ks=floppy
```

You can edit the `sysconfig.cfg` file on the boot floppy to automatically enter this information at boot time so you won't have to. Change the `default` line to read `ks` and the `prompt` setting to `0`:

```
default ks
  prompt 0
```

Append a `ks` label to the file so that the default uses this rather than another label:

```
label ks
   kernel vmlinuz
   append ks=floppy initrd=initrd.img
```

You can also keep the Kickstart configuration file on the NFS volume itself if you're installing with that method. The format is `linux ks=nfs:server:/path`. For example, you'd enter the following:

```
linux ks=nfs:matrix.server.com:/mount/nfs/RedHat
```

Setting Up NFS for Kickstart

The Network File System protocol has been a staple of UNIX that allows for sharing of directories across networks. Invented by Sun Microsystems in the early 1980s, the protocol was made publicly available from its onset. Many UNIX vendors were quick to jump on the bandwagon in adopting the protocol to their own versions.

Setting up the NFS for Kickstart is first done by starting the daemons in `/etc/rc.d/init.d`. As root, start the `portmap` and `nfs` daemons:

```
[root@matrix init.d]# ./portmap start
Starting portmapper: [  OK  ]
[root@matrix init.d]# ./nfs start
Starting NFS services:  [  OK  ]
Starting NFS quotas: [  OK  ]
```

```
Starting NFS mountd: [  OK  ]
Starting NFS daemon: [  OK  ]
```

To check the status of NFS, use `/usr/sbin/rpcinfo -p`. You should get output
similar to the following:

```
[root@matrix init.d]# /usr/sbin/rpcinfo -p
   program vers proto   port
    100000    2   tcp    111  portmapper
    100000    2   udp    111  portmapper
    100011    1   udp    829  rquotad
    100011    2   udp    829  rquotad
    100005    1   udp   1041  mountd
    100005    1   tcp   1879  mountd
    100005    2   udp   1041  mountd
    100005    2   tcp   1879  mountd
    100005    3   udp   1041  mountd
    100005    3   tcp   1879  mountd
    100021    1   udp   1042  nlockmgr
    100021    3   udp   1042  nlockmgr
    100021    4   udp   1042  nlockmgr
```

Put the directory that you want to share (hopefully, the directory that houses
your entire Red Hat distribution) in `/etc/exports`. This ensures that your files
are shared over the network to allow for remote installs. The format for
`/etc/exports` is `/directory/to/export host1(permissions) host2(permissions)`
`host3(permissions)`. Use one directory per line. For example:

```
/usr/share/redhat cthulhu(ro)
/export/share/files *(rw)
```

The first line shares over NFS the directory `/usr/share/redhat` to host `cthulhu`
read-only. The second line also shares `/export/share/files` to all hosts, with read
and write permissions.

To get the server to reread changes to `/etc/exports`, use the `/usr/sbin/`
`exportfs -r` command.

Sample Kickstart File

After a few tries, you'll get a feeling for Kickstart and what it can do for you.
The first few times you start, the install will probably turn interactive, meaning
that you didn't set up the Kickstart file correctly. Don't lose heart; it happens
to the best of us. It just takes getting used to. One of the most common mis-
takes is that you've set up X wrong in the configuration file. If that happens a
few times, it's easier to skip the X configuration altogether and run `setup` after
the install finishes. Chances are that you won't need it in the first place if

you're installing most types of clusters. Here's an example of a Kickstart configuration that might be used to install a cluster:

```
#Kickstart for Parallel Cluster
#These first configuration selections are mandatory
lang en_US
keyboard us
mouse generic3ps/2
timezone —utc America/Tijuana
rootpw —iscrypted 3BVrRSeDD2vvE
network —bootproto dhcp —device eth0
install
nfs —server matrix —dir /usr/kickstart/redhat7/
auth —useshadow —enablemd5
zerombr yes
# Partitioning Information
part /boot   —size 35
part swap —size 128
part /   —size 1000 —grow
lilo —location mbr
reboot
skipx
# Install the RPM's here
%packages
@Development
@Kernel Development
@NFS Server
@Networked Workstation
@Printer Support
@Utilities
@Web Server
# Post Install Configuration
% post —nochroot
echo "Kickstart finished successfully at `date`" | sbin/sendmail
cbookman@uop.edu
echo "/usr/local/bin/wmaker" > /root/.xinitrc
echo "uop.edu" > /etc/sendmail.cw
```

SystemImager

SystemImager was initially designed to do automated installs of Solaris, yet its current incarnation allows for unattended installs of virtually any Linux distribution. The premise behind SystemImager is that it takes an image of a Linux distribution, uploads it to a master server, and houses that image for use on any future machine. Basically, it's a front end to rsync. It's been tested with Debian, Kondura, Red Hat, Storm, Mandrake, and Turbo Linux, although the manual says that it doesn't work with 2.0 kernels and below. SystemImager also can be run over SSH for encrypted installs. SystemImager also works with ext3 and reiserfs partitions.

What separates this image program from others is the ability to push updates to clients. After the image is sent to the master server, each update can be pushed to the clients. Only the files that have changed are pushed out.

Installing SystemImager is fairly straightforward. After installing and configuring your favorite distribution on a "golden client" with the SystemImager software on it, the entire distribution is pushed to the image server. After an update of the configuration file on the image server telling which clients can access which image, the program can then automatically install the desired image on the client.

Preparing SystemImager

SystemImager needs to have nasm (`www.kernel.org/pub/software/devel/ nasm/source/`), syslinux (`www.kernel.org/pub/Linux/utils/boot/syslinux/`), rsync (`http://rsync.samba.org/ftp/rsync/`), and tftp-hpa (`www.kernel.org/pub/ software/network/tftp`) installed as prerequisites. Tftp-hpa is only needed if you're planning on booting off the network. You can download and install these from source or rpm; it's your call. SystemImager also needs its client and server software installed. You can find these at `http://systemimager.org/ download/`.

Redhat 7.1 ships with tftp enabled in `/etc/services` as a TCP service. Tftp is based on UDP. Commenting out tftp's TCP service will fix the bug.

Uncompress the `systemimager-server` software with `bzcat systemimager-server- <version>.tar.bz2 |tar xf -`.

Change to the install directory and run the install script to setup the program:

```
cd systemimager-server-<version>
./install
```

This starts the install script (obviously) and installs the program. Be sure that you've got enough space on your image server to handle a few complete images.

To prepare the golden client, you need to first install a supported distribution of Linux to a separate client. After the initial install of the distribution, you must tweak, patch, and upgrade it to the finished product. The SystemImager client software uses this install as the image itself, and once it's transferred to the image server, it is pushed out to subsequent clients upon request.

Download the SystemImager client software to the client, uncompress it, change into the client directory, and run the install program. The installer will run through its setup program and then ask to prepare the client. Running the prepare client is a good idea at this stage because you'll just have to run it if you're not finished configuring the client. To run `prepareclient` after the initial install, just run `/usr/sbin/prepareclient`. This process simply prepares your system to run rsync as needed by the image server.

After the client install, you have to run `getimage` on the image server. Be sure that you run this program with the destination directory option (`-directory PATH`), or you might run into some space problems down the road (if your partition is small). This enables rsync to pull the entire client to the image server. The format of `getimage` is

```
getimage <options> -g <client hostname> -image <imagename>
```

For example,

```
getimage -directory /export -g venom -image venom_Linux_image
```

runs `getimage` and puts the `venom_Linux_image` file from client `venom` in the `/export` directory. The default directory for SystemImager is `/var/spool/systemimager/images`.

Don't forget that you can also substitute the client's IP for the hostname. `/usr/sbin/getimage -help` will list options. SystemImager doesn't have the ability to use an exclude list, so be sure that the distribution you transfer over is prepared exactly the way you'd like to replicate.

If you're going to prepare the client with SystemImager, the golden client needs to be patched before you pull the distribution to the image server.

After `getimage` transfers the image over with rsync, the program prompts you for four different methods to assign IP addresses to the clients for future installs. SystemImager manipulates the subsequent installs to include the different IP and hostname information. The first option is to give a static IP. This will offer the same address each time from the client that was backed up. The second option, `dynamic_dhcp`, will use a DHCP server to assign a different address to each installed client. The third method, static, will configure a static address to the client. The fourth method will not edit the network settings at all.

The install script offers to run `addclients` (`/usr/sbin/addclients`) once you select a method to assign IP addresses. The `addclients` script will configure the way each subsequent client is installed. The script will ask for your domain name, the base hostname, a beginning number, and an ending number. This allows SystemImager to populate `/etc/hosts` and `/tftpboot/systemimager/hosts` with subsequent client information.

SystemImager comes with a utility called makedhcpserver, which is housed in /usr/sbin/. This script will take user-defined values and propagate /etc/dhcpd.conf with the values that you give it. If you have an existing dhcpd.conf file, it will back it up before installing its own. The utility /usr/sbin/makedhcpstatic is similar, yet will assign static address to all the hosts.

Installing Clients with SystemImager

After the image is pushed to the image server, the next step is to be able to create different clients with the precreated image. SystemImager comes with three different methods to install the image: namely, creation of a boot disk, creation of an ISO from the image that can be burned onto CD-ROM, or by enabling an update of a pre-existing distribution.

Making an install floppy is done with the /usr/sbin/makeautoinstalldiskette command (SystemImager's robust functionality comes through in the strength of its long filenames). Take a floppy, insert it in the drive, and don't bother mounting it. The diskette command automatically formats the floppy, mounts it, copies the necessary files over to it, then unmounts it.

SystemImager will automatically install the image based on the selection criteria done at image creation time with getimage. If you're not satisfied with your settings, you can always change them by running /usr/sbin/updateclient. Settings for the install are kept in /tftpboot/systemimager and are based on DHCP addresses soft-linked to the install image.

Creating a CD-ROM install from the image is done with /usr/sbin/makeautoinstallcd. This script makes an ISO file that can then be burned to a CD-ROM. The image will still be kept on the image server; the CD-ROM just contains the boot information should you prefer booting off CD-ROM rather than a floppy.

Updating Clients with SystemImager

Making changes to the client image on the image server is done either by making changes to the golden client and running /usr/sbin/getimage again on the client, or by changing into the directory that you want to manipulate on the image server and modifying those files directly.

According to the SystemImager FAQ (http://systemimager.org/manual/html/faq.html), you can use getimage to upload using a different image name. This allows for a makeshift version control, although this takes up space for each install.

If you modify the files on the image server directly, you can change into the root directory of the image and execute the chroot . sh command as root to change your root directory to the current directory. You can then run rpm commands to add or remove software from the subsequent image.

Post-Installation Procedures

After the clusters are set up with the correct Linux distribution, it's a good idea to go through and start patching the system if you haven't done so already. For most programs on Linux, this means upgrading the packages that you're going to use on your production systems.

If you're installing from SystemImager, it's a good idea to patch the golden image before creating the other clients. It's not difficult to keep the master copy well patched and then distribute the updated image to the other clients.

Similarly, it's easy to keep patches up with a Kickstart-based install. Red Hat keeps a list of updated packages, which you can download to your master imager. Simply replacing the old packages might not work due to dependencies, although all you'll have to do is create a separate directory under NFS share, place the updated packages in there, and update your finish script to mount that directory and update the scripts.

If you're doing an install from CD-ROM, don't connect the ethernet card until your server is tightened up. Many servers have been hit and compromised as soon as they come up.

The first stop you should hit for your install is the distribution homepage itself. Times arise when the program itself won't be buggy, although the vendor's implementation might pose a security risk. Next, check out your favorite mirror of bugtraq or subscribe to the mailing list by sending any kind of mail to bugtraq-subscribe@securityfocus.com.

Here's a list of things to keep in mind for the post installation:

- Make sure that your /etc/resolv.conf is populated with the correct DNS servers.
- Check for updates, security holes, and bug fixes.
- Close down all unneeded service ports by commenting out /etc/services.
- Consider populating /etc/hosts.allow and hosts.deny to limit access at the protocol level.
- Remove unnecessary accounts and groups.
- Install TCP Wrappers and the latest version of SSH.
- Disable all remote logins by root, especially with SSH.
- Change the start up scripts so that only the desired programs start at boot.

- If you're running Red Hat or Mandrake, consider running Bastille-Linux (`www.bastille-linux.org`). This user configurable script will tighten down the server to your specifications. Also consider tripwire (`www.tripwire.org`), which is a tool that detects if system files have changed.

Go through the server on a periodic basis, starting with directly after install. Find out which files are set SUID and make sure the bit is actually needed. You can find the SUID files with

```
find / -type f -perm +6000 -exec ls -l {} \; > suidfiles
```

This creates a file called `suidfiles` and populates it with all the files on your system that contain the SUID bit. If you want, you can remove the bit from the program with

```
chmod -s <programname>
```

After all the configuration and installations are done, plug the ethernet cables back in, fire up the primary interfaces, and play another game of ping-pong. You've earned it.

Summary

Linux installs don't have to be painful if you plan accordingly. There's a method for installing Linux on a large amount of machines, with a minimum of preparation, and some trial and error, so there's no reason why you can't replicate many servers with an unattended install. Add a scripting to the finished product, and you've got a powerful tool to help with the preparation and install of many servers. With the addition of unattended installs, you'll never want to install a server by hand again.

4

Alternative File Systems

THE MOST COMMON FILE SYSTEM FOR Linux is currently the ext2 file system, written by Réme Card as an alternative to the Minix file system. It is used as the basis for most distributions and appliances; anything that needs a file system can use ext2. Ext2 as a file system is robust and mature enough to be the back end for stable production use.

Ext2, although stable for most needs, does not support journaling. *Journaling*, basically, is the process of recording changes made by file system writes. When implemented properly, journaling can enable the system to avoid fsck altogether when coming up from a sudden reboot or ungraceful shutdown. Many different file systems, including ones that have been ported over from other manufacturers, such as SGI and IBM, handle journaling. Both SGI's XFS and IBM's OS/2 JFS, even the newer ext2 revision, ext3, and reiserFS are available under the GPL for integration under most any environment.

Other file-system tools enhance both ext2 and alternate file systems. The Network Block Device (NBD), essentially a loopback file system that can be mounted over the network, is an add-on that can easily enhance file-system functionality in a clustered environment. Sistina Corporation's Global File System (GFS) provides similar functionality to NBD, but includes built-in high availability (HA) utilities. Sistina also has an implementation of HP's Logical Volume Manager (LVM), which is a file system layer abstraction that allows for volume management similar to Veritas Volume Manager and Sun's Solstice Disksuite.

Ext2 Under a Microscope

To understand why alternative file systems might give you better performance and features, it's helpful to get a better understanding of what makes up the ext2 file system. This will hopefully introduce a better understanding of what's capable with such an operating system (OS) and what to expect in the future when choosing an alternate file system to implement.

You might assume that, if there's a second extended file system, there would be a first extended file system, wouldn't you? And if there were an extended file system in the first place, there might be an initial file system that was neither extended nor second. Well, the initial file system was based off of the Minix OS, which had a filename limit of 14 characters and had a maximum file size of 64 megabytes. The extended file system was born when Réme Card discovered that the 6-megabyte limitation was too small to rip MP3s with. Although the extended file system introduced a 255-character limit, larger file support, and increased performance, he was still taunted by the bigger kernel developers down the street. To appease them and keep his lunch money, Réme introduced the ext2 file system. (Okay, so I might be stretching the truth just a little.)

The Virtual File System Layer

The extended file system introduced a virtual file system (VFS), a sort of abstract caching layer that allowed for support of many different file systems. The VFS sits on top of the block-level file system to keep track of which file system is mounted at any one time. Loaded at boot, the VFS has its own virtual inode and block table that corresponds to the underlying file system. Each different file system appears to the kernel itself as ext or ext2 to maintain compatibility.

At boot, the OS loads the root and other partitions, which the VFS interprets. The information about the file systems are either loaded into the kernel or, optionally, as loadable modules for file systems such as VFAT, NTFS, or perhaps Minix. When such a file system is mounted, the VFS reads the superblock information about that file system and maps that file system's topology, associating its own inodes to reference that system. The resulting structure is kept in cache for easier access.

The buffer cache keeps the file access in memory until it's queued to disk. The VFS also keeps track of frequently used directories. The more times a certain directory is accessed, the longer it's kept in memory. The buffer cache also helps manage the asynchronous interface with the block device drivers. If a call is made to write data to disk, the VFS doesn't handle the actual write. That's the job of the underlying file system.

One problem of such an asynchronous system is that it can report that writes have taken place when, in fact, they haven't. This can lead to file-system corruption. In normal circumstances, a user wouldn't have to worry about asynchronous write problems. However, problems do occur; for example, a drive can be forcibly unmounted or the server can suddenly lose power when writes haven't taken place. Those circumstances can lead to data corruption.

Playing with Blocks and Inodes

The ext2 file system, similar to many file systems, is made up of a certain number of blocks that happen to be all the same size. You can determine the amount of bytes per block during file system creation by using the mke2fs command (using the -b switch). Files are created starting on block boundaries. If a file system is made up of 1,024 byte blocks, a 1,025-byte file will take up two blocks. The next file that is created will start on block three, which means most of the space on block two is wasted. This isn't a highly effective means of space allocation, but it strikes a balance between processing time, memory, and file system access time. Blocks are placed in block groups with allocation from 1 to 32 blocks.

Not all the blocks contain simply data. Parts of the blocks are dedicated to inode and block metadata. The *superblock*, which is illustrated in Figure 4.1, contains the basic information of the file system and its components. The superblock is backed up across block groups in case the master becomes corrupted. The superblock contains such information as the magic number, ext2 revision level, number of free inodes, number of blocks per block group, and group size.

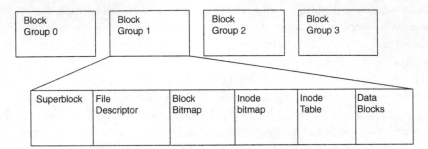

Figure 4.1   The superblock contains the basic
information for the file system and components.

What's in that block, anyway? The magic number for the current version of
the ext2 file system is 0xEF53. This tells the mounting software that, yes, this is
an ext2 file system. The revision level tells the software which features of the
file system are available at any one time. The mount count and maximum
mount count are numbers that determine the number of mounts of any particular file system. The mount count is an incremental number, and when it
reaches the maximum mount count, an fsck is recommended. The block size is
the setting for the number of bytes per block, and valid values include 1,024,
2,048, and 4,096. The first inode record points to the first inode (who would
have thought?), which just happens to be /.

Inodes are essentially records of blocks and files. Each file system unit has a
corresponding inode, with data recorded about file creation, last access time,
user permissions, type of the file, and so on. One inode exists for each directory, link, file, and device on the system. (This means that thousands of inodes
exist, not just one.) The inode stores information records about file types such
as who owns information, the size of the file, last accessed, and the pointer to
the data blocks themselves. By looking at Figure 4.2, you can see that the first
12 are pointers to the first 12 data blocks. If the file takes up more than 12
data blocks, another group of pointers takes over, and the first group will have
a set of secondary pointers, which will point to that extra set. If the file is large
enough, many redundant, as well as secondary and tertiary pointers, can be
used for extra large files. The larger the file, the more pointers there are to the
file and the slower the access to the file. (The file system keeps it in cache, so
the performance isn't too poor.) There's a limit to the amount of inodes in
each file system, so you don't want to overdo it with large amounts of small
files and directories. The inodes, at least in ext2, are created when the file

system itself is created, although it's possible to specify the amount of bytes per inode under `mke2fs` with the `-I` option. Got it? Good. The command `/sbin/dumpe2fs` displays block, block group, inode, and other information about the created file system.

The problem with file systems is that people tend to put files wherever there's free space because putting files where data already exists can be construed as a bad thing. The ext2 file system, which is similar to other UNIX file systems, tries to allocate new files in the same block group or adjacent to other blocks to minimize the seek time. The OS allows only one process to write to the file system at any one time, so it's done on a first come, first served basis. When writing to the block group, the process of doing so locks the superblock so no other process can write to the same place. After the process is done with the file write, it frees it up for another process to repeat (from the *Second Extended File System (EXT2)*; `www.science.unitn.it/~fiorella/guidelinux/ tlk/node95.html#ext2fsfigure`). The kernel also tries to group writes for better performance, as well as block allocation across the disk platter.

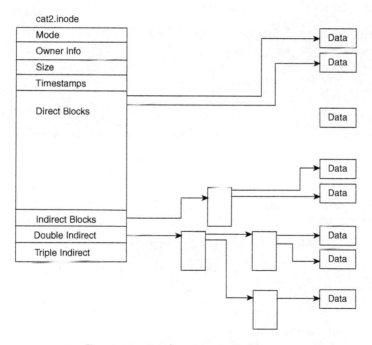

Figure 4.2   Inode structure and layout.

Loopback File Systems

Now that you have a greater understanding of how the ext2 file system works (and pretty much most UNIX file systems in general), take a look at other file systems and see how they differ in structure and design.

A *loopback file system* is a file that can mimic a device and can be formatted with any file system available before being mounted. Entire distributions have been created on loopback file systems, even ones that can start under Microsoft Windows. Loopback file systems enable you to share them over the network as a block device, mount an .ISO image to behave similarly to a CD-ROM, create bootable floppies, burn toast, and change the cat litter.

Creating a basic loopback file system is easy and done with the /sbin/ losetup command. losetup creates and manages loopback devices, after which you can mount, format, and use the file as a file system.

The first thing you need to do if you're using the loadable modules is load the module loop.o:

```
# insmod `path_to_module/` loop
```

Substitute path_to_module with the correct location of your loop.o module, of course. Make the file itself with dd, then tell make it's a loopback file:

```
# dd if=/dev/zero of=/<path_to_file> bs=1024 count=<size_of_filesystem>
# losetup /dev/loop0 /<file>
```

> **Warning**
> Leaving off the count attribute causes the dd creation to use the rest of the entire file system. Be careful and use this at your own risk.

After that's done, make a file system on it and mount it:

```
# mkfs -t ext2 /dev/loop0
# mount /dev/loop0 /mnt
```

To unmount and delete the loopback file, unmount the file system and run losetup against it with the -d switch:

```
# umount/dev/loop0
# losetup -d /dev/loop0
```

Loopback with Encryption

You can add encryption to the loopback file system by running losetup with the -e switch and adding the type of encryption that you want, assuming that you've got the algorithm compiled in the kernel in the first place. For example, use the following:

```
# losetup -e blowfish /dev/loop0 /file
```

Adding encryption to the kernel is a good way to store valuable data in the file system; however, remember that any encryption is dependent on the strength of the encryption scheme itself and the passwords involved. It doesn't do any good to mount the encrypted loopback file system in your HA cluster and make it accessible by a simple .htaccess file. Keep in mind that you might not be in an area that can use all the available ciphers because of export restrictions.

According to the *Loopback Encrypted Filesystem How-To* (www.kerneli.org/loopback-encrypted-filesystem.html), you have to download the kernel patch through FTP at ftp.kerneli.org, in /pub/kerneli/crypto/ <kernelversion>:

1. Patch the kernel.

2. Make config (or your favorite config).

3. Enable Prompt For Development and/or Incomplete Code/Drivers under Code Maturity Level Options.

4. Under Crypto Options, enable Crypto Ciphers and your choice of encryption.

5. Under Block Devices include Loopback Device Support, use Relative Block Numbers As Basis For Transfer Functions (recommended), and General Encryption Support.

6. Recompile the kernel.

7. Run lilo to add the kernel into the boot up sequence.

8. Download the newest source for util-linux from ftp.kernel.org/pub/ linux/utils/util-linux and extract it.

9. Apply the patch that's found in /usr/src/linux/Documentation/crypto/.

10. Read the INSTALL file carefully, and compile and install according to the instructions.

11. Reboot the machine with the new kernel.

12. Set up the loopback as previously described by using the desired encryption.

After that's done, you'll have a decently encrypted file system where you can store sensitive data, such as the antidote to Aunt Lola's fruitcake. Taking things a step further, you can actually use this file for a shared storage cluster solution using the NBD.

Browsing an Image with a Loopback File System
One of the handier things that a loopback file system can do is let you browse image files (.img, .iso, and so on) as if they were a regular file system. This is great if you're trying to set up or edit such things as a boot disk or a CD-ROM image. The creation also is done similarly with losetup. Instead of creating a file with /dev/zero, you simply take the preexisting image and mount that on a loopback device:

```
# losetup /dev/loop0 /home/user/file.iso
# mount /dev/loop0 /mnt
# cd loop; ls
```

The Network Block Device

The Network Block Device (NBD) is essentially a loopback file system that is shared over the network by a daemon and mounted by a client file system. "Ah," you say, "But can't I also do this with NFS?" You can, of course. The NBD has a buffer size of 1.5k as opposed to just 1k for NFS, which translates into faster speeds. This loopback file system can be formatted and used in a software RAID just like any other file system.

First, download the NBD packages from http://atrey.karlin.mff.cuni.cz/~pavel/nbd/. Some versions allow a Microsoft Windows machine to act as a server. Make sure that you get the appropriate versions for both server and client, which are usually encapsulated in a single tar file. If you decide to use the Windows version, you'll have to get the GNU Cygwin tools (http://sources.redhat.com/cygwin/index.html) to compile it on your system.

Uncompress, un-tar the file, and change into the resulting directory. Run the ol' configure, make, make install. make install installs nbd-client and nbd-server into /usr/local/bin. You can easily skip make install and put these files wherever you'd like, although nbd-client has to be copied over to the client machine.

As soon as you have those installed, you'll have to create a loopback device differently than described due to the fact that you'll be sharing it over the network rather than attaching it to a local device.

```
# dd if=/dev/zero of=/mnt/loopback_file bs=1024 count=1000k
```

This creates a loopback file just a bit larger than a gig for testing. Next, initialize the loopback for use across the network with nbd-server. The format is /us/local/bin/nbd-server <port> <filetoserve>. For example,

```
# /usr/local/bin/nbd-server 1024 /mnt/loopback
```

shares /mnt/loopback on port 1024. Next, run nbd-client on the client. Don't try this on only one machine! Severe consequences might result, including being forced to watch endless reruns of "Leave it to Beaver." The syntax is /usr/local/bin/nbd-client <server> <port> <device>.

```
# /usr/local/bin/nbd-client matrix.domain.com 1024 /dev/nb0
```

Next, make a file system on the new device and mount it:

```
# mkfs /dev/nb0
# fsck /dev/nb0
# mkdir /mnt
# mount /dev/nb0 /mnt
```

The Ext3 File System

The ext3 file system is an alternative file system created by Dr. Stephen Tweedie. The ext3 file system is based on the ext2 file system, yet with a forked code base so that development can proceed with a pristine code base in the same kernel. The addition of the ext3 file system to the development tree was made basic so that compatibility can be addressed. The goal of the ext3 project wasn't to make a more efficient file system, but to avoid the problems that a hard shutdown or reboot could cause.

Ext3 introduces another virtual layer similar to VFS, called *JFS*. This virtual layer is an API, responsible for handling the journaling transactions independently of the ext3 layer. Like VFS, it takes block transactions in the cache and executes them in an arbitrary way. It can handle journaling for alternative file structures like loopback file systems or logical volumes, just as long as it's formatted with ext2. Ext3 doesn't know anything about journaling; it passes everything on to the JFS layer. On that note, the JFS doesn't know anything about file systems—that's done by ext3.

This method of implementation enables the user to flip back and forth from ext2 to ext3 just by using mount options at boot.

Ext3 is still in development, as are most of the new journaling file systems. Ext3 has a mailing list and archive at http://listman.redhat.com/mailman/listinfo/ext3-users. The list is quite active, and the developers are quick to respond and share.

Installing and Configuring Ext3

The first thing you're going to do is download the latest kernel source and the appropriate ext3 patches. You can find patches for 2.2 version kernels at ftp.kernel.org, while 2.4 patches are found at www.uow.edu.au/~andrewm/linux/ext3/.

Quick and Dirty Guide to Kernel Recompilation

Kernel compiling is an art. Although it's not that difficult to do, it takes a few tries to get it right without too many errors. For those of you who haven't already done it a zillion times, a little reminder might be helpful to ensure that you know how it's done. The first thing that you have to do is grab the source code from ftp.kernel.org/pub/linux/kernel/<kernel version>/. Next,

```
# cd /usr/src
# rm -rf link_to_linux
# tar xzvf /<path_to_source>/<Linux_src.tar.gz>
# cd linux
#make xconfig # (or config, or..)
save xconfig
# make dep
# make bzImage (or zImage)
# make modules
# mv /lib/modules/ /lib/modules.old
# make modules_install          #don't forget, this is important!
# vi /etc/lilo.conf   #add image to lilo
# lilo                #run lilo to add image to bootup
reboot
```

Uncompress the kernel and the ext3 patch. Change into the Linux directory and run the ext3 patch against the current kernel. When recompiling the kernel, be sure to include "enable second extended FS development code."

Add the new image to lilo, run lilo, and reboot with the new kernel.

You'll have to get an updated copy of e2fsprogs. You can find this at ftp://download.sourceforge.net/pub/sourceforge/e2fsprogs/. Download the program, uncompress, and install it. The install procedures are a little different; you've got to make a "build" directory and install from that. Otherwise, configure, make, make install as usual. Also, for e2fsprogs to work correctly, you must make sure that your fstab fields are set up correctly (that is, six entries instead of four). If the fstab isn't set up correctly, you must add entries to it—perhaps add a few 1s to make up for the difference.

For example, here's a /etc/fstab that has four entries in two of its file systems:

```
/dev/hda1   /      ext3    defaults
/dev/hda2   /boot  ext2    defaults   1 1
/dev/sda1   /export ext3   defaults
```

The first field refers to the block device or remote device to be mounted. The second field is the mount point for the block device. The third field refers to the type of file system. The fourth field refers to extra options associated with the file system.

The fifth field, which is sometimes forgotten, specifies whether or not that file system is to be called during dump. If the field is not present or is set to 0, dump passes that file system and does not call it for a backup. The sixth field, also forgotten at times, specifies the order of preference when an fsck is not present. Although ext3 and related journaling file system don't need to fsck, the entry still needs to be in your /etc/fstab file. Here's what it might look like:

```
/dev/hda1    /    ext3   defaults 1 1
/dev/hda2    /boot   ext2   defaults   0 2
/dev/sda1    /export ext3   defaults   1 2
```

Having the fstab set up this way allows the root file system to undergo fsck first—only if field three is set up with ext2 as an option. The way it stands, it would normally be backed up with dump and would not undergo fsck simply because ext3 handles journaling. The second line refers to the boot partition, which is still set up with no journaling (because it's marked ext2). It will not be backed up with dump, and it has a lesser fsck priority than the root file system. The third line refers to an scsi device mounted on /export and will not generally undergo a fsck simply because it's ext3. It will get backed up with dump, however.

After you reboot and work out the bugs, if there are any, initialize ext3 by creating a journal on it. This is done with tune2fs:

```
tune2fs -j /dev/<device>
```

Mount it with the following:

```
mount -t ext3 /dev/<device> /mnt #or wherever it goes
```

Now, you are completely set up with a journaling file system. The good thing about adding a journal in this method is that you can instantly convert all of your partitions to ext3, including your root and boot partitions. At this point, you should be feeling brave enough to do a power cycle to try out the journaling feature. Go ahead and do a few reads and writes, get some entries in the journal, and hit the power switch. If it's set up correctly, your system will rebound without fsck in a matter of seconds.

A journaling file system is critical when you implement an HA cluster because of the response time while recovering from a crash. Large file systems can take hours to recover, potentially costing thousands of dollars in lost revenue. Although it's still in development, ext3 is still a production quality file system capable of running production applications.

ReiserFS

The *Reiser File System (ReiserFS)* is another alternative file system for Linux that not only introduces journaling, but is also a sophisticated method of allocating inodes that is a departure from the previous ext2 file system.

Hans Reiser, the chief developer, graduated from eighth grade and went directly into the computer science program at UC Berkeley (like most of us). Hans currently runs a company called Namesys (www.namesys.com) where he employs a small group of programmers to write the code for ReiserFS.

ReiserFS uses a balanced tree (Btree) method of creating inodes as opposed to a fixed block method. Similar to the way a relational database handles its data, ReiserFS sorts its data by keys. Because the file system doesn't create fixed block sizes, each file can be placed next to each other with a corresponding inode attached. This means that each file doesn't have to start on a block boundary, saving a great deal of space. ReiserFS also features journaling and support for quotas, which, combined with the tree allocation, makes for quite an improvement over ext2. ReiserFS also has the ability to be resized, depending on your needs.

ReiserFS is designed to be user extended with the use of plug-ins. Currently in development, ReiserFS has plug-ins planned for such things as security, backup, and node and item search.

Remember that, although ReiserFS takes a great leap ahead of ext2 and similar journaling file systems, it does have limitations. Due to the nature of the way Linux dump and restore are intertwined with ext2, they cannot be used with ReiserFS. However, you can still get around many limitations by using GNU tar, which is superior to straight UNIX tar. ReiserFS also has problems interacting with qmail, although a patch is available.

Although it is possible to change your root file system to ReiserFS (and we show you how to do it), you might ask yourself if it's actually worth the trouble. Actually, changing the root file system isn't that difficult. You must understand, however, that the changes you're about to make are to a file system that doesn't see much of a data change and is, therefore, unlikely to benefit much from ReiserFS. You might be better off considering implementing ext3, which simply adds a journal rather than a more complex file system.

Implementing ReiserFS

To implement ReiserFS, you need to recompile the kernel yet again. Be sure to grab the latest copy of the kernel at ftp.kernel.org; ReiserFS will work with 2.2 and 2.4 versions of Linux. As of Mandrake 8, ReiserFS as a root partition was included as a install option, and Red Hat as of 7.1 comes with ReiserFS already compiled. SuSE has included ReiserFS support for quite some time as well. ReiserFS support also is included in the standard kernel release tree as of 2.4.1-pre4, so be sure and see if your distribution includes it as part of its default setup.

Patches for the kernel need to be applied. You can find these at `ftp.namesys.com/pub/reiserfs-for-2.2 or 2.4`. You can apply these with `patch -p0 linux-2.4.5-reiserfs-umount-fix.patch` or similar.

The trick to using `patch` is knowing how to incorporate the `-p` option. The `-p<number>` refers to stripping the number of slashes off of the patch to define the correct destination for the patch. For instance, let's say the filename in the patch is `/foo/bar/baz/boff/woof.c`. If you refer to `-p0`, that will give you the entire patch. Using `-p1` will strip the first `/`, resulting in `foo/bar/baz/boff/woof.c`. Using `-p3` will result in `baz/boff/woof.c`. Do you see how just using a little change in number can affect where the patch will be applied? The wrong number can completely throw your patch off.

If you're planning to use ReiserFS with RAID, be sure you're using 2.4.1 or greater. The folks at Namesys recommend a 2.4 kernel, although 2.2. kernels still work nicely.

After patching the kernel, you need to compile it. If you're compiling it from scratch, include the following (from the configuration page on `www.namesys.com`):

- **CONFIG_REISERFS_FS**—Either compiled in the kernel or insert as a module.

- **CONFIG_REISERFS_CHECK**—Used for debugging.

- **CONFIG_REISERFS_RAW**—Provides a raw interface to the ReiserFS tree and automatically removes aged files. Designed for a backend to Squid.

After configuring and making the kernel, get the latest ReiserFS utils from `ftp.namesys.com /pub/reiserfsprogs/pre/`. Download, uncompress, `configure`, `make`, `make install` as root. You also can download and install ReiserFS utils as an rpm from `http://rpmfind.net/linux/RPM/mandrake/RByName.html`.

After you install the utilities and reboot with the correct kernel, you can format a file system with `mkreiserfs`:

```
# mkreiserfs /dev/<device>
```

The `reiserfs-utils` package contains `reiserfsck` to repair inconsistencies in file systems; `mkreiserfs`, to initialize the Reiser File System on a raw partition; and `debugreiserfs` used to examine the internal structure of a file system.

You also can resize ReiserFS by using the `resize_reiserfs` command. You can either shrink or grow the file system, but be aware that, if you change the file system, the block device doesn't change. This means that you have to repartition or change the partition table of the hard drive underneath. You can remap the partitions with `cfdisk` or repartition with `fdisk`.

You can grow the file system with `resize_reiserfs` without a problem, but if you shrink the file system, you need to make sure to unmount it before doing so. Resizing ReiserFS is done with a size parameter, `-s` and `+` or `-` the size. Take this, for example:

```
# resize_reiserfs -s +1G /dev/sda1
# resize_reiserfs -s -500M /dev/hdb2
```

Installing ReiserFS on the Root Partition

Normally, making a file system on the root partition isn't recommended after the initial install because of the loss of all data on the partition when formatting. However, if your distribution won't format the root partition with ReiserFS before installation, it still can be done—provided you follow a few simple steps. Be careful, however. If you don't follow the procedures here, it might result in loss of data or worse—an unbootable system. It's best to test this first on a system that's not in production.

Make sure your default kernel supports ReiserFS. There's nothing like redoing your entire partition, trying to reboot, and finding out that your kernel won't even support its own file system. That is a bad thing. So be sure to recompile if necessary. It might not hurt to convert the rest of your partitions to ReiserFS before doing this.

Next, `tar` all the data from /bin, /etc, /lib, and /sbin to a spare partition. If you're hurting for space, you can use `gzip` to copy the partitions over. Make sure that you've also got `mkreiserfs` copied to the spare partition. Things might be more difficult if you've installed your system with one big uber-partition and installed everything on there. If you did that, make sure to either copy everything over to a different disk or see that you've got at least a different partition to copy everything over to. This is a destructive process that *will* kill all of your existing data if you don't have it backed up.

Make a boot disk for your system or download a ReiserFS aware image and create a boot disk with that. Using it to boot from, run `mkreiserfs` against your root partition, erasing all the data. You'll also be erasing /bin, /etc, /lib, and /sbin.

Mount the backup partition as a ReiserFS partition and change into that directory. You should be able to un-tar all the data back into the root file system and uncompress if needed. Be sure to run lilo again to get everything set up correctly. Also change the entries from /etc/fstab from ext2 to ReiserFS and make sure that the last two fields for fsck frequency and pass are 0 0. After this, you should be able to reboot and have everything set up properly.

You can also make /boot a ReiserFS partition if you mount it with the - notail option.

The Logical Volume Manager

The *Logical Volume Manager (LVM)* is a method of handling block devices through disk volumes and volume groups. Written by Heinz Mauelshagen of Sistina Software, LVM brings to Linux what companies such as Veritas brought to the UNIX world with their Volume Manager product. LVM brings Linux into the fray, competing head-to-head with the corporate UNIX environments (not that it wasn't there already) and their volume management.

LVM offers the ability to take hard drive partitions and basically make virtual drives out of them. Not only does LVM offer the ability to resize volume groups on the fly, but it also offers disk concatenation, which enables the system administrator to make one volume out of many smaller drives or partitions. In place of /dev/sda1 and /dev/sdb1, you can actually call them "development" or "backup." You also can add or subtract drives into the volume as the need arises. LVM also allows for hot snapshots of data. This is incredibly useful for HA systems that can't be taken down for backups. A snapshot can be taken of a live data volume and be replicated over to a standby volume to back up formerly live data.

LVM works similar to other disk tools because it incorporates another abstraction layer into the mix. The volume group (VG) is comprised of number of physical drives or partitions. The VG presents these as a single drive or resource. On top of that layer, there exists a logical volume (LV), which can be mapped with a logical name that the system administrator can assign. These LVs can be formatted with any file system, including ext3, ReiserFS, and XFS.

Installing LVM

LVM is incorporated in the standard Linux kernel tree as of 2.4.3, although you should still incorporate the latest patches before implementing your production software on it. Unfortunately, implementing LVM requires a kernel reconfiguration.

It's a good idea to follow the mailing lists for a few days before starting an implementation of LVM. There are certain caveats that must be followed for both kernel and file system to play nicely. These are discussed often in the mailing list, and it's always nice to get a feel for possible problems.

You can get the latest source code by FTP. LVM is located at Sistina's FTP site (`ftp.sistina.com/pub/<currentLVMdirectory>`).

You can build LVM against either 2.2 or 2.4 series kernels. If you're going to build against the 2.2 series, you're going to need Stephen Tweedie's IO patch (remember him?) from `www.kernel.org/pub/linux/kernel/people/sct/raw-io`. There's also a LVM patch for the kernel in the PATCHES subdirectory of the LVM distribution. You can apply these patches to the source code with the patch command (`patch p0 <patchname>`).

For 2.4 version kernels, LVM might already be included. You should be able to see a LVM entry in /proc, or be able to run any LVM command with the `-h` (help) switch. You still need to download all the correct patches from the Sistina FTP site. When recompiling your kernel, you need to check the proper settings in Multi-Device Support (RAID and LVM) and compile this in the kernel itself or a module. You'll want namely the Multiple Devices Driver Support (RAID and LVM) and Logical Volume Manager (LVM) Support enabled.

Download the LVM software tools from `ftp.sistina.com` or from a mirror listed on the `http://www.sistina.com`. You'll need to apply the current patches to the kernel, probably regardless of the kernel revision. There is also a patch in the LVM source code for ReiserFS. If you're using ReiserFS, apply the `linux-2.4.x-VFS-lock` patch in the source PATCHES directory. Running `configure` in the top level directory also creates the proper makefile for addressing the patches. In the PATCH/ directory, look in the makefile for the proper location of the kernel (if it's not in /usr/src/linux, you'll have to point it to the right place). Typing **make** from here will create the patches. You'll want to add at least the patch for the current version of LVM, if not the proper patches for the 2.2 or early 2.4 kernels.

Add the proper patches, such as the following, compile, and boot off of the new kernel:

```
# cd /usr/src/Linux
# patch -p1 < /root/LVM/1.0/PATCHES/lvm-1.0-2.4.9.patch
```

Next comes installation of the software tools. That's done within the LVM directory. See if you can guess how to do it? Yes, you're right: `./configure`, `make`, `make install`. But wait—there's more. LVM also comes with a `make remove` script should you want to uninstall.

Starting the software requires two commands: vgscan and vgchange -ay. These have to be placed in the startup scripts, right after / is mounted and before the other file systems are. You can change this in your Red Hat start up scripts in /etc/rc.d/rc.sysinit. Debian users can just make a startup script in /etc/init.d.

Creating Disk Groups and Volumes

After you reboot with the correct kernel, you need to tell LVM to initialize either the disk or the partition. Both are done with the pcreate command. To initialize the entire disk, use pcreate <device> or the partition, pcreate <partition>. For example,

```
# pcreate /dev/hdb
# pcreate /dev/hdb1
```

prepares the entire disk for LVM, while the latter prepares the partition for LVM. Remember that if you're only using an individual partition, set that partition type to 8e; Linux LVM, using fdisk. If your version of fdisk doesn't support 8e, Linux LVM, you would need to upgrade.

After you prepare the disk or partition for LVM, you must create a volume group. To do this, use the vgcreate command and include the disks or partitions that you want to include in the initial volume group. The format is vgcreate <volumename> <firstdisk> <seconddisk> <etc>. For example,

```
# vgcreate myvolume /dev/hda1 /dev/hdb1 /dev/hdc1
```

After creating the volume group, you now have to activate it. Either reboot or reread the configuration with vgchange -an. If you want to reactivate it, you'll do that with

```
# vgchange -a y my_volume_group
```

Run vgdisplay to make sure that everything looks correct. Make certain that this reflects your environment. After you're satisfied with the way things are looking, the next step is to make a logical volume group on top of what we already have:

```
# lvcreate -L1G -nmy_logical_volume myvolume
```

After you make the logical volume, you must format it. Format with your favorite file system, even ext2. According to the documentation, there can't be any spaces after the -n switch, or lvcreate automatically generates the name. You wouldn't want your mother-in-law picking your child's name, would you? This is kind of like that.

```
# mke2fs /dev/my_volume_group/myvolume
```

Mount the volume, and you're good to go:

```
# mount /dev/my_volume_group/myvolume /mnt
```

Instead of just setting up the three disks in one normal logical volume, you can add striping to the disks simply by adding options to lvcreate. For instance,

```
# lvcreate -i3 -I4 -L1G -nmy_logical_volume myvolume
```

The lowercase -i sets up the number of stripes. This reflects the number of physical disks or media in the set. The uppercase -I refers to the kilobytes for the granularity of the stripes.

Resizing a Volume

You can even add to the volume on the fly by using the lvextend command. Running the following will grow the mymount volume to 5 gigs:

```
# lvextend -L5G /dev/mylogicalvolume/mymount
```

The following will grow the mymount volume an extra gig:

```
# lvextend -L+1G /dev/mylogicalvolume/mymount
```

Remember that only the volume here will change and that you'll have to extend the overlaying file system as well. If you're going to shrink the volume, you first need to unmount it and then use the lvreduce command. The following shrinks the volume by 1 gig:

```
# lvreduce -L-1G /dev/mylogicalvolume/mymount
```

If you're going to reduce the volume size, remember that you also have to either reduce the file system on it or reformat it. If you're using ext2, you can use e2fsadm to reduce it. ReiserFS users can use resize2fs. Be sure to unmount it, or weird things can happen as a result.

Removing a Volume Group

Removing a VG is accomplished first with removing the logical volume on top of it. After unmounting the volume, use the lvremove command:

```
# umount /mount
# lvremove /dev/my_logical_volume/myvolume
```

Deactivate the volume group:

```
# vg_change -a n myvolume
```

Remove the volume group:

```
# vgremove myvolume
```

Backing Up with LVM: A Live Snapshot in Progress

LVM offers the capacity to take a snapshot of a live file system at any point in time, then replicating it for a live backup. LVM does this by creating a sub partition inside of the partition that you're going to be making the snapshot of. The volume that is created is a read-only copy of the live volume so that you don't have to take your HA cluster or load balancing solution offline.

A snapshot volume can be as small as you like but only a maximum of 1.1 times the size of the original volume. The volume also has to be large enough to hold the entire snapshot for the lifetime of the backup. If the snapshot volume becomes full, it's unusable, so calculate wisely. Running lvcreate creates a volume group, but the addition of the -s switch tells it that it will be created as a snapshot file system:

```
# lvcreate -L400M -s -n dbsnapshot /dev/hr/database
```

This creates a volume of 400 megs in /dev/hr/dbsnapshot. After the snapshot is created, place it on a mount point:

```
# mkdir /home/hr/database
# mount /dev/hr/database /home/hr/database
```

The volume will be mounted read-only. Take a backup of the file system and then umount it. Remove it with the lvremove command:

```
# umount /home/hr/database
# lvremove /dev/hr/database
```

The LVM is a great addition to any clustered solution because it enhances the Linux block device. Not only can it concatenate drives, but it can strip them for performance. You can resize the groups on the fly—not to mention the capacity you'll have for file system snapshots. This in itself is a great reason to include LVM in any HA cluster—you don't have to take it down for backups.

Sistina Software offers a mailing list for issues regarding LVM. You can subscribe by heading over to http://lists.sistina.com/mailman/listinfo/linux-lvm/.

Summary

The attractiveness of using Linux in a clustering environment really shines as new file systems and methods of handling these file systems become available. The goal of higher availability becomes more easily obtainable with journaling and redundant file systems. These features that you can implement freely within Linux were only available on other UNIX programs for a hefty fee. Although some of these features are still in development, many are suitable for production use.

II

Building Clusters

5

High Availability and Fault-Tolerant Clusters

SERVER DOWNTIME IS GENERALLY A BAD thing. Losing access to vital resources can cost a company millions of dollars in lost revenue, and result in decreased worker productivity. A business or resource that relies on the uptime of a particular service can be crippled by lost connectivity. Imagine what might happen if an application with no redundancy fails.

Let's say that you're the system administrator for a bank in your small town. You create a secure web server to allow the customers real-time access to their bank accounts. Having services such as this potentially allows the bank to grow their business because of the greater freedom it allows customers. But what happens if the web server loses a vital piece of hardware? You have to deal with downtime.

Downtime in a business-critical server environment means that customers can't access their data. Because customers are fickle people, who won't tolerate not being able to access services, they're more than likely to become someone else's customers. Having fewer customers might also lead to a reduction in your labor force, which just might mean the unemployment line for you.

It's imperative to have a backup plan. Each second that your servers are down means lost customers and a halt in productivity. What good is email if your email server is down? What good is a web site if it's not available to your customers? Each minute that you spend rebuilding data from backups or restoring hardware is another minute that your users won't be able to access your services.

That's where high availability comes in. High availability is the science of creating redundancy in every system and subsystem to ensure that a service remains up and available. As mentioned in Chapter 1, "Clustering Fundamentals," the perfect highly available service runs on more than one computer, has redundant networks, a generator, and backup ISPs. A highly available server essentially places one or more backup servers in standby mode, which are able to come online within mere moments after they discover a failure on the primary system. What does this mean to average system administrators? It means that they'll fear their job less because there's always a standby server to take over just in case the primary happens to fail.

Creating a highly available solution to run your application means that you have to decide how much availability is acceptable for your environment. Depending on the design and infrastructure, there's got to be a threshold of acceptable downtime due to unforeseen circumstances. Anything could happen to take down a server or application. Power failures, security breaches, and viruses can all take their toll on a server or network.

Highly available services are measured by percentages of uptime. When designing your solution, you need to decide on a measurement of reliability that you can provide for your network. Having an uptime of 98 percent might be reasonable for a smaller organization that can afford almost three and a half hours a week of scheduled downtime; however, this amount of downtime is unacceptable in most financial institutions or large e-commerce sites. (See Table 5.1.)

Table 5.1 **The Nines of Availability**

Uptime in Nines	**Downtime (%)**	**Downtime Per Year**	**Downtime Per Week**
One (98%)	2	7.3 days	3 hours, 22 minutes
Two (99%)	1	3.65 days	1 hour, 41 minutes
Three (99.9%)	0.1	8 hours, 45 minutes	10 minutes, 5 seconds
Four (99.99%)	0.01	52.5 minutes	1 minute
Five (99.999%)	0.001	5.25 minutes	6 seconds

These uptime requirements are referred to as the theory of nines. If you have 99.999 percent availability, you call it five nines. Having five nines of availability is almost impossible without some sort of realistic redundancy in the form of a high availability solution.

There are different types of high availability scenarios that all involve some kind of standby server. One of the more common scenarios is to have a standby server that takes over when there's a loss of connectivity or service if the primary server fails. You can also use pools of servers that jump at the chance to become the primary, with the remaining working as standby servers. This might mean a different pool of servers being configured to take over when the first pool dies. Finally, you can use a weighted solution that forces the most powerful server to replace the primary, followed by the secondary servers.

Often, such a solution involves some sort of shared storage because of the need to access dynamic data. Unless each server is serving up static data, there has to be some method of storing current data. These servers must be configured to not only gain control of the shared storage, but to relinquish access when the server dies. Following is an example of an optimal high availability configuration that uses shared storage:

Figure 5.1 shows a totally redundant server configuration. There's basically two of everything here, for redundancy. The only single point of failure (SPOF) in this network is the electricity, so it's a good thing that you've got several backup generators, right?

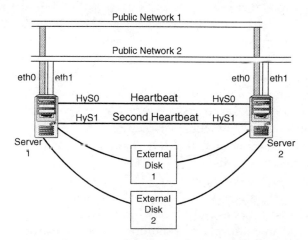

Figure 5.1 Optimal high availability configuration.

Although the servers in this picture might be going a bit overboard, this illustrates the kind of redundancy that can easily be achieved with a little know how and a decent budget. Each server has two interfaces attached to different networks in case one or the other goes down. The interfaces are programmed with a virtual IP (VIP) that can be moved from interface to interface. The servers are attached to each other by means of two heartbeat cables in case one dies. In this illustration, they use two null modem cables on /dev/ttyS0 and /dev/ttyS1. In actual practice, you might install a third network card instead of /dev/ttyS1, for redundancy. Each server has to be attached to redundant external disks. This is necessary for the backup servers to take control of the data after the primary goes down. You also need a second disk group in case the primary goes down. Ideally, these are all connected to a hub by fibre connections or by a shared SCSI bus.

Haven't We Heard of This Somewhere Before?

Hopefully by this time, the idea of redundant systems is firmly placed in your mind. There can never be too many backup systems. There are systems that you can purchase with totally redundant systems; in fact, you can buy an individual system with two motherboards, two power supplies, two controllers per machine, but those systems can get pretty pricey. It's a good thing that you're looking at Linux to provide you with that functionality. And always remember to avoid the SPOF.

Having two servers that can talk to each other, with the understanding that a secondary (or a tertiary) can take over if the primary fails, is a tried and true method for achieving a decent level of high availability. However, any time that you fail over to a redundant box, there are risks involved. Although the servers are set up to monitor each other and fail over to a backup should anything happen, there's always a chance that something strange might happen, which is why it's a good idea to make sure that your servers are filled with redundant architecture. Using redundant architecture can mean dual power supplies, redundant array of disks (RAID) controllers on separate channels, and even redundant network cards on separate networks.

Remember to implement a journaling file system on your drives. Although this added feature might cost a small hit on performance because of journal writes on drives that are constantly accessed, you save a great deal of time when rebooting from a non-graceful shutdown. The experienced administrator remembers the hours spent in front of the computer waiting for large file systems to finish with their fsck checks. Imagine if this happened on a file system that is terabytes in size? Do you remember the discussion of journaling file systems in Chapter 4, "Alternative File Systems"? This is one of the most important things you can do for your high availability systems.

Heartbeat Connectivity

Imagine that you run a business that sells widgets, and that the lifeblood of your business is the online sale of these widgets. Your business becomes successful and you start moving thousands of widgets an hour. And because of the critical nature of your business network, you decide to implement a high availability solution that allows you to keep up your web servers.

Remember that the main feature of a high availability solution is at least one redundant system. The more redundant systems you have, the greater chance you have for recovery if one of those systems goes down. One of the easiest things you can do to develop a high availability solution is to have a totally redundant system on standby in case of failure. When one system goes down, you've got another to take its place. With no other high availability options, you have a backup server to put in place if the primary server fails. Although this is a decent solution to a potential problem, there's no automatic failover.

Without automatic failover, moving to the secondary server has to be done by hand, and if it is done in the middle of the night when nobody is around, it might be a while before someone responds. All of this downtime can result in lost productivity and sales.

Another layer of high availability is adding a way to fail over automatically, if the primary server fails. Any automatic failover device has to have some way of determining if the primary server has lost its ability to deliver services. Fortunately, through the use of a technology called a heartbeat, you can tell if a system is up or down. The heartbeat is either a separate program or included in the primary functionality of the clustered application. Its purpose is to continually poll the servers in a cluster configuration to ensure that they're up and responding. It continually asks, "Are you there? Are you there? Are you there?" If the servers respond with a "Yes, I'm here," the backup servers don't have to do anything. If the backups don't receive a response, the heartbeat has to be configured to take certain steps to bring up the backup server.

Attaching Hardware for Heartbeat Connectivity

For the Heartbeat application to run, it needs a method of contacting the other computers. Theoretically, you can run the application over the same network as the public interfaces, but it's highly recommended that you have a private dedicated network specifically for the task. Putting a Heartbeat on a public network can be intercepted and blocked, which causes automatic unwanted failover. A private dedicated network can take the form of basically whatever you can use to get two computers to talk to each other. Most often, you use a second Ethernet card on each node on a separate private subnet, an infrared (IrDA) connection, or a dedicated serial connection. Because the goal here is high availability, remember that the SPOF is something that is to be avoided at all costs. Therefore, some combination of connectivity between the servers is recommended.

The serial connection is perhaps the most robust route. Attaching a serial cable between servers is relatively easy, in that all you have to do is attach a null modem cable between the serial ports on two computers. This allows for reliable connectivity between nodes. If you have more than two nodes, you can daisy chain the serial ports together by using two serial connections on the nodes. You connect one end to the first computer on the first serial port, and to the second computer on its second serial port. You can repeat the process by hooking a null modem cable from the second computer's first serial port to the third's second port. To test serial connectivity between the nodes, you can set up a quick check after the cables have been strung between the first serial port on each computer. Assuming that /dev/ttys0 is your first serial connection, type the following as the root:

```
# cat < /dev/ttys0
```

Then, on the secondary computer, type the following:

```
# echo "This is a test." > /dev/ttys0
```

On the primary computer, you see a "This is a test." echo on the screen.

You can also build your own null modem cable for connectivity, as shown in Figure 5.2. All you need are two DB-9 to RJ-45 connectors so that you can string normal Cat-5 cable between them. You can build your own connectors by simply making sure that your transmit and receive connections cross, and that Clear To Send (CTS) and Request To Send (RTS) circuits cross.

If you choose connectivity based on an Ethernet route, it is advisable to dedicate a separate Ethernet card with its own internal subnets. You can attach a switch between more than one computer, or a crossover cable if you're simply replicating services over a backup server. You can pick up your own cable from any number of sources, or create your own. Creating your own crossover cable is relatively easy, as shown in Figure 5.3.

	25 Pin	9 Pin		9 Pin	25 Pin	
FG (Frame Ground)	1	—	X	—	1	FG
TD (Transmit Data)	2	3	—	2	3	RD
RD (Receive Data)	3	2	—	3	2	TD
RTS (Request To Send)	4	7	—	8	5	CTS
CTS (Clear To Send)	5	8	—	7	4	RTS
SG (Signal Ground)	7	5	—	5	7	SG
DSR (Data Set Ready)	6	6	—	4	20	DTR
DTR (Data Terminal Ready)	20	4	—	6	6	DSR

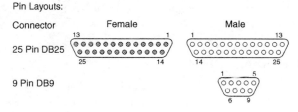

Pin Layouts:

Figure 5.2   Null modem pinouts.

Connector A
Pin 1 - White with Orange
    2 - Orange with White Stripe
    3 - White with Green Stripe
    4 - Blue with White Stripe
    5 - White with Blue Stripe
    6 - Green with White Stripe
    7 - White with Brown Stripe
    8 - Brown with White Stripe

Connector B
Pin 3 - White with Green Stripe
    6 - Green with White Stripe
    1 - White with Orange Stripe
    2 - Orange with White Stripe
    7 - White with Brown Stripe
    8 - Brown with White Stripe
    4 - Blue with Blue Stripe
    5 - White with Blue Stripe

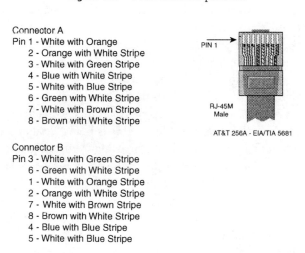

Figure 5.3   Crossover cable diagram.

If you add a secondary network to your computer, you need to add routes so that the computers can talk to each other on the secondary subnet, and keep the primary subnet and the primary gateway. First, bring up the secondary interface with something similar to the following example, (depending on your network):

```
# /sbin/ifconfig eth1 10.0.0.2 netmask 255.255.255.0 up
```

Next, add a route statement that allows the kernel to talk to the secondary network from the secondary Ethernet card:

```
# /sbin/route add -net 10.0.0.0 netmask 255.255.255.0 eth1
```

Be sure to add routes on each computer that has a secondary interface. To test connectivity, perform a straight ping from the command prompt to the secondary interface. It's also a good idea to place this secondary interface in the /etc/hosts table, and optionally, to add a second hostname such as hostname-priv1.

Configuring the Heartbeat Code

You start your examination of a heartbeat with an application called Heartbeat. This program is an open-source application that is found at the Linux High Availability web site (www.linux-ha.org). This application is designed to do IP takeover for any number of servers. Heartbeat can handle both serial and Ethernet connectivity either by crossover cable or a private network. Although most programs that achieve high availability service include a Heartbeat program, this application is designed as a basis for server monitoring, and it serves as the core for other utilities.

Before installing, be sure that you've got the hardware configured correctly, as in the previous section. You need either two subnets over Ethernet or serial ports attached with a null modem cable. As this is being designed for high availability, it is a good idea to include both so that you can avoid the SPOF.

Download the heartbeat code from the web site at www.linux-ha.org/download/. To install, uncompress and type **make install**. There are three files that you need to configure. They are called ha.cf, haresources, and authkeys. These files and the heartbeat code have to be installed on both servers in /etc/ha.d.

First, edit these files, and make sure that only the internal addresses are configured. Don't configure the external addresses yet; Heartbeat does that for you. This means that you select a VIP for configuration. If your external addresses are 138.9.1.1 and 138.9.1.2, you want to make your VIP something similar to 138.9.1.12.

Editing the *ha.cf* File

The following is a sample `ha.cf` file, without comments:

```
debugfile /var/log/ha-debug
logfile /var/log/ha-log
logfacility      local0
keepalive 5
deadtime 30
udpport 694
watchdog /dev/watchdog
bcast    eth0
node     matrix
node     aenima
```

The first two lines tell Heartbeat where to write the debug and log messages to. The third is a resource that configures the syslog.

The `keepalive` parameter sets the time between heartbeats. Because this value allows for a User Datagram Protocol (UDP) connection on a private network, there's no reason why you can't set this value lower; however, you do increase the chances of a potential false reading. If you set it too high, you might lose valuable seconds of uptime.

Deadtime refers to the amount of time to wait before a node is considered dead and failover begins to happen.

The `udpport` setting tells Heartbeat which port to use for UDP communication.

The watchdog parameter always points to `/dev/watchdog`. This is a software implementation of the kernel module softdog. If `/dev/watchdog` is written to, it calls the softdog kernel module and reboots the system. To enable `/dev/watchdog`, perform the following steps:

1. Load the softdog module, `softdog.o` with `insmod softdog` as the root. This loads the module into the running kernel. The location of the module varies, but it should be in `/lib/modules/<kernel number>/misc`.

2. Make sure that `grep misc /proc/devices` is `10` and that `cat /proc/misc | grep watchdog` is `130`.

3. Make a character `/dev/watchdog` file with `mknod /dev/watchdog c 10 130`.

The `bcast` setting tells Heartbeat which port to listen on. In this case, `eth0` is the public interface, while `eth1` is the private, crossover cable-connected interface.

The node listing refers to each node in the cluster. This has to be taken directly from `uname -n`. If you configured your hostname to be something different, use whatever's taken directly from `uname`. More nodes are obviously available, but in this scenario, you only use two nodes connected through crossover.

Heartbeat can also use a serial connection by adding the following settings:

```
serial /dev/ttyS0
```

The serial setting tells Heartbeat which serial port to use for its heartbeat connection.

Creating *haresources*

The `haresources` file has to be the same on each computer, and it's only comprised of one line (after taking out the comments). The only thing it contains is the hostname, the IP address, and the service(s). It should read something similar to the following:

```
aenima  IPaddr::172.16.0.12/8 httpd mysql
```

This tells Heartbeat that the available hostname is `aenima`, that its address is `172.16.0.2` with a `/8` netmask, and that it must stop and restart the `httpd` and `mysqld` processes upon `death/reboot`. Heartbeat looks for these scripts in both `/etc/rc.d/init.d` and `/etc/ha.d/ha.resource.d`. They have to be called with either start or stop parameters passed to them, which is similar to the run-time level scripts for Heartbeat to understand them.

Heartbeat also takes arguments and passes them onto the script, such as `httpd::foobar`, or whatever you need passed onto the initial program, if you need something that has that functionality.

In the case of servers with multiple interfaces, Heartbeat consults the routing tables to determine the shortest route to the other server(s) to be taken over. If there's more than one route selected, Heartbeat chooses the first one.

Setting Up Authentication

The final part of setting up Heartbeat is deciding which version of authentication to use. Heartbeat currently supports cyclic redundancy check (CRC), Message Digest 5 (MD5), and Secure Hash Algorith 1 (SHA-1) authentications. The one that is best for you depends on the resources that you're using. According to the documentation, you want to use CRC if the network you're on consists of a straight crossover cable. MD5 offers more protection, and SH-1 uses better security, although it's got more overhead in terms of CPU.

The only reason that you might need anything but CRC authentication is if you send the heartbeat over a public, non-switched network. Then again, the only resources that are passed are the heartbeat commands. If you care who sees the heartbeats saying, "Are you there? Are you there? Are you there?," you'll want to use SH-1 authentication.

The format of the file is as follows:

```
auth <number>
<number> <authmethod> <authkey>
```

For example:

```
auth 1
1 sha1 this_is_an_authentication_key
```

Authentication keys can be just about anything, but CRC doesn't need an authentication key. In the preceding example, substitute SHA-1 with CRC and leave off the authentication key. The file also has to be set to mode 600.

Starting Heartbeat

Make sure that you've installed Heartbeat on both (all) your servers, and that they're configured with the correct `ha.cf`, `haresources`, and `authkeys` settings. Starting Heartbeat is as simple as running the Heartbeat program and letting it take over.

You want Heartbeat to start at boot time, so be sure to place it in your startup scripts. If you use Heartbeat with the watchdog function, you also need to insert the softdog kernel module at boottime, along with `insmod` and your local startup scripts.

To test it, type `/etc/ha.d/heartbeat` on both servers, or reboot. Check the output of the logs where you've defined them in the `ha.cf` file. Take down one of the servers, and watch the other one seamlessly attempt to take over.

Heartbeat starts the node by looking at `haresources` and bringing up a virtual interface, `eth0:0`, with the IP defined in the virtual interface. When the one heartbeat can't connect to the other machine, it starts up the services as listed in the `haresources` file, and assigns itself the virtual address.

Heartbeat provides a decent solution for monitoring processes and brings a secondary server up if the primary one(s) fail. Not only does this provide a decent failure mechanism for high availability servers, but it also provides the core technology for an entire variety of other Linux-based projects.

Houston: We Have a Problem

The high availability scenario seems rather simple on the surface. One server monitors the other server, and assumes the place of the other server if there's a problem. However, underneath the surface things never run that smoothly. Although there doesn't seem to be much involved in having a server come up when another one is down, doing so automatically, and in a matter of seconds, can be a bit tricky.

In an ideal world, having the time to guess what went wrong and to diagnose the problem is preferable to another server deciding when to do that for you. There's not much of an issue when the primary server fails because of a blown power supply, yet sometimes services appear to be failing when they're not. Sometimes, there's a fine line between what passes between a downed service and one that needs a tweak.

Problems with IP Connectivity

When a secondary server takes over the address of a downed primary server, the traffic destined for that address doesn't automatically follow the IP because the switch has the port in its cache. This causes a lag between fail over and restoration of connectivity. This is affectionately known as the Address Resolution Protocol (ARP) problem. What happens essentially is the following:

Server A is chugging along, happily being the server that could. Server B plays standby, jumping at the bit for a chance to prove itself, similar to a backup quarterback in a playoff game. The silly computer operator, who is too busy watching his latest hentai flick, kicks the power cord out of the primary server and downs his company's web server. But he doesn't have to worry. Server B comes up, takes over, and Mr. Operator doesn't have to worry about missing his flick because it's all apparently seamless.

But behind the scenes, here's what happens. Replaying the scene back in slow motion, you see Mr. Operator kick the cord out of the server while his attention is elsewhere.

Server A instantly goes down. Server B, seeing its chance, starts into takeover mode, after waiting the configured time. After a certain number of seconds, Server B assigns itself a VIP address, and starts the web server. But how does the switch know where to send the traffic?

Meanwhile, back at the switch, it sends an ARP request to find out which address to send the traffic to. It basically asks, "Which machine owns this IP address of the web server?" It keeps asking until it finds a response. The server that holds the IP responds, "Yes, I own that IP address. Here is my Media Access Control (MAC) address, which you know me by." Because each machine has its own unique MAC address, the switch stores it in cache so that it knows exactly which port to direct traffic to.

The problem comes in when the switch has the MAC address in cache, and then the server dies. The secondary server assumes the IP address, yet the switch says, "Um, dude, all traffic destined for this IP goes here." It doesn't know about the secondary server until its cache expires. And that can take upwards of fifteen minutes or so. So the problem then is that high availability isn't so available if someone has to wait fifteen minutes for a service to come back up. You can refresh the cache manually by means of a script, or do it by hand, although that's not a great scenario because it might mean waking up your network administrator at three in the morning. Often, refreshing the cache is the cleanest method of solving the ARP problem, although it might not be the simplest.

So, what can be done about this problem? There are several things, including hacks that can be set up on the fly so that this scenario doesn't happen. One is to have the new interface assume the MAC of the downed server. This method is almost instantaneous, but a problem can occur when the initial server comes back online. It's not as potentially clean as refreshing the ARP tables on the switch. Although Linux itself supports this behavior, you need to find a card that also supports it.

Another possible method is to use Network Address Translation (NAT, discussed further in Chapter 6, "Load Balancing"). A server that uses NAT can act as a front end to a web server or similar service and direct traffic itself, without having a messy switch in the way to second-guess itself. To avoid the SPOF, you also want at least one standby for the NAT server.

Another method is to implement dynamic Domain Name System (DNS) entries. Although this method can potentially solve the problem with assigning different names at servers when needed, the method is rather slow for any amount of true high availability.

Although ARP (not to be confused with AppleTalk Address Resolution Protocol or the American Association of Retired Persons (AARP)) continues to be a problem in achieving high availability, it's not unobtainable. It is something to be considered when dealing with high availability services. The method is up to you; and the amount of uptime that you're willing to sacrifice for a clean transition to a new server.

Shoot The Other Machine In The Head

There lies another possible bump in the high availability roadmap, and that's the possibility that the secondary node might come up while the primary node is still active. There are a few scenarios in which this can happen.

First, if the heart beat cable is somehow disconnected, both machines lose connectivity to each other, and they won't hear a response to their "are you there" query. The primary machine no longer thinks that the secondary machine is around, but that's not much of an issue, as it's already in control of the IP, serving up web pages. Where the problem comes in is when the secondary server can't reach the primary IP and tells itself that it has to take control. You can imagine what happens next. That's right, two machines with the same IP serving up web pages.

Things could be worse. Let's say you've got a high availability situation that has two servers sharing the same storage. Server one is in control of the array, and the heartbeat cable goes down. After the specified period of time, server two thinks that it's supposed to come up and take control of the array, so it mounts the file system and assigns itself the VIP of the primary web server. Now you've got two machines that have mounted the same file system and that have the same IP. This is an almost sure fire way to ensure file system corruption. This is known as a split-brain condition; when both systems are acting independently of each other, and each is trying to take control of the cluster. This is a bad thing.

What can be done about such a situation? Well, you can Shoot The Other Machine In The Head (STOMITH) to avoid the split-brain situation. When the secondary server detects a problem with the primary server, it downs the primary server so that it doesn't come back up. No reboot, nothing. This ensures that the primary server can't come up and try to take over the storage or IP, or if it's still up, that it goes down and relinquishes all resources.

Something else to think about is that, although it's a little slower, you might consider a Network File System (NFS) share rather than a shared Small Computer System Interface (SCSI) solution. This way, having two or more servers accessing the same data won't corrupt the file system. However, if the machine sharing the data goes down, the secondary server has to unmount the data and wait for the NFS to time out. Along with NFS, you might also want to think about a storage area network (SAN) solution. A SAN allows you to access data from across the network for your other applications, and it provides a decent resource for housing shared storage between servers that need to access the same data.

Putting It All Together

Now that you understand what's involved in putting it all together, you can work on an imaginary setup to see just what it takes to put a high availability cluster in place. (This imaginary setup also includes an imaginary budget and an imaginary management, which assumes that money isn't an object.) For this highly available solution, you're going to need at least two servers, dual storage devices for maximum availability, and a mess of extra parts such as cables and stuff to hook everything together. It's also a good idea to have some sort of KVM solution to access the multiple servers, in case anything happens to them. KVM over IP solutions allow you to monitor your machines from anywhere on the network.

The dual storage devices are best served with a hardware RAID that is connected by SCSI or a Fibre Channel interconnect. In case of a RAID controller failure, you also need dual raid controllers. For SCSI devices, consider a single-initiator SCSI bus or single-initiator Fibre Channel interconnects to a RAID array. You need the controller to provide simultaneous access to all the Logical Unit Numbers (LUNs) on the host ports so that a failover isn't seen by the operating system. The trick here is to provide a solution that allows multisystem access to storage. You also need two SCSI controllers or Fibre Channel bus adapters in each system, and cables to connect them. The SCSI cables also need terminators. If you're going fibre, you need a fibre hub or switch unless the storage has two ports and you can directly connect the fibre from the systems to those ports.

On the network side, for full availability, you need three networks. You need two public networks for redundancy on two Ethernet cards, and a third private network for a heartbeat connection. The heartbeat connection can be hooked up with a crossover cable. For a redundant heartbeat network, you need a serial connection with a null modem cable. Remember that each network card has a different IP address, and shares a virtual address between them. Look at Figure 5.4. If your web server address to mybusiness.com is 192.168.0.1 (this is a private, non-routable address, but we're pretending here), you might configure your four network interfaces to be, 0.2, 0.3, 0.4, and 0.5, starting with 192.168. The .0.1 is a virtual address that is attached to `eth0:1` of .0.2 to begin with, but can flit from server to server as it's needed.

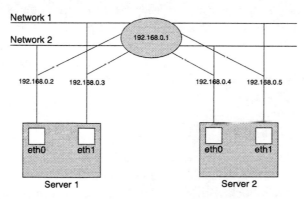

Figure 5.4   Placement of virtual addresses on a high availability server.

You also want to include an Uninterruptible Power Supply (UPS) with as much battery life as you can possibly afford. You won't have connectivity to the humming server if your network goes down. The power supply to the switches and routers has to remain up.

Now that you've got your hardware purchased, you need to configure your servers and start piecing the cluster together. How you do it is up to you; either connect al the hardware at once, or piece it together as you go. The latter might save a little time and effort; however, troubleshooting might be difficult over the long term.

When setting up the initial operating system, imaging technologies can't be stressed enough, if not for initial setup, for disaster recovery. It's recommended to have some sort of image available, whether through Kickstart, System-Imager, Ghost, or some other service or program.

After installation of the operating system, you configure the servers to recognize the RAID arrays, dual networks, internal heartbeat network, and serial connectivity.

Install the services to be run: the web server, databases, ftp sites, and any other services that you plan on running. Make sure they're up and working fine.

The last thing that you have to do is to put a high availability service up to monitor the network. Heartbeat is a decent, basic, open-source solution that works well enough as a standalone product, or integrates well with other products. Consider using a combination of Heartbeat with the Linux Virtual Server, as discussed in Chapter 6, or perhaps with another open source solution such as from Mission Critical Linux. For a non-free solution (which isn't a bad avenue at all, considering the resulting technical support you get with the products), Red Hat sells their Piranha high availability solution, and the Lifekeeper product from SteelEye technologies is recommended. Legato even offers clustering products for Linux.

Summary

High availability isn't all just about clustering programs that can catch a server that has failed over. High availability is the science of ensuring that services are accessible around the clock. Although redundant servers can be made available, it's a good idea to make sure that the initial server doesn't go down in the first place. How can you do this? By incorporating things such as a RAID on the drives, redundant controllers, and redundant power supplies. The more backups you can have in place, the better off you are in the long run.

After the primary server is in place with all the redundant capacity you can reasonably manage, consider a backup server that can switch in at a moment's notice. Often, a secondary server that can switch in is less expensive than a primary system with all redundant parts. This allows you to fix the primary if it ever goes down. If your secondary system goes down, it's time to break out the emergency sysadmin resume kit.

A backup server isn't the single answer to high availability. Remember that, in trying to avoid the SPOF, redundant switches, redundant cabling, redundant routers, and possibly even redundant LANS are all issues when planning high availability networks.

6

Load Balancing

IT'S DAY ONE OF YOUR NEW PRODUCT launch, and your marketing people have done the best job they can of promoting your company's widgets. As system administrator, you've done the best job you can bringing the company's infra-structure up to speed. The web site runs on the latest and greatest multiproces-sor system, and you have a brand-new File Transfer Protocol (FTP) site. You've even been thoughtful enough to put up a chat room so that people can talk about your new widget.

Everything goes well during the first few days of the launch. The word gets spread quickly, and the marketing blitz kicks into full gear. Your servers can handle the load, although traffic at certain times of the day tends to put a strain on both the servers and the network that supports them.

Because of pressure from the venture capitalists, management tells the mar-keting department to come up with an even better plan of attack. They decide to purchase pop-up ads all over the Internet, including sound! And as manage-ment is prone to do, they notify everyone but your department. Your servers are taken by storm because as everyone knows, nobody can resist an annoying pop up, much less one that plays music at you.

"Help us," you cry. "Our servers are overloaded! They just can't take it any-more," you exclaim to your boss.

Seeing that your company broke all their sales goals, your manager decides to increase the budget for your infrastructure (I might be stretching the truth here, management never gives money for extra servers when they're war-ranted). This allows you to buy more servers to spread the load, which allows traffic to be distributed evenly throughout. This results in lower load averages on your servers throughout the load balanced cluster and a raise in salary for your entire staff, just because you read this book.

What Is This Load Balancing Thing, Anyway?

Load balancing takes communications and distributes them across the network. So what does this mean in English? Load balancing can distribute applications across the network. Even though the majority of load-balancing applications handle web servers, load balancing can distribute practically any service across any number of computers and geographic locations.

Traditionally, Hypertext Transfer Protocol (HTTP) requests can only be addressed by the computer that the user or service is accessing without load balancing. For example, if a user sends an HTTP request to a web address, the request is directed to the web server that is specified by the Domain Name System (DNS). Sending a request to www.domain.com is handled by a machine called www. All requests are handled by this machine. Services can be offloaded and distributed by sending subsequent requests to different servers. Services such as FTP are more difficult to spread out, as FTP requests cannot be redirected across different machines. One enables an FTP session to one machine, and that's that.

Sessions are defined by the time that an individual user spends on a particu-lar site. Sessions can be one request, where an individual loads a page from your site and moves on to a different one. A single session can also entail multiple requests as users browse your site. Sites that include e-commerce process data throughout the length of the request, and have to keep track of each session as the user moves through the site. An order placed through a web site shows a session with multiple hits. The user has to browse the catalog, add items to the catalog, and pay for those items. All these sessions must be kept track of.

One can spread out the sessions to different machines by using the round-robin DNS hack, as described in Chapter 1, "Clustering Fundamentals." By associating the same domain name with different addresses, one can spread the sessions across many servers. This brings up several issues; namely that you must have access to either the same file system, or have file systems that had the data replicated across each server to have access to the same data. You can introduce a network-based solution, such as NFS, or implement storage area networks (SANs). You cannot use session management because each request is sent to a different server. The individual server cannot keep track of sessions on other servers, which limits the effectiveness of this type of web serving.

Enter load balancing. With load balancing, requests for services destined for a specific address can be spread across virtually any number of servers. Load balancing can take place across any geographical location, which allows traffic to be managed locally across global regions. Load balancing can be handled by application service providers, routers and switches, load-balancing applications, and Linux.

Most load balancers use some form of admission control. *Admission control* is the process of controlling the rate at which each session is passed onto those services that handle those requests. Basically, it's a way to ensure quality of service (QoS). Under admission control, everyone that accesses these services can optimally achieve sessions in an acceptable period of time. The servers that ensure admission control make sure that everyone involved gets an equal, enjoyable, and uninterrupted experience. Without admission control, everyone's access is processed on a first come, first serve basis, with preference being given to those who have been there a shorter period of time. This is because of the way a web server handles requests.

There are a few methods of enabling admission control in a load balancing device. One is by measuring the number of sessions that a particular server can handle. The load-balancing device or program sends a specific number of sessions to each server that is based on a predetermined number. Another way is for the load balancer to keep track of the CPU cycles of the servers in question. If the server has more CPU to spare, it's interpreted to mean that it can handle more requests.

Zen and the Art of Algorithms

Being able to take the incoming load and distribute it across the cluster farm is only the first step. This question then remains: how best to distribute the load across the different servers? Balancing by load is only one method of distributing requests. The correct method for your organization depends on the type of service that is offered, the size of your network, and the number of computers in your cluster. Many different algorithms exist that allocate connections depending on the topology of the cluster.

Round Robin

One of the easiest methods to distribute services across your load-balanced cluster is to use a round-robin method. This simple method can be achieved with straight DNS, although more efficient methods exist. In a cluster with three servers, round-robin load balancing passes the first request to Server A, the second request to Server B, and the third request to Server C, before starting over at Server A with the fourth request. In Figure 6.1, requests are generated by a single client and spread across three different web servers by means of round-robin load balancing.

This method works well if all your servers are the same, although this might not be a good strategy if you're trying to balance your load across servers with different requirements. If Server A can handle more requests than either B or C, this method is not an effective solution.

Other algorithms include a weighted round-robin solution, which gives special precedence to selected servers. If the server that is weighted is Server B, the requests might be A, B, B, C, A, B, B, C, and so on. Plain round-robin scheduling is similar to this, with all servers having the same weight. Figure 6.2 shows a client requesting services from a weighted solution.

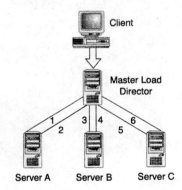

Figure 6.1   Round-robin load balancing.

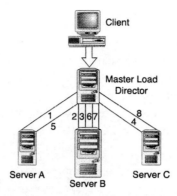

Figure 6.2   Weighted round-robin load-balancing scheduling.

Load-Based Balancing

A load-based balancing solution is arguably one of the more popular solutions. That's why they call the cluster solution load balancing in the first place. Load-based connections can either be measured in processes or connections per server. A load-balanced cluster takes requests and distributes them across the cluster based on the amount of load that a particular server has, and sends requests based on available resources.

A server that uses an algorithm based on load typically has a daemon running in the background, which tells the master load-balancing server about the given resources. This allows the master server to make decisions about each subsequent request for service, which allows for each individual server in the cluster to reach a certain threshold.

Least-connection scheduling balances the number of connections to each server. It relies on the master server to count the connections of each server and distributes them accordingly. This isn't the greatest method when you have machines of different processing capabilities because of limitations with the Transmission Control Protocol (TCP).

There's also weighted least connection scheduling, where you can assign weight to a server that can handle a certain number of connections. Similar to weighted round robin, this algorithm gives a larger percentage to a particular server or servers with connections.

Different load-balancing applications, such as the Linux Virtual Server (LVS) project, offer algorithms for location, and for destination and source hashing scheduling. However, not all load-balancing programs or devices offer such diverse algorithms. When evaluating a load balancing product, decide which kind of load balancing best suits your needs before settling on one that doesn't fit. You'll be thankful later. The next sections show different load-balancing solutions, which cover a variety of solutions—from the quick and dirty load balancer to the eminently configurable solution.

Balance

Balance is a simple TCP proxy that offers round-robin load balancing and failover. This allows for any service to benefit from load balancing, not just HTTP requests. Balance runs on most UNIX platforms, including Linux, BSD, and Solaris.

Balance works by organizing connections into what the developers call channels and channel groups. The default setting is up to 16 channels in up to 16 groups. Balance attempts to route a connection beginning with the first channel in the first group, which is 0. If more channels are defined in the first group, Balance affects load-balancing solutions between the defined hosts.

Balance is a simple load-balancing solution in that it's not stateful, which means that it's not going to keep track of user sessions. Similar to the round-robin load-balancing solution, Balance treats all sessions as single serving sessions, and it doesn't keep track of previous hits. Balance simply plays traffic cop, passing off individual requests to whichever server it's supposed to be load balancing for.

Balance can monitor and load balance any application that connects to a port. It can be either balanced by the port name or by the named reference in /etc/services. You can use popular applications such as Telnet, Secure Shell (SSH) Security, and FTP with Balance to either limit the amount of connections, forward ports, or do simple round-robin load balancing, including failover.

Groups are collections of channels that are designed for failover. You can use Balance to redirect and load balance connections to different servers at any given time. If none of the services happen to be available, you can set up failover groups that redirect the service to other machines. You can also limit the number of connections to any given service. The default setting is an unlimited number of connections, but you can throttle that back to any number you want, even to one session at a time.

Failover is achieved if Balance cannot make a connection to any of the channels in a specified group. In this case, the program defaults to the next group. If all channels and groups are down, Balance shuts down all connections to the specified resource.

Balance can be downloaded from the homepage at `http://balance.` `sourceforge.net` in binary and source rpm format, and as a `.tar.gz` file.

Installation and Configuration

There currently aren't any configuration options for Balance at compile time. To install, uncompress the program, type **make**, then **make install**. The `make` `install` command copies the executable to `/usr/sbin/`, and the man page into `/usr/man/man1`.

You start Balance at the command line, either by a fixed set of options, or interactively. The most basic form of balance is invoked with `/usr/sbin/balance` `<protocol> <address>`. For example,

```
# /usr/sbin/balance ftp ftp.domain.com
```

simply redirects all FTP connections from the balance machine to the server at `ftp.domain.com`. To use load balancing, all you have to do is add another address. For example,

```
# /usr/sbin/balance ftp ftp.domain.com ftp.domain2.com ftp.domain3.com
```

creates a round-robin FTP connection server and spreads them between three hosts.

Balance settings can optionally use different ports on different servers, and specify the default number of connections. The first number after the host is the port, and the second refers to the number of connections that Balance can maintain to the server. Setting `balance 80 host1:8080:10` redirects HTTP requests from the balance server to host1 on port 8080 with up to 10 connections.

Groups are added from the command line by using the ! switch. Following is an example of a load-balanced cluster setup that uses two groups for failover:

```
# /usr/sbin/balance 80 host1::10 host2::10 host3!host4::10 host5:8080:10
host6:8080
```

Using this setting, balance forwards all port 80 requests to host1, host2, and host3 in a round-robin configuration. If the first three hosts fail, Balance uses the second group. Balance redirects port 80 requests to host1, host2, and host3. If Balance has to failover to group two, it uses port 80 on host4, but port 8080 on both host5 and host6. Balance serves 10 connections to all servers each, except for host3 and host6, which are served unlimited connections.

You can also use Balance in an interactive mode by using the -i switch. Adding the -t switch sets a timeout value to the connection before balance decides the host is down. The default value is five seconds.

You can use Balance as a quick and easy method for load balancing. The program is small and lightweight, and extremely easy to set up.

Eddie Mission

The *Eddie Mission* is a load balancing solution for web services, which expands the scope of load balancing from a simple round-robin solution. The goal of the Eddie Mission is to provide open source load balancing on a global scale. Eddie works as a stateful (keeping track of user sessions) load-balancing solution, and is designed to be scalable on the fly.

Eddie is based on Erlang, an open-sourced programming language developed by the Ericcson's Computer Science Laboratory. On a side note, Ericsson uses the language in embedded devices, such as switches and digital subscriber line (DSL) solutions. Because Eddie is written in Erlang, each server that is included in the load-balancing solution must have the language installed.

The Eddie Mission server also works on introducing QoS through admission control. QoS is a networking term that refers to a guaranteed throughput level. Eddie tries to implement this to maintain fast load times, and attempts to redirect to a server with enough of a load to actually process the request within an acceptable period of time. If enough resources are not found, a user request can either be queued or rejected.

Similar to Balance, the Eddie front-end server can detect downed web nodes and redirect traffic to alternate servers if needed. A node can take the IP of another node and process requests for that server. Eddie can be scalable simply by adding entries to the configuration file. Eddie automatically determines the capacity of the server and assigns load requests as needed.

Load-balancing clusters that take advantage of the Eddie Mission environment include an intelligent HTTP gateway package (or front-end master server), client servers, and an enhanced DNS server. The DNS server is based on Berkeley Internet Name Domain version 4 (BIND 4), and is specially designed to load balance a heterogeneous cluster over a large geographically distributed network.

Eddie is targeted to medium to large corporations, or Internet service providers (ISPs). The typical Eddie consumer is someone who houses globally distributed web infrastructures because of the overhead of the DNS server. Eddie supports Apache and Netscape servers.

Installing Eddie

Eddie requires a few components to run correctly. The first thing that you must do is install Ericsson's Erlang. The installation process is discussed later in this section. Install Erlang on each computer that you're going to be load balancing with the Eddie Mission.

You also need the basic Eddie Mission installed on each server. If you're not going to install Eddie on each system, you're left with simple DNS round-robin load balancing.

You also need BIND 4. Unfortunately, Eddie doesn't currently support versions 8 or 9, which can have drawbacks. Be sure to secure your implementation as well as possible, because of potential flaws with BIND 4. Eddie integrates its own server with BIND to affect its enhanced load balancing. Configuring BIND is beyond the scope of this book; one of the best books on the market for DNS is O'Reilly's *DNS & BIND*. Eddie integrates its own enhanced DNS with BIND, which results in a dynamic DNS that helps serve load-balanced requests.

For the configuration to be complete, Eddie also uses an HTTP gateway to direct web requests. Not only does this allow for load balancing, but it also provides a certain amount of fault tolerance as Eddie can reroute requests around downed nodes.

Configuring Erlang

The download site from the Eddie Mission currently only has .rpm binaries pre-built. You can grab the preconfigured binaries at http://eddie.sourceforge.net/erlang.html. If you're the type who wants to build Erlang from scratch, you need to grab it from www.erlang.org/download.html. You can also grab binaries for Windows, Linux and FreeBSD.

To install a binary from rpm, remember to use rpm -i <program name>. Users who use .deb-based distributions such as Debian can use Alien to convert rpms. There's also a great package for slackware that converts rpms, which is called rpm2tgz. Configuring Erlang isn't difficult, although you might be interested in some extra options. To install from source, first download and uncompress the image. Then, you can run ./configure, make, make install. Compiling Erlang can take some time on a slower machine because of the complexity of the makefile. To install, you need GNU make, a GNU C compiler (gcc does nicely), and Perl 5. Optionally, you can build with nawk, openSSL/ssleay for ssl and crypto; Sun's Java jdk-1.2.2 for the interface application; X Windows for gs, sed; and m4.

Compiling the Eddie Mission

You can download the Eddie Mission source at http://eddie.sourceforge.net/ release.html. Grab the latest edition, and uncompress. Change into the source directory, and make sure that Erlang's erl and erlc are in your path. You need these to compile Eddie. These must be installed by default in /usr/local/bin. You can make sure that these are in the path by using the which command (for example, which erl, or which erlc).

Next, type **./configure, make, make install**. Eddie installs into /usr/local/sbin, /usr/local/etc, and /usr/local/lib/eddie. You can change the install prefix directory by adding the --prefix tag to the configure option, as in the following example:

```
./configure --prefix=/usr/src
```

This uses /usr/src as the base directory. Be sure to run make install as root. Make sure that the prefix directories are in your path.

Eddie needs those files for each server that you intend to load balance on. So you can either build that from scratch each time, or use rsync to transfer the files from one computer to the others. You also must have SSH installed on each machine with authorization keys installed for each user that is running Eddie, or use remote shell protocol (rsh) enabled with .rhosts for each user. Be sure that Eddie is in the user's path.

Configuring the Enhanced DNS Server

The server that runs the DNS server needs to have Eddie on it. You also need the special Eddie Enhanced DNS configuration file for load balancing, lb_dns.boot. A template is found in $DNS_ROOT/examples/.

```
## Example of a load balancing DNS boot file.
#
Port 4567
Cookie YourSecretCookieHere
TTL 123
#
Netmask 173.20.128.0/24
Netmask 173
#
Domain www.foobarcorp.com
Domain www.foobarcorp.com.au
```

Eddie uses the port listed here to listen for load information for other load-balanced servers in the network. This same port has to be enabled in the default Eddie configuration.

The Cookie information tells Eddie to check the md5 signatures on the load data that were sent to it for security.

Time to live (TTL) refers to a setting for load-balanced domains. According to the documentation, you have to balance your TTL between short-term changes and constant refreshes against your DNS.

The third entry refers to the subnet(s) that Eddie accepts changes from. Eddie accepts several network parameters. If you don't enter a valid network with the netmask parameter, Eddie cannot accept load information.

The last entry is the list of domains for which Eddie can load balance. The domains entry can take simple wildcard notation for finer granularity.

With that simple configuration done, the enhanced DNS server can be started with the lbdns command. Be sure that you've already got BIND 4 configured and running. The syntax for lbdns is the following:

```
lbdns [-b Boot-file] [-p Port] [-l ConfigFile ] [-i Directory] [-d Level] [-rv]
```

For example,

```
# lbdns -l lb_dns.boot
```

sets up load balancing by using the configuration in the lb_dns.boot file. Using the other options allows you to specify alternate DNS ports, alternate named.boot files and log directories.

```
# lbdns -b /var/named/named.boot -l /etc/lb_dns.boot -i \ /var/tmp/ -r
```

This uses the DNS file named.boot with the configuration file lb_dns.boot. The -i switch tells Eddie to use the alternate logging directory /var/tmp. The -r switch restarts the server if something happens.

Configuring the HTTP Gateway

After the enhanced DNS portion is completed, it's time to configure the next portion of the Eddie Mission, namely, the enhanced HTTP gateway. You can, of course, install this portion first; however, both must be completed before you have a working Eddie Mission load balancer.

Although it's possible for the gateway to run on one of the web servers, it's recommended to dedicate a master node to it because of the effectiveness of the admission control.

The HTTP gateway uses three configuration files: a .conf, .mig, and .gate, each stored in /etc/eddie/. If this directory doesn't exist, you can either make one, or point the configuration files somewhere else. These files are an Eddie configuration file, a configuration file for the gateway, and a migration configuration file.

Eddie Main Configuration File

This file is the master configuration of the Eddie Mission load-balancing server. Although not a complex file, it tells the HTTP gateway where to find its initialization files and how to start itself up.

Following is a sample configuration file, as shown in the documentation:

```
## Sample Configuration File
Cookie=YourSecretCookieHere
MnesiaDirectory=/usr/tmp
CallbackDirectory=/usr/local/lib/eddie/conf
DNSonly=false
ClusterConfig=/etc/eddie/eddie.mpg
GatewayConfig=/etc/eddie/eddie.gate
```

Remember that Eddie uses the cookie information between the nodes for security information. Keep the cookie name the same as in the DNS configuration file.

The next lines specify where the Mnesia database is located, along with the directory for callback modules that Eddie uses. The DNSonly line specifies if the program is to run in Enhanced DNS only.

The last two lines specify where the cluster configuration and the gateway configuration files lie.

Eddie Gateway Configuration

The Gateway configuration basically tells Eddie how to interact with the back-end web servers. Its job is to tell the HTTP gateway how to implement the admission control, and sets up which ports to talk to the web servers on. This configuration takes a format similar to XML, with the sections encased in brackets. Following is a sample configuration from the documentation at the site http://eddie.sourceforge.net/txt/Gateway_Install_1.3.1.html:

```
#------------------------------------------------------------------
# File    : ex3.gate
# Purpose : A configuration with one front end running on europa,
#           one back end running on eva and one back end running on erika.
#------------------------------------------------------------------

<Frontend http>

 ProtocolModule http

 <EndpointConfig http_tcp>
 Port 80
 ReadTimeout 480
 KeepAliveTimeout 20
 ExternalProxy /usr/local/lib/eddie/bin/relay @control_port @ip @port
 </EndpointConfig>
```

```
AdmitControl true
AdmitTime 600
AdmitAlways 150.236.14.*
AdmitNever 150.236.20.*
AdmitQueuePlaces 1000
AdmitMaxSessions 100
AdmitBlockedPage /eddie_admit_blocked
AdmitRejectPage /eddie_admit_reject
AdmitQueuePage /eddie_admit_queue

<Erlets admit_control>
<Erlet erlet_admit_ctrl>
</Erlet>
        </Erlets>

<Erlets status>
<Erlet erlet_status>
</Erlet>
</Erlets>

<Backend http_tcp eddieBE@eva>
<Schedule>
Patterns uri /
Proxy 10.0.1.171 8001
</Schedule>

<Schedule>
Patterns uri /eddie_status
Erlets status
</Schedule>

<Schedule>
Patterns uri /eddie_admit
Erlets admit_control
</Schedule>
</Backend>

<Backend http_tcp eddieBE@erika>
<Schedule>
Patterns uri /
Proxy 10.0.1.170 8001
</Schedule>

<Schedule>
Patterns uri /eddie_status
Erlets status
</Schedule>
```

```
<Schedule>
Patterns uri /eddie_admit
   Erlets admit_control
   </Schedule>
   </Backend>
   </Frontend>
```

The endpoint configuration file listed is responsible for handling sockets, and tells what ports to listen in on.

The next section handles admission control, which guarantees service if the servers become overloaded. The AdmitControl attribute handles whether the attribute is used, and secondly, which clients already admittedly have access to the server. An admit time of 600 seconds gives the user 10 minutes to browse your site before being passed through the admission control again. Adjust as necessary. The admit control attribute always bypasses admission control and ensures that the IPs listed are always granted access.

The AdmitBlocked page is shown to the user if he or she is not accepted because of the AdmitNever directive. Likewise, the AdmitRejectPage directive is shown to the user if the admission control is put in place because of high overhead and the user is rejected. It's a good idea to make this file as small as possible because of already high bandwidth concerns. You don't want a reject message taking up too much of your already high bandwidth. If a client is placed in the queue, the client is sent the AdmitQueuePage. Eddie assumes that it's sending a cgi script while the session is placed in queue.

Eddie also needs a configuration directive for each of the back-end nodes. All nodes need to start with a lowercase letter because of limitations in Erlang.

IP Migration Configuration

The IP migration configuration file tells Eddie which DNS server(s) exist, and keeps information on all the nodes and how they cluster in failover groups. Following is a sample configuration from the documentation:

```
#------------------------------------------------------------------------
# File    : ex2.mig
# Purpose : A configuration with one front end running on europa
#           and one back end running on eva.
#------------------------------------------------------------------------

DNSServer eddieware.org 4567

<Node eddieFE@europa>
 Interfaces eth0
 LoadThreshold 0.8 2.0
 </Node>
```

```
<Node eddieBE@eva>
 Interfaces eth0
 LoadThreshold 0.8 3.0
</Node>

Netmask 255.255.255.255

<Cluster www0101.eddieware.org>
 ClusterType Frontend

 FailoverNodes eddieFE@europa
 BackendClusters backend0101.eddieware.org

 <Server eddieFE@europa>
   AutoConfig On
   Interface eth0
   IPAddress 10.0.0.164
   Port 80
   Start generic module eddie start @IPAddress @Port http
   Stop generic module eddie stop @IPAddress @Port http
 </Server>
</Cluster>

<Cluster backend0101.eddieware.org>
 ClusterType Backend

 <Server eddieBE@eva>
 AutoConfig Off
 IPAddress 10.0.1.171
 Port 8001

 Start generic exec /usr/local/lib/eddie/bin/start_httpd @IPAddress @Port
  /usr/sbin/httpd /usr/local/lib/eddie/conf/conf

 Stop generic exec /usr/local/lib/eddie/bin/stop_httpd @IPAddress @Port

 </Server>
</Cluster>
```

The first thing that you must put in your configuration file is the names of your enhanced DNS servers. Secondly, the names of the web back ends have to be defined, along with their interfaces. The Netmask directive determines which machines are allowed to communicate.

Eddie has two types of clusters: front and back end. The front-end clusters are set up as the gateways and they direct traffic to the back-end clusters, which are the web servers. These configuration directives map front-end to back-end clusters.

Initializing Eddie

Starting the gateway can be done by running `eddie`. You can also start Eddie in verbose mode with `eddie start -v`. Stopping all Eddie nodes can be done with `eddie stop`, or you can stop a single Eddie node with `eddie stop <node name>`. Another node cannot be added on the fly; you have to stop and restart Eddie. Entering `eddie status <nodename>` enables you to find the status of a single node.

Linux Virtual Server

The goal of the Linux Virtual Server project (LVS) is to build "highly scalable and high available network services." LVS encompasses a group of solutions that provide mission-critical applications a framework to achieve load balancing and high availability. LVS provides load balancing by implementing either Network Address Translation (NAT), IP tunneling, or direct routing (DR).

The virtual server in LVS is described by the master node, or director, which serves requests to more than one machine in the back-end cluster. The LVS load balancer can handle requests in a local-area network (LAN), or a large, dispersed wide-area network (WAN).

LVS makes use of the IPVS kernel module to multiplex incoming TCP/IP connections to back-end servers over Layer-4 topology. LVS can handle load balancing over multiple ports such as FTP, Telnet, and common HTTP requests. Although LVS doesn't need a sophisticated program to implement load balancing, a kernel recompile is necessary if your distribution doesn't already have it enabled.

Sites such as www.linux.com, www.sourceforge.net, www.valinux.com, and others all use LVS for their public infrastructure.

Load Balancing by any Other Method

LVS implements load balancing through NAT with a single, public IP that is accessible from the public Internet or LAN, while serving requests over a cluster of servers in an internal network. Packets from these internal servers are translated into the public IP at the NAT machine.

Although effective for a small number of translated servers, as the cluster begins to increase in load, it starts to put a strain on the server that is doing the translation. Each packet header has to be re-written with the public IP. One way to solve this problem is to have multiple load-balanced clusters accessible by either a simple round-robin DNS solution, or by having a cluster of LVS clusters accessible through a master node.

LVS implemented through IP tunneling is similar to NAT, in that the master director is the only server to have a public IP, with the rest of the cluster nicely residing with their own private address, safe from public routing. The difference is that instead of sending the resulting packet through the master node to be re-written, the packet is sent directly back to the clients. This method saves the master node valuable processing time, which enables it to route more requests to the internal network.

The direct routing approach to LVS saves even more overhead, but it requires that all the servers share a physical network segment. There isn't much overhead between the network or the master node, yet it allows for greater scalability.

Implementing LVS

For the initial install of LVS, you need a minimum of four machines; a director, at least two back-end servers, and a client to simulate actual requests. You need the client machine to handle testing and troubleshooting; after the installation works, it's not needed. Others can supply their own clients.

The kernel module can be downloaded from www.linuxvirtualserver.org/software/index.html. You can find patches for either 2.4 or 2.2 series kernels. The good thing is that only the master director needs to be patched. You can grab the latest source kernel from ftp.kernel.org, as the source in your distribution might already have the patch applied. If you try to patch an already patched kernel, you get errors, and won't be able to completely redo your kernel. According to the LVS mini-HOWTO (www.linuxvirtualserver.org/Joseph.Mack/mini-HOWTO/LVS-mini-HOWTO-4.html), the kernel options for 2.2 are different from 2.4. Following are the options that you must select to enable LVS:

```
    [*] Kernel/User netlink socket
            [*] Routing messages
            < > Netlink device emulation
    *       [*] Network firewalls
            [*] Socket Filtering
            <*> Unix domain sockets
    *       [*] TCP/IP networking
            [*] IP: multicasting
            [*] IP: advanced router
            [ ] IP: policy routing
            [ ] IP: equal cost multipath
            [ ] IP: use TOS value as routing key
            [ ] IP: verbose route monitoring
            [ ] IP: large routing tables
            [ ] IP: kernel level autoconfiguration
```

```
*            [*] IP: firewalling
             [ ] IP: firewall packet netlink device
*            [*] IP: transparent proxy support
*            [*] IP: masquerading
             --- Protocol-specific masquerading support will be built as modules.
*            [*] IP: ICMP masquerading
             --- Protocol-specific masquerading support will be built as modules.
*            [*] IP: masquerading special modules support
*            <M> IP: ipautofw masq support (EXPERIMENTAL)
*            <M> IP: ipportfw masq support (EXPERIMENTAL)
*            <M> IP: ip fwmark masq-forwarding support (EXPERIMENTAL)
*            [*] IP: masquerading virtual server support (EXPERIMENTAL)
*            (12) IP masquerading VS table size (the Nth power of 2)
*            <M> IPVS: round-robin scheduling
*            <M> IPVS: weighted round-robin scheduling
*            <M> IPVS: least-connection scheduling
*            <M> IPVS: weighted least-connection scheduling
*            [*] IP: optimize as router not host
*            <M> IP: tunneling
             <M> IP: GRE tunnels over IP
             [*] IP: broadcast GRE over IP
             [*] IP: multicast routing
             [*] IP: PIM-SM version 1 support
             [*] IP: PIM-SM version 2 support
*            [*] IP: aliasing support
             [ ] IP: ARP daemon support (EXPERIMENTAL)
*            [*] IP: TCP syncookie support (not enabled per default)
             --- (it is safe to leave these untouched)
             < > IP: Reverse ARP
             [*] IP: Allow large windows (not recommended if <16Mb of memory)
```

For the 2.4 kernel version, the following options are enabled:

```
<*> Packet socket
[ ]    Packet socket: mmapped IO
[*] Kernel/User netlink socket
[*]    Routing messages
<*>    Netlink device emulation
[*] Network packet filtering (replaces ipchains)
[*]    Network packet filtering debugging
[*] Socket Filtering
<*> Unix domain sockets
[*] TCP/IP networking
[*]    IP: multicasting
[*]    IP: advanced router
[*]    IP: policy routing
[*]    IP: use netfilter MARK value as routing key
[*]    IP: fast network address translation
[*]    IP: equal cost multipath
[*]    IP: use TOS value as routing key
[*]    IP: verbose route monitoring
[*]    IP: large routing tables
```

```
[*]    IP: kernel level autoconfiguration
[ ]    IP: BOOTP support
[ ]    IP: RARP support
<M>    IP: tunneling
< >    IP: GRE tunnels over IP
[ ]    IP: multicast routing
[ ]    IP: ARP daemon support (EXPERIMENTAL)
[ ]    IP: TCP Explicit Congestion Notification support
[ ]    IP: TCP syncookie support (disabled per default)
IP: Netfilter Configuration  --->
IP: Virtual Server Configuration  --->
< >    The IPv6 protocol (EXPERIMENTAL)
< >    Kernel httpd acceleration (EXPERIMENTAL)
[ ] Asynchronous Transfer Mode (ATM) (EXPERIMENTAL)
```

The configuration from the mini-HOWTO suggests that you pretty much run
everything as a module:

```
<M> virtual server support (EXPERIMENTAL)
[*]    IP virtual server debugging (NEW)
(12)   IPVS connection table size (the Nth power of 2) (NEW)
       IPVS scheduler
<M>    round-robin scheduling (NEW)
<M>    weighted round-robin scheduling (NEW)
<M>    least-connection scheduling scheduling (NEW)
<M>    weighted least-connection scheduling (NEW)
   <M>    locality-based least-connection scheduling (NEW)
   <M>    locality-based least-connection with replication scheduling (NEW)
   <M>    destination hashing scheduling (NEW)
   <M>    source hashing scheduling (NEW)
          --- IPVS application helper
   <M>    FTP protocol helper (NEW)
```

For the netfilter section, you need to enable the following:

```
<M> Connection tracking (required for masq/NAT)
<M>    FTP protocol support
<M> Userspace queueing via NETLINK (EXPERIMENTAL)
<M> IP tables support (required for filtering/masq/NAT)
<M>    limit match support
<M>    MAC address match support
<M>    netfilter MARK match support
<M>    Multiple port match support
<M>    TOS match support
<M>    Connection state match support
<M>    Unclean match support (EXPERIMENTAL)
<M>    Owner match support (EXPERIMENTAL)
<M>    Packet filtering
<M>    REJECT target support
<M>    MIRROR target support (EXPERIMENTAL)
<M>    Full NAT
<M>    MASQUERADE target support
```

```
<M>    REDIRECT target support
<M>    Packet mangling
<M>    TOS target support
<M>    MARK target support
<M>    LOG target support
< >    ipchains (2.2-style) support
< >    ipfwadm (2.0-style) support
```

Next comes the install of `ipvsadm`, which is the user interface to LVS. You can grab `ipvsadm` from the software page of LVM at `www.linuxvirtualserver.org/software/index.html`. To install, uncompress it, change into the resulting directory, and type **make install**. Be sure that you've already rebooted with the new kernel or the install will fail.

You also have to get the configure scripts from the LVS web site, which is the same URL that's shown in the previous paragraph. These are a set of Perl scripts that configure the LVS code. Unfortunately, the scripts need extra modules not included in the code distribution.

You also need to get `Net::DNS` for one, which is a Perl module that enables you to make DNS queries. You can find `Net::DNS` at `www.perl.org/CPAN/modules/by-module/Net/`. Download and uncompress the file. `Net::DNS` requires Perl 5.003 or higher, and IO-1.15. To install the Perl module, use the following:

```
# perl Makefile.PL
# make
# make test
# make install
```

Perl complains if the modules aren't correct.

Configuring the Director

Within the Perl script directory lies a configure script that you use to configure the version of LVS; either NAT, IP forwarding, or DR. Included in the current release of the scripts lie pre-written configure scripts that you can use to try out different aspects of LVS. These scripts include preconfigured configurations of both NAT and DR load balancing.

To set up LVS, you must configure it with either one of these pre-configured scripts or create your own. To use a pre-configured script, look in the `perl` directory that you downloaded and select one of those. The syntax for configuring LVS is `./configure <script>`. If you set up your kernel correctly, it installs without a problem.

Setting Up LVS to Use NAT

A basic NAT model needs at least three computers to install everything on, and at least one other computer to try out the configuration. This sample configuration uses the ability of the Linux kernel to rewrite packets that access two internal web servers. For this example, you configure the LVS cluster to use HTTP.

You need to make your cluster with the master director having only one interface card with two IPs; one being an alias.

As in a normal NAT setup, the two internal web servers must have the director's IP assigned as their primary gateway. Both web servers also must have a web server up and running, preferably with slightly different content so that you can see to which server you're attaching.

In this configuration, you assign the primary external address as 138.9.200.20 (eth0:1). The internal address on the primary server is 172.16.0.1, and the two internal web servers are 172.16.0.2, and 172.16.0.3, respectively. You set up a configure file to reflect the configuration called lvs_nat.conf, or something similar. The following example is from the LVS mini-HOWTO:

```
#----------lvs_nat.conf---------------
LVSCONF_FORMAT=1.0
LVS_TYPE=VS_NAT
INITIAL_STATE=on
CLEAR_IPVS_TABLES=yes
#note: VIP, netmask, broadcast are from a /24 network (unlike VS-DR)
VIP=eth0 138 9.200.20 255.255.255.0 138.9.200.255
DIRECTOR_INSIDEIP=eth0:1 172.16.0.1 172.16.0.0 255.255.255.0 172.16.0.255
DIRECTOR_GW=172.16.0.254
SERVICE=t http rr 192.168.1.2:http 192.168.1.3:http
SERVER_NET_DEVICE=eth0:1
SERVER_GW=172.16.0.1
#----------end lvs_nat.conf------------
```

This configuration tells the configuration file which servers are included in the cluster, and defines the netmasks, the broadcasts, and the network configuration. To get the ball rolling, you need to run it through the configure script. Enter ./configure lvs_nat.conf after you save the configuration to a file. You also have to run lvs_nat.conf on each of the two web servers that you've got clustered.

Run ipvsadm after that.

Bring up the director's address with a web browser. Now hit Shift Refresh. If you installed everything correctly, you can see the other web server's content. If you still see the primary server's content, consider running ipvsadm again.

LVS NAT for Telnet

You can also use LVS NAT with other services, such as Telnet. Instead of using the exact configuration previously shown, substitute the service line with one that looks similar to the following:

```
SERVICE=t telnet rr 192.168.1.2:telnet 192.168.1.3:telnet
```

You have to rerun ./configure lvs_nat.conf before running it as an executable on each server that is included in the cluster. After that, run ipvsadm on the director, and you can Telnet right to the director and have it load balanced to each server.

LVS supports all major versions of load balancing, such as round-robin scheduling, weighted round-robin scheduling, least-connection scheduling, weighted least-connection scheduling, locality-based least-connection scheduling, destination hashing scheduling, and source hashing scheduling.

The nice folks at VA Linux have written a graphical front end for configuring LVS. You can find either a .tar.gz- or .rpm-based tool at www.ca.us.ver-genet.net/linux/lvs-gui/. Currently, the only LVS method supported is the direct routing approach. Netparse, a throughput testing tool for LVS, is at http://linuxvirtualserver.org/~julian/.

Summary

Although this isn't a complete list of possible solutions for load balancing with Linux, a brief explanation of load balancing and how you can effectively use it was presented. The master nodes of any of these load balancers can easily be turned into a redundant, highly available load-balancing server with the use of any HA code discussed in Chapter 5, "High Availability and Fault-Tolerant Clusters."

Plenty of decent hardware devices and applications can do the job of the Linux server, and with much greater efficiency. Load-balancing networks and ISPs that perform global load balancing are also good and should be considered for large networks, although they're not typically as Linux solution.

7

Distributed Computing

DISTRIBUTED COMPUTING IS THE ABILITY to run various jobs through the processing power of primarily heterogeneous environments. Although distributed computing can easily be covered under homogenous systems, what differentiates parallel computing from distributed computing is that it's not necessarily tied to one type of machine or dedicated cluster.

To illustrate this fact, imagine that you're going to the store to get some milk. It's right after work and the store is crowded. Not only do you have to fight your way through the back forty to find an open spot in the parking lot, but you have to walk all the way to the back of the store to get your single bottle of milk. When you get back to the front of the store you realize that there's only one checkout stand! So, there you are, with your one bottle of milk, behind all these people who have crammed their carts chock full of food. The line crawls along.

Enter the distributed computing model. With distributed checkout, the store has numerous checkout lines, which enables each person to go to the shortest line and speed through without worrying about their milk spoiling.

Distributed computing works in exactly the same way. Instead of a single overly large computer doing all the processing, chunks of data are broken up for several systems to process. The data is distributed throughout the computer farm, depending on the ability of the individual processor to process units of data. As soon as a computer finishes processing the data, it sends the results back to the master server and is offered a new packet. Of course, the faster the computer, the faster it can burn through data and receive new packets. Distributed computing can speed up processing by enabling computers to share in the workload of one or more jobs. Unlike parallel computing, some distributed models are designed to handle the unused CPU cycles of several machines; many of which aren't dedicated to a single task. Other distributed models are similar to parallel computing methodologies, in which the environments are primarily homogenous and dedicated. In theory, you can harness the power of every spare computer in your workforce after hours to play Quake. Business models that most profit from this form of computing are those that require an amount of processing power that is too large for a single dedicated machine. This is what makes distributed computing so attractive; you don't have to purchase a million dollar server. Chances are, your company has enough computing resources right under its nose. You just have to learn how to take advantage of all the wasted CPU cycles. Financial institutions, oil companies, pharmaceutical companies, and even the census bureau can all benefit from this technology.

The beauty of distributed computing is that it can perform its processing either in the background, or it can wait until a specified period of idle time has elapsed before spawning. A common method of harnessing idle processing is to embed the distributed application into a screensaver. Not only does this ensure that the computer is idle, but it also gives the user a sense that their computer is actually doing something productive. When the user returns to their workstation, the application stops, returns control to the user, and waits again for the specified idle time.

One For All, and All For One

The massive growth of the Internet and the availability of low cost, high speed processing power has spawned a multitude of projects that follow the distributed model. Any project that requires a massive amount of number crunching can be made into a popular project. All that a project needs is a large number of volunteers who are willing to share their idle processing time, a way of transmitting the data back and forth, and a server that's dedicated to putting all the units together.

The projects shared here are indicative of how individuals, companies, and non-profit organizations can use the Internet as a massive distributed computer.

Distributed Net

Taking part in a project with a cow as a mascot might seem like a silly idea at first, but the folks at Distributed Net share in many of the Internet's more popular distributed projects, such as cracking encryption. The goal of Distributed Net is to popularize and further the notions of distributed computing by offering several projects at once and optionally sharing prizes to the individual or team that processes the winning data.

Distributed Net works on such projects as the RC5 challenge, which is currently involved in finding a key with 2^{64} combinations. The Optimal Golomb Ruler project, which searches for certain mathematical pairs, is running at over 182 billion nodes a second.

You can download the distributed net application for almost any operating system, including Linux, BEOS, VMS, IBM OS/390, and QNX. You can find and download the client at `www.distributed.net/download/clients.html`.

Search for Extraterrestrial Life

You too can join your friends in the search for extraterrestrial life by using the wonders of distributed computing technology. No longer do you have to invest millions in your own radio telescope. With SETI at Home, you can use your computer to analyze seemingly random noise in the hopes of discovering an entire new civilization that is too far away for any physical contact.

The SETI at Home project works in a distributed manner by using data taken from the Arecibo radio telescope in Puerto Rico and sending out the different packets to host computers that are participating in the program. The host program runs as a screensaver while analyzing the data. Most of the processing power that is needed by the distributed clients is spent micromanaging the data and separating known sounds from other white noise. Unfortunately, the Arecibo telescope is only able to sample a fraction of the sky, and because of the popularity of the program, the same data has been sent out multiple times for analysis.

You can find the SETI at Home project at `http://setiathome.ssl.berkeley.edu/`, including a client for Unices. The current project isn't multi-threaded, so it won't support symmetric multiprocessor (SMP) machines, nor does it benefit each user to distribute it, or run the data in parallel.

Using Distributed Computing to Fight AIDS

Although it's not a Linux distributed computing program, the folks at fight-aids@home are using distributed computing methods to process data to achieve a greater understanding of how genetics play a role in our lives. As the title states, one of the projects involved uses distributed computing to assist in AIDS research.

Fightaids@home uses distributed computing software from Entropia (www.entropia.com) software, which processes data to collect information for potential drug discoveries. The extracted data is taken by Olson laboratory at the Scripps Research Institute, and modeled with a program called AutoDock (www.scripps.edu/pub/olson-web/doc/autodock/index.html). This modeling program helps scientists understand how molecules dock with each other. This research helps them understand how certain medicines can best be synthesized to help in drug research.

Entropia's software occasionally uses a part of CPU cycles to fund other profit applications to fund its research on the AIDS project. The client software is only available for Windows platforms with greater than 98MB of memory. It can be downloaded securely from www.entropia.com/FAAH/join-FAAH.asp.

Distributed File Sharing

Instead of using distributed computing algorithms to solve complex applications, file-sharing programs such as Napster and Gnutella use distributed files and databases to serve music and video files. These programs are essentially a group of distributed databases that are linked to provide a file-sharing network. Within these databases are lists of files (most notably mp3 songs) that are served on the client's computer.

Each file-sharing system has its own protocol, which lies at the heart of the application. When a user installs the client, the program uploads the desired list of songs to the server, which enters the file information into the database. Subsequent client requests for the uploaded files can tell exactly where the files are and on which client computer they can be retrieved from the quickest. This provides for a quick and efficient means of file distribution.

Distributed Denial of Service

The darker side of distributed computing lies in the ability of crackers to perpetrate Distributed Denial of Service (DDOS) attacks and viruses.

Traditionally, the malicious cracker uses a network scanner to rapidly locate a large number of hosts for an easily penetrable service in which to install a client. Common culprits include systems that haven't been hardened yet, or that contain the latest Microsoft IIS vulnerability. After a system is compromised, the cracker installs the distributed application and moves onto the next system. After enough systems have been compromised, the cracker starts them off, perhaps running a simple Internet Control Message Protocol (ICMP) flood, or a smurf attack.

Today's crackers can program viruses that look for other hosts to infect by themselves. After several hosts have been infected, they can begin their rampage by starting a DDOS attack, or by having the program start sending malicious packets as soon as a host has been infected.

Condor

Condor is a program that runs on many UNIX-type platforms, including Linux. Essentially a complex front end for batch jobs, the Condor team at the University of Wisconsin-Madison started development of the distributed computing resource over 10 years ago. Condor is designed to take any number of jobs and distribute them across any number of machines that are also running Condor. This distributed application maintains a database of running machines and their specifications. Users can specify which type of machine to run their jobs on, and Condor distributes the jobs accordingly. Similar to most distributed applications, Condor suspends its processing when user activity is detected, and regains control after a certain amount of time.

Condor implements checkpoints, which is the ability for the distributed application to restart jobs if the remote computer loses communication or goes down. The server takes snapshots of the remote job so that it isn't lost, but rolls back if required by the user. This is an important idea behind distributed computing; the data from the master node must be able to be tracked or resent to different computers if the data is lost or can't be resent back to the originating node.

The architecture of Condor is laid out around a master server, which is referred to as the *Central Manager*. This Central Manager serves as the information collector, and negotiates resources and resource requests. The Central Manager shares information with the submit server, which organizes the jobs and maintains all the checkpoint information. Each job that is run on the remote machines creates a process on the machine, so that you need a great deal of random-access memory (RAM) or Swap Space to manage a large environment. All checkpoint data lives on this machine, unless you decide to dedicate a server to the task. The submit machine can also reside on the Central Manager. Each machine, including the Central Manager, can run jobs. If there's a problem on the machine, the job is stored on the local disk until it can send the job back to the submit machine.

Condor jobs have to be run in the background, without user input. The jobs can be redirected to standard input or output, depending on the needs of the user. This means that you must plan for the batch jobs that are being run to be set up in advance to read or write to a file instead of to stdout.

Installing Condor

Condor can be downloaded from the binaries page at www.cs.wisc.edu/condor/downloads/. You can get binaries for Linux, Solaris, Digital UNIX, SGI, and Windows NT. Condor recommends Red Hat Linux, and although other distributions might work, they're not supported or tested.

It's a good idea to plan the topology before installing Condor for the first time so that you have a plan of attack. Knowing which machine in your environment can best handle the resources assigned to it helps in the long run. It also helps if youcan assign a dedicated machine to tasks, if your environment is large. Condor can be installed with either static or dynamic linking binaries. The source code is not available publicly, but on a case-by-case basis.

You can use Condor to handle certain applications differently in four different environments, which are called universes. There's a standard universe, a vanilla universe, universes that you use with Parallel Virtual Machine (PVM), and Globus. The vanilla universe can be run with any job, although it doesn't support checkpointing; jobs that are run with the standard universe must be linked with Condor, but can support checkpointing. Shell scripts are a good example of jobs that you can use with a vanilla universe; they can run, but they can't be linked with Condor.

Although you can install Condor as any user, it's suggested that you run it as root because of the lack of permission restrictions. The manual suggests that running as root allows the program to access certain parameters from the kernel, rather than calling on other programs to get parameters. By default, condor installs in /usr/local/condor. The setup script allows you to change this location. In general, running things as root isn't such a great idea, but you make a trade off for a system that is dedicated to Condor.

The first step to running Condor is to grab the binaries and extract them to a temporary directory. This initial install is done on the Central Manager.

Make a condor account on the local install machine. The install script will fail if it's not set up. You can get around making a condor account if you set the CONDOR_IDS environment variable to the uid.gid settings that condor uses.

Run condor_install. The setup script asks you a set of questions that are self-explanatory. Answer them to suit your environment. The setup presents a list of default values, if you're not sure. The Condor install script places it's binaries and scripts in /usr/local/condor/bin, although it links other existing directories if you want to include those. The installation asks if you want to perform a full install, submit only, or define a Central Manager. Remember that you cannot run jobs on a submit-only machine. You must run a full install on each machine, unless you want only a Central Manager. You can define a shared directory where all condor machines can retrieve their files from, including a set of scripts installed to manage your environment.

Condor has to get its files to run jobs from somewhere. You might consider a Network File System (NFS) shared directory specifically for this use. Step two of the install asks that you run the script on the machine that you are using as your file server; in this case, it is the machine that is also the Central Manager. You don't have to distinctly set it up this way, as this is just for demonstration purposes. You also must enter in the names of the machines that you are setting up.

After the script finishes, you must run condor_init on all machines in your pool before you can run Condor jobs on them, even the master. It reminds you of this as it goes through its list of default questions. Or you can adjust these depending on where you installed the binary files. Although the initialization script populates condor_config for you, you might want to double check and make sure that everything fits your environment. That information is placed in /<condor root>/etc/condor_config. Don't forget to also create the startup scripts; a sample script is placed in /<condor root>/etc/examples/condor.boot. Edit the script to your taste and merge it with your current startup scripts.

Starting Condor is done by executing /usr/local/condor/sbin/condor_master. If everything goes fine, you see five processes running as follows:

```
condor   18650     1   0 22:44 ?      00:00:00 ./condor_master
condor   18651 18650   0 22:44 ?      00:00:00 condor_collector -f
condor   18652 18650   0 22:44 ?      00:00:00 condor_negotiator -f
condor   18653 18650   1 22:44 ?      00:00:06 condor_startd -f
condor   18654 18650   0 22:44 ?      00:00:00 condor_schedd -f
```

If you want to run condor jobs on more than one machine, you have to run condor_install on each, unless you created a shared directory that contains all the executable files.

Allocating Resources with ClassAds

Condor's ClassAds mechanism acts as a gatekeeper for resources, which interacts between the job submissions and the servers who advertise their resources. The ClassAds enable the clients to send specific jobs to those servers that match the resource requirements of each job.

When Condor is installed on the remote servers, they advertise their resources so that they can best serve the needs of the server farm. The ClassAds mechanism displays the relevant attributes of the machines in the class pool, such as memory, CPU usage, and load average, so that each job can go to the machine that best suits its needs. As a machine owner (one whose machine accepts jobs), you can tweak the ClassAd to suit your machine, the jobs that it accepts, and your own computing resources. You can specify if the machine is to accept only certain jobs, if it runs only with no keyboard activity, at certain times, or other similar specifications.

Running condor-status gives you a good idea of the status of the Condor environment. If Condor is set up correctly, it displays something similar to the following:

```
Name       OpSys     Arch   State   Activity   LoadAv  Mem  ActvtyTime

matrix     LINUX     INTEL  Owner   Idle       0.000   123  0+00:15:04
stomith    LINUX     INTEL  Owner   Idle       0.000   123  0+00:00:04
```

Running condor-status -l <server> gives you configuration details of the individual servers and shows their status. The output is similar to the following:

```
MyType = "Machine"
TargetType = "Job"
Name = "matrix.stomith.com"
Machine = "matrix.stomith.com"
Rank = 0.000000
CpuBusy = ((LoadAvg - CondorLoadAvg) >= 0.500000)
CondorVersion = "$CondorVersion: 6.2.1 Jul 27 2001 $"
CondorPlatform = "$CondorPlatform: INTEL-LINUX-GLIBC21 $"
VirtualMachineID = 1
VirtualMemory = 2088108
Disk = 10518096
CondorLoadAvg = 0.000000
LoadAvg = 0.000000
KeyboardIdle = 2359
ConsoleIdle = 9597550
Memory = 123
Cpus = 1
StartdIpAddr = "<172.16.0.6:1035>"
Arch = "INTEL"
OpSys = "LINUX"
UidDomain = "matrix.etopian.net"
FileSystemDomain = "etopian.net"
Subnet = "172.16.0"
TotalVirtualMemory = 2088108
TotalDisk = 10518096
KFlops = 30068
Mips = 368
LastBenchmark = 1006382711
```

```
TotalLoadAvg = 0.000000
TotalCondorLoadAvg = 0.000000
ClockMin = 1040
ClockDay = 3
TotalVirtualMachines = 1
CpuBusyTime = 0
CpuIsBusy = FALSE
State = "Unclaimed"
EnteredCurrentState = 1006390812
Activity = "Idle"
EnteredCurrentActivity = 1006390812
Start = ((LoadAvg - CondorLoadAvg) <= 0.300000) && KeyboardIdle > 15 * 60
Requirements = START
CurrentRank = -1.000000
LastHeardFrom = 1006392016
```

To show a list of current jobs, use condor_status-run.

After you get a listing of your environment and the type of machines that are in it, you can select which server or types of servers that your jobs run on. The condor_status command keeps you up to date with the current environment. The only thing that you have to do is build your job and submit it.

Submitting Condor Jobs

Submitting jobs to Condor is done through four easy steps. The first thing you must do is prepare your code to actually work with Condor. Remember that these jobs have to work independently in the background with no user input, although you can pass data to and from Condor jobs to choose which type of universe the job runs in. Next, you select a universe for the code to run in, and relink if necessary. Third, you set up a control file to tell Condor what to do with the code it's dealing with. Lastly, you submit the job to Condor with the control file.

Remember that Condor can run in four different types of universes: standard, vanilla, PVM, and Globus. To run Standard jobs, you must link them to Condor by relinking them with condor_compile. To do this, prepend the gcc command (or whatever compiler you use with condor_compile), as in the following example:

```
# condor-compile gcc foo.o bar.o -o myprogram
```

Vanilla jobs are designed for projects that can't be relinked, or shell scripts. The only difference between standard and vanilla jobs is that vanilla jobs can't use check points or remote system calls. Remember that if your script calls certain files, they're easily accessible. Remember to set your file and NFS permissions correctly.

Submitting jobs through Condor is done by preparing a control file, which is called a *submit description file*. Condor uses this file to determine the requirements of the specific job. With the control file, you can specify such things as the class requirements of the job, the number of times the job is to be run, stdout (standard output) and stdin (standard input) attributes. Following is a basic example from the documentation:

```
###################
#
# Example 1
# Simple condor job description file
#
###################

Executable    = foo
Log           = foo.log
Queue
```

In this example, the script is named foo, and all data from the job goes into foo.log. Without an attribute for the Queue parameter, the job is only run once. You don't have to have a log file, but it's recommended.

As a second example, a Mathematica job is run through Condor:

```
###################
#
# Example 2: demonstrate use of multiple
# directories for data organization.
#
###################

Executable    = mathematica
Universe = vanilla
input    = test.data
output   = loop.out
error    = loop.error
Log      = loop.log
Initialdir    = run1
Queue

Initialdir    = run2
Queue
```

The executable here is mathematica, and it's a vanilla universe job. If the job is submitted as in example one, with no universe, a standard universe is assumed. If there are no machine-specific requirements, a machine of the same type is assumed to be requested. The data file that the mathematica file uses is test.data, stdout is loop.out, and stderr is loop.error. In this scenario, two different sets of data are required as evidenced by the queue attributes; each needs its own directory to store data in. Each data directory isn't absolutely necessary, but it depends on the job. The directories are called with the `initialdir` attribute, and are stored in the `run1` and `run2` directories.

You can specify the type of machines that your job runs on by specifying the `Requirements` attribute. Remember that the attributes are case-sensitive. Your job might not run if you're passing information that doesn't match up to a job resource. In the previous case, you can tell job two to only run on a Sun UltraSparc machine, Solaris 2.8, with greater than or equal to 128MB of RAM, by specifying the following:

```
Requirements    = Memory >= 128 && OpSys == "SOLARIS28" && Arch =="SUN4u"
```

For a complete list of attributes, see Appendix D, "Condor ClassAd Machine Attributes."

Submitting the job is done with the `condor_submit` command. The syntax is `condor_submit <control-file>`. For example,

```
#condor_submit -v control-file
```

runs the job according to the control file. The -v switch forces `condor_submit` to show the `class_ad` attributes.

Even though Condor can also link jobs for use with PVM and Globus, that's beyond the scope of this book. More information on PVM and parallel clustering is covered in Chapter 8, "Parallel Computing," and Chapter 9, "Programming a Parallel Cluster." For a quick reference to Condor's class attributes, see Appendix D.

Mosix, Kernel–Based Distributed Computing

Taking distributed computing a step in a different direction, the multicomputer Operating System for UNIX *(Mosix)* introduces job processing directly to the kernel, which makes the operating system part of the cluster. Approaching distributed computing in this manner allows jobs to run without linking or submitting them. Amaze your friends as you run simple commands such as `ps` and `ls` across a large cluster.

Mosix is designed to run on any Intel platform computer as a true adaptive distributed clustering environment. This allows it to run in any number of configurations, similar to Condor. You can run it with a dedicated pool of machines, or have machines join the cluster during off hours without intruding on users' work.

Mosix takes care of its load balancing transparently to the user. It assigns jobs on its own, based on its own resource monitoring without intervention. Basically, Mosix treats the cluster as an extended SMP machine, which forks processes to other Mosix-enabled kernels.

Mosix is designed to work with a dedicated cluster. Mosix currently doesn't have the ability to sense whether or not a workstation is idle. You have to tell a Mosix node when to join the cluster, or write a script to detect lack of workstation usage to join the cluster.

Installing Mosix

You can get the latest version of Mosix from www.mosix.org/txt_distribution.html. Because Mosix is kernel-dependent, you want to get the version of Mosix that's designed for use with the specific kernel sources. You also must recompile the kernel to include Mosix. Don't use the kernel sources that come with the distribution that you're using; often they've been rewritten for the version of Linux that you're using. Instead, spend the time and download the vanilla sources from kernel.org.

Mosix can be installed by hand, or for the rushed administrator, it comes with a script that does the installation for you. The first thing you must do is download the recommended kernel and unzip it into /usr/src/linux, optimally, /usr/src/linux-<kernelversion>. Uncompress Mosix into its own directory and install.

If you choose to run the install script that comes with the Mosix package, you must run the mosix.install script in the directory that you just uncompressed.

The script first has you point to the correct kernel source directory. The script also asks if it should include the new kernel in the lilo boot loader, and which default run levels it should be included in. If you're using a distribution without run levels, be sure to check the -for none setting and add Mosix to your startup scripts. Mosix also asks you to set a MFS mount point for the Mosix file system. This is currently in the experimental stages.

If you look at the install FAQ, you can see that the following files are replaced, and that the old files are saved with a .pre_mosix extension.

```
/etc/inittab
/etc/inetd.conf and/or /etc/xidentd.d/*
/etc/lilo
/etc/rc.d/init.d/atd
/etc/cron.daily/slocate.cron
```

The install script then asks for the version of the kernel configuration methods that you'd like to take part in (namely config, xconfig, or menuconfig), patches the kernel, and runs the configuration method that you've chosen. Take advantage of the kernel compilation; Mosix can only incorporate the options that it needs for itself; it can't guess which options you want. Mosix recommends that you keep the kernel configuration options of `CONFIG_BINFMT_ELF` and `CONFIG_PROC_FS`. After you save the kernel sources, Mosix attempts to compile the kernel for you based on the options that you've given it.

If you need other kernel options besides the ones that Mosix gives you, you must patch the kernel before running `mosix.install`. Be sure that, if you're running alternate file systems, such as ext3 or ReiserFS, you modify your kernel to be configured with these. Mosix does not include these other options by default.

Manual installation isn't that much harder, but you do have to install everything by hand, rather than have Mosix scripts do everything for you. If you're brave enough to try to install Mosix by hand, you gain a much greater level of control and finer granularity. You can find detailed instructions within the man pages that are created from within `manuals.tar`.

After configuring the kernel, be sure that the entry is placed within `lilo` and reboot.

Configuring your Mosix Cluster

After you let Mosix compile the kernel by using your choices, you need to edit/create `/etc/mosix.map`, or it prompts you right after booting with the new kernel. This file has three fields per line: any node number that's associated with the node itself, the IP of the first node in the network, and the number of hosts in the cluster. Following is an example configuration:

```
1      172.16.0.1    6
7      172.16.5.1    3
10     172.16.10.1   7
17     172.16.30.5   2
```

In this configuration, the first column of numbers represents the unique nodes number in the first part of the subnet. The second column represents the IP of that node, and the third represents the number of hosts in the subnet. Each subnet has to have its own entry. If the Mosix node is a gateway between subnets, you use the word `ALIAS` in place of the third column. If your cluster is separated by subnets, you have to create the file `/etc/mosgates`, and enter the number **1**. If there are two more gateways between a node and others, enter the number **2**.

If all the nodes are on the same subnet, you don't need an `/etc/mosgates` entry. However, if the node number of the local node isn't in the list, that node number must be written to `/etc/mospe`.

After that is set up and Mosix is started, Mosix takes over and shares processes over the different computers in the cluster. You can type complex scripts or commands, such as ls, and have them replicated over the entire cluster. Well, ls might not require the entire cluster, but you get the idea.

Mosix at the Command Line

Mosix has several utilities that you can use to configure and tune Mosix, so as to gain information about the running kernel. You can use the setpe command to configure a Mosix cluster. By using the setpe command with the -w switch, you can configure Mosix to use new commands to add hosts to the cluster. The setpe command with the -r switch rereads the current configuration from /etc/mosix.map. This resets the configuration, if you want to start over and reset the cluster back to its original state. The setpe -o command shuts down Mosix by removing the configuration.

The Mosix configuration also includes utilities called tune, mtune, tune_kernel, and prep_tune. These utilities direct output that you can use to include in the kernel to optimize Mosix.

The Mosix tool mosctl allows the administrator greater control over how Mosix works, and allows control over the processes. For example, using mosctl stay forces the current processes to stay on the current node, and not be migrated. This is cancelled by using mosctl nostay or -stay.

You can use the migrate utility to move processes to any machine in the cluster, to the home machine that spawned it, or perhaps to a more powerful machine that is better suited for the task. The syntax for migrating a job is migrate <pid> <mosix machine id> | <home> | <balance>. In this syntax, you can choose the machine ID to move the process to; home, where you can send the process back to its home machine; or balance, which finds the best machine to load balance the process. For example,

```
# migrate 1024 16
```

migrates pid 1024 to node 16.

Administrating Mosix

The system administrator can make changes to the running Mosix configuration and to the running jobs. The administrator can maintain the kernel parameters with the setpe command, and manipulate /proc directly.

The file /proc/mosix/admin/gateways handles how processes from guest nodes are migrated into the current node. By changing the number to a 1 in that file, Mosix blocks guest processes from entering. If that number is 0, guest processes are free to enter.

By entering a 1 into /proc/mosix/admin/expel, Mosix expels the guest processes that are currently running in the host machine.

To run the tune_kernel command, you must enter a 1 into /proc/mosix/admin/quiet. It is recommended that you do this kernel-tuning directly after installation of the Mosix cluster, or when changing networks or CPU.

More information about the current processes are available in /proc/<pid>/. This tells you which process runs where, with 0 being the home node. The entries in /proc/<pid>/lock state whether or not the process has been locked against auto migration from its home node. The entries in /proc/<pid>nmigs show the number of times that the process has been migrated.

Entries in /proc/<pid>/cantmove list the reasons why a process can't migrate from its home directory. Some possible reasons are that the process is using files as shared memory, the process is using device-memory, the process is in 8086 mode, or the process is a kernel-daemon.

Information about all the configured nodes in the cluster are in /proc/mosix/nodes/<node-number>.

Using Diskless Clients with Mosix

A fully functional Linux workstation or cluster node can easily run without hard drives, CD-ROMs, or floppies, which saves administration time and maintenance. One of the benefits of having these diskless clients is that they can also harness their spare CPU cycles into a distributed cluster.

Diskless appliances can be bought for less than half the price of today's cheapest workstations, or easily built from commodity parts. The only moving part in such a workstation is the fan from the power supply. Not having moving parts greatly reduces the amount of equipment that can fail, which reduces downtime. Diskless clients share the processing power of distributed and parallel clusters by sharing CPU cycles with the master nodes.

A diskless client can ease administration time and maintenance by not only reducing the amount of parts in a computer, but by centralizing all the necessary files on a single server. The single server environment allows for such things as the simplification of printer management, centralized backup, the restore of user files, and the elimination of costly trips to the user's desktop. With the addition of Linux as the choice of OS, the risk of virus infection is greatly reduced, and with the advent of programs such as Star Office, the cost of the applications is almost nil. Add solitaire and a chat program or two, and your users have the same functionality as with Microsoft Windows. Both the server and the users are managed more effectively.

Although diskless appliances and XServers can reduce maintenance costs, the price of disks has gone down so much recently that implementing diskless workstations might not be worth the effort. It's a judgment call, which is based mainly on the ability of the support staff to manage multiple systems.

Installing a Diskless Client with Mosix

Diskless clients are simple machines that rely on a network card with pre-installed read-only memory (ROM) attached, a kernel, and a NFS share. After the system is turned on, the network card gets its IP from a Bootstrap Protocol (BOOTP) or Dynamic Host Configuration Protocol (DHCP) server. Remember that the BOOTP or DHCP server has to be on the same subnet or have a protocol-like spanning tree enabled on the routers. The server transfers the kernel image to the client over Trivial File Transfer Protocol (TFTP), and upon boot it offers up a root file system that the client can mount through NFS. Optionally, the root server loads a XServer into memory and executes X Display Manager (XDM) for a remote log in to the server. These services often are offered from the same server, although it's entirely possible to separate these services according to function.

The Linux Terminal Server Project (LTSP) is a concrete example of diskless clients. This is an implementation of an X-Terminal Server that runs an XServer, although most operations run on the server itself. Because of limited client requirements, it's possible for the client to be no faster than a 486 with 16MB of RAM.

The LTSP makes use of the Etherboot (http://etherboot.sourceforge.net) program to serve a kernel through TFTP to the individual clients. The program allows the transfer of boot images and other programs through the network.

For quick installation, LTSP requires Red Hat, Mandrake, or compatible distribution. Debian is functional, although it's still in beta. LTSP assumes that you're using an IP address of 192.168.0.254, and it populates DHCP with a range that includes that address. If your server uses anything different than that, you have to edit a few files back to your original IP scheme. You also have to be running DHCP on the server, as described earlier in this chapter.

Remember that for this implementation, all programs run on the server, and therefore it uses the CPU of the server. A decent SMP-based server with a hefty bit of RAM (about a gig or so) can easily handle upwards of 80-100 clients. You can download the RPM packages from http://sourceforge.net/project/showfiles.php?group_id=17723. You need the most recent core package, lts_core-2.xx-xx.i386.rpm, and the corresponding kernel made for your network card. If you're using the terminal server with Mosix support, you can get

the client kernel from www.nl.linux.org/~jelmer/vmlinuz-mosix.ne2000, or
www.nl.linux.org/~jelmer/vmlinuz-mosix.all. Otherwise, you can grab a client
kernel such as lts_kernel_eepro100-2.2-0.i386.rpm. You also need an XServer to
match your video card, such as lts_xsvga-2.xx-xx.i386.rpm. Install the three files
with rpm -i <package>.

The core Route Processor Module (RPM) installs files in /tftpboot/lts/.
Make sure that the kernel you download lies within this file. Execute the main
install file with the following:

```
/tftpboot/lts/templates/ltsp_initialize
```

The initialization script creates an /etc/dhcpd.conf.example file. Edit the script
to reflect your environment, and copy it to /etc/dhcpd.conf. Edit the dhcpd.conf
file to include the Media Access Control (MAC) address of the workstation,
then add the workstation names and associated IPs to /etc/hosts. For instance,
if /etc/dhcpd.conf contains a host ws001 parameter and a fixed-address option of
192.168.0.1, you add

```
192.168.0.1   ws001   ws001.fqdn.com
```

to /etc/hosts. Edit the /tftpboot/lts/ltsroot/etc/lts.conf file to reflect changes
to your configuration.

You also need to make sure that the XServer process on the client isn't
migrated from there. To the beginning of /tftpboot/lts/ltsroot/etc/rc.local,
add

```
echo 1 > /proc/mosix/admin/stay
```

after the line with PATH=. You also need to link the mosix.map file so that the
clients can access it.

```
# ln -s /etc/mosix.map /tftpboot/lts/ltsroot/etc/mosix.map
```

Make sure that the client is able to use the Mosix files by copying them into
the tftpboot directories, and add the Mosix startup to the client init scripts.

Reboot the server, turn on the client, and watch as it comes up cleanly.

Following is an example /etc/dhcpd.conf file that is set up with two workstations for the LTSP:

```
default-lease-time          21600;
max-lease-time              21600;
ddns-update-style ad-hoc;
option subnet-mask          255.255.255.0;
option broadcast-address    172.16.0.255;
option routers              172.16.0.1;
option domain-name-servers  24.130.1.32;
option domain-name          "domain.com";
option root-path            "/tftpboot/lts/ltsroot";
```

```
shared-network WORKSTATIONS {
    subnet 172.16.0.0 netmask 255.255.255.0 {
    }
}

group {
    use-host-decl-names        on;
    option log-servers         172.16.0.6;

    host ws001 {
        hardware ethernet      00:E0:06:E8:00:84;
        fixed-address          192.168.0.1;
        filename               "lts/vmlinuz.eepro100";
    }
    host ws002 {
        hardware ethernet      00:D0:B7:23:C0:5E;
        fixed-address          172.16.0.50;
        filename               "lts/vmlinuz.eepro100";
    }
}
```

If you have problems with the installation of LTSP, you can check a few places to make sure that you configured everything correctly. Make sure that `tcp_wrappers` is configured to accept connections, and that `hosts.deny` and `hosts.allow` are set up correctly for the clients. Make sure that the TFTP server is set up correctly; some tweaks might be needed. Error messages are kept in `/var/log/messages`, as usual. If you can't get an X display, remember to look in `/var/log/xdm-error`. If all else fails, the LTSP has a quick troubleshooting FAQ. Check out `www.ltsp.org/documentation/lts_ig_v2.4/lts_ig_v2.4-15.html` for more information.

Summary

Distributed computing takes information from one computer and shares the data or process load throughout a cluster of computers. Distributed computing can process large amounts of data in a short amount of time; much faster than any single computer or perhaps even supercomputer because of the number of potential nodes in each cluster.

The cluster doesn't have to be dedicated; sometimes, it only uses nodes during times when the user is not at their desk.

Distributed computing is similar to parallel computing; in fact, sometimes their lines overlap. The distributed computing environment takes more advantage of heterogenous environments, but it isn't necessarily limited by them (for example, they do just fine with homogenous networks). A distributed computing environment can be preferable if you have to use the computers for workstations and to compute nodes.

Parallel Computing

8

WHEN MOST PEOPLE THINK ABOUT COMPUTER clustering, they're reminded of large machines in datacenters processing immense amounts of data. In these pictures, large, well-funded organizations employ men in white jackets who must always carry around clipboards and nod solemnly before entering a mark of some sort on the clipboard. And it's obvious, of course, that all these billions of dollars are being spent on some seemingly insurmountable task, such as where to go out to eat for dinner.

Linux clustering refers to many different types of situations where computers act in unison with each other, passing data and acting on it. You've already seen how load balancing is one of the simplest forms of clustering, in which one computer segregates data that is based on a certain rule set and passes it off to other computers. You've seen how high-availability type clusters use a simple heartbeat to make each computer aware of each other and how one computer can take over when another computer fails. You've also seen a greater amount of communication take place in distributed computing and its ability to solve jobs and pass them back onto a master node.

Parallel computing, although similar to distributed computing, in its simplest form distributes tasks between processors and returns a result. Of course, that's the abridged definition. What actually happens behind the scenes is much more complex.

There are literally hundreds of books written on parallel computing, and thousands of documents and web pages devoted to every task imaginable on the subject. In this chapter, you won't be looking at programming the cluster, or even optimizing the code for it. As part of a book written for system administrators, this chapter focuses on the theories behind parallel computing, the background behind it, and how to think about getting a parallel computer up and working quickly.

Parallel Computing in a Nutshell

As discussed in Chapter 1, "Clustering Fundamentals," parallel computing allows you to take data or processes and spread them across processors or nodes. This comes in handy for organizations or people who have large amounts of data that they need to process, and who can benefit from having their data run in parallel.

Running several computers in parallel isn't enough to guarantee that your application benefits from running on several different nodes or processors at once. The data that you process must be appropriate for the parallel cluster. The setup program might be serial, instead of parallel, as it's composed of gathering data and is being set up for processing. However, the data resulting from the setup program might be applicable for a parallel cluster.

Let's say that you have an application that you want to run on a parallel cluster. The first thing to do is ask yourself if it will benefit from being run in parallel. The logic goes that if one computer can run a program well enough, why can't several? If Quake is great on a single processor system, it should be absolutely wicked on a cluster. Unfortunately, this is seldom the case. The program has to be optimized for the environment. These first person shooter games are designed for single processor environments because of the fact that they don't benefit from having a second CPU take the load off of a decent game. However, it does benefit from offloading a good deal of the graphic work onto a separate video chip, which is parallelism at its most basic level. One chip does the graphics processing, while the CPU on the motherboard handles the game engine.

What does benefit from a parallel cluster is an application that offloads much of the same thing to many different processors. If you had a search engine, and the search engine was designed to access data from millions, if

not billions, of pages, the master node offloads each request that is being generated to each node in the cluster; however, each node in the cluster performs
the exact same task, which is churning through the exact same algorithms to
bring up each relevant web page.

Many mathematical applications benefit from being run in parallel mode, as
they have components that are parallel. Take a program that parses the movement of quarks. Large subsections of space-time are mapped out on a lattice,
with the behavior of quarks mapped on this grid. Remembering that there
are six types of quarks with different physical properties, you want to map the
behavior of the quarks not only across three dimensions, but a fourth as they
move across time. Because there's a lot of space-time to cover, and numerous
quarks, this type of application is best served by a parallel cluster.

Here's how it works: The master node houses the data and results. It transfers the data to and from storage, and distributes the data across each of the
nodes or CPUs. Because there are potentially thousands of lattices to run data
against, each node in the cluster is given the same formula, but different data
to run against. Each node returns the result to the master node, which stores
the result in a different database. The database is composed of data from many
different sites that are doing the exact same thing. This other cluster takes the
results of all these different clusters, and by project end, returns the answer to
life the universe and everything, which is close to forty-two.

The problem with parallel code is that to achieve solid results the code has
to be optimized for the cluster in which it's intended. This is why, as a general
rule, there's no commodity software available for parallel computing environments. What works for one cluster is most likely not optimized for another
because of network design and hardware. When designing your parallel cluster
you have to take into consideration the number of nodes, if they're symmetric
multiprocessor (SMP) machines, if you're using hubs or switches, if you're
using one master node or more, or perhaps a single Network File System
(NFS) server or more. And the code has to be fine-tuned to work over the
specific network topology.

A Beowulf by Any Other Name

To some, the term *Beowulf* is synonymous with parallel computing. The work
that the original team did to promote supercomputer-like performance with
commodity parts is now almost legendary. It needs to be said, however, that
parallel computing had been around for some time, and vector computing
even longer. The Beowulf project broke new ground by doing so with Linux
and on commodity hardware.

Thomas Sterling and Don Becker started the project in 1994 at NASA-Goddard (CESDIS, The Center of Excellence in Space Data and Information Sciences) under the sponsorship of the ESS project, which comprised 16 486 DX4 processors connected by channel bonded Ethernet (www.beowulf.org/intro.html), for which he wrote the drivers. The project grew into what they called Beowulf. It was built primarily because of the dissatisfaction of established vendors and the lack of support. Today, Don Becker sits on the board of Scyld Corporation, still writes many of the drivers for Linux Ethernet, and contributes code to the Linux kernel.

Typically, a Beowulf computer is composed of a cluster of commodity network components. There's been strict religious debate over this on the Beowulf mailing lists; some say that a cluster is only a Beowulf if it meets the following requirements:

- The nodes are composed of strictly open-source software.
- The nodes and network are dedicated to the cluster and are used only for high-performance computing (parallel computing).
- The nodes are composed of only commodity, off-the-shelf components.

Some take this to mean that a Beowulf cluster can only run on Linux. However, there are other open-source operating systems that run on commodity hardware, such as FreeBSD. Why open-source software? Cluster development requires a good deal of custom code, and open kernels allow the freedom to change whatever doesn't work. Closed source monolithic kernels, such as those on Windows NT, don't allow for changes, so you're limited in what you can do. Seeing what's happening in the kernel allows you to rule out problems and to fine tune the existing code. If you're not familiar with the kernel tweaks, it's more than likely that someone on the Beowulf list or a fellow parallel programmer can help modify this. Programs such as Mosix have been written specifically through the ability to work with custom kernels.

The low cost of commodity hardware and the high cost of supercomputers helped to make projects such as Beowulf succeed. The availability of free software such as Linux, Parallel Virtual Machine (PVM), and Message Passing Interface (MPI), and a decent compiler such as gcc also served to make this type of computing readily accessible.

Scyld Linux and its Beowulf roots aren't the only parallel software available. Many other models and software programs exist. What makes their software attractive is that they make installation, configuration, and monitoring a snap with their distributions. You can make your own high-performance cluster simply by adding the right network, hardware topology, and message-passing software, such as LAM, MPICH or PVM. Or you can take the same shell script and run it over each node a few thousand times.

PVM and MPI are software packages that allow you to write parallel programs that run on a cluster. These extensions allow you to write in Fortran or C. PVM was the de facto standard in parallel development until MPI came along, although both are still widely used. MPI is standardized and has now taken the lead in portable programs across all parallel computers. More information on these are covered in Chapter 9, "Programming a Parallel Cluster."

High-Performance Topology

The theory behind a cluster is that messages (data) are passed back and forth between nodes so that it is appraised of what each node is doing, and it can send data to be processed. These message-passing nodes are handled like letters sent by the post office. It tries to pass letters to the nodes through the most effective means necessary. It tries to pass a message to the node that it's destined for, and it doesn't tie up any routes in getting the message through the nodes, or router, if it's on a different subnet. If most of your nodes are internal and happen to be composed of CPUs, the only thing stopping the system is the speed of the bus and the speed of the processors. When the server contains 20 or so processors, you have an effective and robust medium to pass messages between.

When each CPU lies on a different server, a more effective method has to be devised to pass data or messages between them. Instead of the bus being the primary means of transport between the CPUs, the network takes its place. The speed on the bus is much faster than the network, which becomes the primary bottleneck. Way before managed switches were common and affordable (not to mention certain parts of the world where they're not so accessible), the nodes of a cluster had to be specially pieced together so that they benefited from the most performance to pass messages back and forth to each other. This was done primarily through means of a hypercube or mesh diagram configuration. Nowadays, with fast Ethernet (FE) and switches being so common and inexpensive, these old topologies are outdated.

Some parallel machines have been designed in a mesh that you can visualize as lines on a sheet of graph paper. Each node is laid out with nodes spread to on right angles to each other. To pass messages to different nodes across the grid, each node in turn must relay messages through other nodes to get their message through. It's not all that effective, but it gets the job done.

Figure 8.1 shows a grid of nodes and the route that the messages are supposed to take. Machine A has to pass messages through three nodes before Machine B can get them. Imagine what it takes to similarly design this in a Linux environment with commodity parts? It's not impossible, but it is a wiring nightmare, with some of the machines in the grid requiring quad Ethernet cards to talk to their neighbors more effectively. The trick here is to get the nodes to talk to each other directly.

A more reasonable fully meshed node takes some of those quad Ethernet cards out and places hubs on the network. This is more cost effective and much less of a wiring nightmare, but you still have the problem of getting the nodes to talk directly to each other, and there is still plenty of hub cross talk. Remember that the network is the single greatest bottleneck. You're not achieving optimal results with 16 computers on one hub.

Enter the hypercube. The hypercube tried to solve the problem of excess chatter in the design level by eliminating the need for hubs, yet not need the overhead of so many network interfaces. Each node in a hypercube only needs up to three interfaces. Figure 8.2 shows an example of a simple four-node cluster. In this example, each node needs only two network interfaces for direct communication with their neighbors. When four more nodes are added, direct communication becomes more difficult. A third network interface needs to be added for direct communication; however, messages still must be passed between nodes. This is more useful than the flat approach, as seen in Figure 8.1, because of the three dimensional design. You don't have to pass through as many nodes.

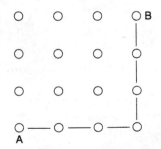

Routing Through Meshed Nodes

Figure 8.1   Routing thorough meshed nodes.

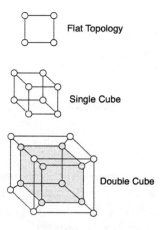

Figure 8.2 Hypercube topologies.

Adding eight more nodes to the hypercube gives you a box within a box, yet you still need only three network interfaces on each node. The number of messages passing increases, as does the complexity of the cube, although you still don't have the issues of a flat topology. In a worst-case scenario with a flat topology, you have a maximum of 6 hops for a 16-node cluster, where you can get a maximum of 4 hops with a hypercube. Similarly, with a 256-node cluster, you have a maximum of 30 hops between nodes as opposed to 8 with a hypercube (*High Performance Computing*, O'Reilly & Associates, June 1993).

Enter the switch. Although in the past, it was common to design parallel clusters with a mesh or hypercube topology, switches are becoming extremely common and the prices are within reach of most budgets. With an initial outlay of a little extra cash, you save yourself a lot of time, effort, and planning. The switch plays traffic director, which makes routing nightmares a thing of the past. The maximum number of hops is dependent now only on the number of switches that you have strung together for the single network. If you can afford it, drop fast ethernet all together, and go with Myrinet. It's becoming the standard in gigabit networking for clustering, and although it is still the bottleneck in your cluster, it definitely won't seem as bad. Myrinet, as you might remember, is a 1.28 Gbps full-duplex interconnection network that was designed by Myricom corporation. Myrinet uses a proprietary interface and switches that result in low latency. You might also consider straight gigabit cards. Although these don't provide the bandwidth of Myrinet, they are less expensive than the Myrinet setup. They do suffer from more latency, although they're still much faster than standard FE cards. If you can afford it, go for the higher bandwidth because it lessens the bottleneck pinch.

Cluster Installation

Up until now you've seen the best practices on how to build a cluster. You've gone over cluster installation and support, how to lay out the datacenter and network, and how to build mass quantities of machines from the ground up. Using tools such as Kickstart, SystemImager, and imaging programs such as Ghost for unix, you can deploy an unlimited number of machines for a parallel cluster in a manner of hours, as opposed to doing it by hand, which takes days.

If you're doing everything from scratch, you must build the network and cluster infrastructure yourself or hire consultants to do it at exorbitant prices. You also need storage, such as a NFS server, storage area network (SAN), Parallel Virtual File System (PVFS), network access server (NAS), or even Internet Small Computer Systems Interface (iSCSI) to serve data and optionally home directories. You need a recommended gateway server to the outside network to shield the cluster, and as many nodes as your budget allows. Your gateway can also serve as the NFS server. Don't forget the switches and cabling. Without connectivity, you're going to have a hard time getting the machines to talk to each other. Power is always another good feature. Now that you have the infrastructure in place and have successfully imaged all the nodes in your cluster (complete with source hashing scheduling [SSH], .rhosts if you like living dangerously, Dynamic Host Configuration Protocol [DHCP], and host table information for all the nodes in your cluster), it's time to incorporate the programming environment. What is a cluster without a programming environment? A POP (Pile of PCs), that's what. Although you can install programs such as Mosix or Condor, as talked about in Chapter 7, "Distributed Computing," a do-it-yourself cluster typically requires either PVM or some sort of MPI (LAM/MPI or MPICH).

Next, you need management software. This is covered in Chapter 10, "Cluster Management." This enables you to view how your systems are doing at a glance. Applying workflow management software helps you to determine who gets access to which resource and when.

You can now either show your friends that you're the most technologically inclined on your block (geek) or hand the system over to your boss with the satisfaction that it didn't take much effort at all to build a parallel cluster.

The other option is to build your hardware infrastructure from the beginning and add a pre-built distribution that is specifically for parallel clustering. There are several pre-built distributions for you to choose from, which contain most of these tools.

Scyld Linux

The Scyld Linux Beowulf distribution is based on Red Hat Linux 6.2 with a custom kernel.

The setup for the Scyld Linux distribution is similar to the Red Hat installation. Scyld Linux needs the creation of a master node. It makes sense that this master node needs to be installed first. From there, you run the `beosetup` and it creates slave nodes for you.

The Scyld Linux distribution is designed to work as a switch setup as opposed to a hypercube where the nodes transmit information. The cluster needs to be set up first with the master node having two interfaces, a public subnet so that it can reach the outside world, and a private subnet that is hooked up to all the nodes in the cluster.

Scyld sells their professional product with varied pricing, depending on the number of CPUs in your cluster. For several thousand dollars, you get a nifty web interface, Alpha processor support, monitoring software, PVFS support, Preboot Execution Environment (PXE) support and a year's support. Or you can buy the basic version from `http://linuxcentral.com` for $2.95 US.

Installation of the Master Node

Scyld Linux is nothing more than a custom Red Hat installation with a few extra packages that specifically refer to parallel clustering. The following is a list of packages that you can install upon setup, according to the install screens:

- **NAMD**—A parallel, object-oriented molecular dynamics code that is designed for the high-performance simulation of large biomolecular systems.
- **Atlas**—Part of the NetLib series of Linear Algebra libraries for high performance computing.
- **Beompi**—MPICH for Beowulf.
- **Beompi-devel**—Static libraries and header files for MPI.
- **Beonss**—glibc nss routines for Beowulf.
- **HPL (High-Performance Linpack)**—Part of the NetLib series of Linear Algebra libraries for high-performance computing. HPL is a software package that solves a (random) dense linear system in double precision (64 bits) arithmetic on distributed–memory computers.
- **MPIBLACS (MPI Basic Linear Algebra Communication Subprograms)** —Part of the NetLib series of Linear Algebra libraries for high-performance computing.

- **Mpirun**—Parallel job launcher for Beowulf-2 systems.
- **Npr**—Demonstration coscheduler that uses the beostatus library.
- **PARPACK**—Part of the NetLib series of Linear Algebra libraries for high-performance computing. PARPACK is a collection of Fortran77 subroutines that are designed to solve large-scale eigenvalue problems.
- **Scalapack**—Part of the NetLib series of Linear Algebra libraries for high-performance computing.

Insert the Scyld CD-ROM and boot from it. Scyld runs the typical Red Hat setup, but gives you three options: You can boot install Beowulf with Gnome, use a controlling, text-only machine, or boot with a custom configuration. Installing with Gnome gives you all the features of a normal workstation, including things such as printer support, synergy advanced multipurpose bus arbiter (SAMBA), and freecell. The only other way that the install differs from the Red Hat default install is that it offers to configure the internal interface and DHCP ranges for the subsequent slave nodes. The Scyld setup program recommends initially that you set up the internal interface on the 192.168 subnet, but of course that's up to you. The install file puts the resulting entries in /etc/beowulf/config, so if you mess up, or need to change things, you can edit this file. At boot, this is called /etc/rc.d/init.d/beowulf.

Select what you want installed, optionally create a boot disk, configure X support, and reboot. You're done installing the master node. If you get stuck, the documentation is on the master node in /usr/doc/beowulf-doc.

Installation of the Slave Nodes

Installing the slave nodes of Scyld is slightly more difficult. Log into the master node as root, and run the beosetup gui. This allows you to make a boot disk for the slave nodes. Run /usr/bin/beosetup on the master node. All configuration is done on the master node, as the main distribution also installs the boot kernel for the slave nodes.

You can either use the CD-ROM to create slave nodes, or create a floppy to get an address and register itself with the master node. After the remote systems are booted, they register themselves with the master node. Drag the node to the configured nodes middle listing, where they register themselves with the cluster and start accepting jobs. Figure 8.3 shows a node being created with beosetup.

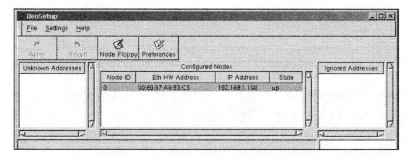

Figure 8.3   Creating a node with beosetup.

Create a floppy so that you can install the nodes, and get them to boot up so that you can indeed drag them with beosetup and register them. Creating a floppy is done by inserting a floppy in the drive, clicking the Node Floppy button, and pointing the destination path to the correct floppy drive, which is usually /dev/fd0.

After beosetup has finished the floppy installations, insert them into the slave computers and boot. The (Media Access Control (MAC) addresses register into the Unknown Addresses section of the beosetup upon startup. Drag these into the Configured Nodes section where they can register themselves into the database. After these are registered, it's time to partition your nodes. If the slaves have a problem coming up, check the error logs on the master node, in /var/log/Beowulf/ node.<node>. If you haven't partitioned the disks yet, you automatically get an error. Don't worry about that, unless you've already partitioned and you're still drawing errors.

If your nodes are already partitioned, record the information into /etc/beowulf/fstab on the master node. If not, you've got two choices: Either you can install default partitioning on the slave nodes, or you can manually partition the slave nodes however you wish. All partitioning is done from the master node. Following is how to quickly partition the slave nodes with a default setup:

```
#/usr/sbin/beofdisk -q

#/usr/sbin/beofdisk -w
#/usr/bin/beoboot-install -a /dev/hda <or /dev/sda, or default boot device>
#/usr/sbin/bpctl -S all -s reboot
```

The first line tells beofdisk to query partitions for the slave nodes. The second line creates default partitions for the nodes. The third line writes the partition table to the drives. The fourth line installs the kernel on /dev/hda (or /dev/sda) and sets the partition as bootable so that you don't have to boot off the floppy each time you bring the cluster up. You can select which node you write to with the `beofdisk -n <node>` option. Remember that the nodes start at n-1, so that the first node is always node 0.

The default partition includes three partitions: a boot partition of 2MB, SWAP Space consisting of twice the amount of physical memory, and the rest is put in as a default root partition.

> **Note**
>
> It's interesting that you can bring up each node in the cluster with just a floppy with the Scyld kernel on it. If you have a notebook with the Scyld distribution installed and a handful of floppies, you can walk right into a lab or classroom, jack into the network, install floppies into the lab machines, and reboot them all. Voila—instant parallel cluster.

If you're not comfortable with the `beofdisk` installing a default partition on each node in your cluster, partition the cluster yourself using `beofdisk`. This is a neat little utility that lets you partition everything at once from the master node.

You can manually partition the disks from the master node with the `bpsh` utility. Running `bpsh <node number>` `fdisk` lets you run the `fdisk` utility on the remote node. Setting your own partition is reflected in `/etc/beowulf/fdisk` by the disk type, position, and geometry (`disktype:position:geometry`).

And don't forget to reboot with the following:

```
#/usr/sbin/bpctl -S all -s reboot
```

You now have a working copy of Scyld Linux after you install the kernel on the slave nodes and reboot. These should all boot easily and register themselves with the master node, ready to accept jobs, assuming that you've registered them as configured nodes.

Channel Bonding

One of the benefits of the Scyld Linux distribution is the `ifenslave` command, which is designed to scale network bandwidth. In its simplest term, channel bonding allows you to take multiple networks and trunk them together as a single network with more bandwidth. The use of the resulting bandwidth is transparent to the cluster, except for the resulting speed gain.

The `ifenslave` program works similar to the `ifconfig` command, although it bonds higher networks to lower ones. For example, it bonds `eth1` and `eth2` to `eth0`. This program doesn't allow for general trunking, however you're not limited to using `ifenslave` on Scyld Linux computers. All computers that talk through this method also must be connected to others that talk through this method. If you're using channel bonding with one node, you must implement it on all nodes, or it doesn't work.

The `ifenslave` program comes standard with the Scyld Linux distribution, or you can build it for other applications at `www.beowulf.org/software/bonding.html`

For example, if you have an eight-node cluster, you're going to implement channel bonding throughout on two channels. Each node in the cluster has two network cards (except for the master node, which needs an extra to talk to the outside network). You also need two different networks, which means two different hubs, switches, or one switch with segregated virtual local-area networks (VLANs).

To start, type

```
#modprobe bonding
#ifconfig bond0 192.168.0.1 netmask 255.255.0.0
#ifenslave bond0 eth0 eth1
```

which first creates `bond0` and then slave `eth0` and `eth1` to `bond0`. You have to bond the slave nodes before the master node. Be careful when using this command; channel bonding the master when the slaves aren't configured correctly can result in the slaves rebooting and being unable to pick up an `arp` request to register themselves back on the cluster.

After your cluster is set up, you're ready to start launching remote jobs from the master node. You'll most likely want to look at programming solutions such as an MPI running code that's distributed with Scyld. MPI and PVM concepts are covered in the next chapter. Have fun; you've got a working Beowulf cluster.

Summary

You can use many different software distributions with clustering. The Scyld distribution happens to be one of the more common distributions, as is PVM. Environments such as these give the user a handy means of running parallel applications across many environments.

With the right planning for your network and hardware topology, you can come up with a decent cluster in no time. And you don't need a dedicated clustered environment to work from, as you see in the next chapter.

The Care and Feeding of a Cluster

9

Programming a Parallel Cluster

AT ITS MOST BASIC LEVEL, A PARALLEL CLUSTER is designed to make use of several processors at once and pass code between them. The combination of nodes, networks, and the monitoring software that runs in integration with each other is only one aspect of running a parallel cluster.

Remember that a parallel cluster is designed to handle a larger data set of code than a single processor system. Where one CPU can handle a small amount of code, many processors can handle that much more processing. However, in actual practice, the code has to be optimized to handle the extra processors. Although Linux can easily handle systems with extra processors, it's not designed to handle clusters right out of the gate, and similarly, there isn't much code written to handle parallel environments because each environment is different. Each environment has different needs.

Putting several nodes together and making sure that they can communicate is only the first step. These nodes are essentially useless without giving them a means to communicate with each other, and that's where message-passing capable languages come into play. Libraries such as Message Passing Interface (MPI) and Private Virtual Machine (PVM) can build upon C and Fortran, which enable code to be passed onto different nodes of a cluster. These libraries were built out of the need for standardization across platforms. Before these standards were put in place, each vendor had its own implementation of parallel programming code. Each environment had to be programmed differently. With the growth of Linux and the maturity of these libraries, parallel computing has taken off as a viable alternative for supercomputer performance.

This chapter doesn't intend to be an exhaustive resource of MPI programming applications. However, by using the material in this chapter, you will be able to install and use MPI in clustered environments that are suitable for problem solving.

Coarse Granularity in a Finely Granular World

The application to be run against the cluster defines the cluster itself, and therefore must be taken into account when designing the cluster and the environment in which it's run under. If you're simply designing an environment in which to run generic and varied applications against, a generic cluster full of single CPUs does nicely. It might be preferable to spend the money on cheaper systems rather than budget the extra money on dedicated symmetric multiprocessor (SMP) machines. The truth is that different types of problems work better with different hardware configurations. This is determined by what's known as granularity.

Granularity is measured by fine, medium, and coarse grades that are similar to sandpaper. Granularity is determined by the amount of possible parallelism in the code, rather than the complete code itself. You must consider three factors when determining the granularity: the structure of the problem, the size of the problem, and the number of CPUs available to handle the problem.

Parallel programs are composed of tasks that are distributed across each processor. The larger the task size, the coarser the granularity. If you assign your cluster the simple task of having each processor add 10 numbers to each other, the task isn't that difficult, and is said to have coarse granularity. Problems arise when the code starts becoming more complex and starts to interact with other nodes. The more interaction, the finer the code.

If there's much interaction between CPUs, you want them to be closer in general. Remember that it's much quicker to communicate over a fast bus speed of a SMP system than a multitude of single processors that are connected over a network. The more finely granulated the code, the faster you want the nodes to talk to each other. It's for this reason that you want to think about a SMP system with more processors. A code base that doesn't see the nodes talking to each other much is said to be very coarse, and suffices just fine with multiple nodes, rather than with multiple CPUs.

For this reason, you also want to tailor your code to the pre-existing environment. In a best-case scenario, you're given a task and are given the opportunity to design your cluster around the problem. In a worst-case scenario, you're given a cluster and have to modify your code around the hardware. Either way, you must write code to fit the environment. This is why pre-written software doesn't fit well into the parallel cluster environment. It's hard to optimize code for every possible scenario.

Programming in a Clustered Environment

When considering writing programs for parallel and high-performance clusters, each particular program has to be evaluated for the type of cluster and problem to be solved.

You might be asking, "Why can't I just install a package with the program I want to run across my cluster?" It's not totally unheard of, but the truth is that the problems that people want to solve typically haven't been solved already. The companies or universities that use parallel clusters use them for research such as weather prediction, genome and pharmaceutical research, even nuclear predictions. It's unlikely that someone has already written a program for a computer, such as ASCI White, to be ported to an elementary school cluster. Each application is best served by knowing the cluster itself. By writing these applications from scratch, you can make the best usage out of your own cluster. You can know where the bottlenecks lie and effectively work around them. By knowing where your Network File System (NFS) server lies, you can write your application to take full advantage of it.

Programming for parallel systems falls into two categories, shared and distributed-memory, depending on the type of architecture you're talking about. SMP clusters, however, have elements of both in a mixed configuration. Message passing is the preferred method for these clusters because of the standardization and ease of the programming environment. Message passing is achieved with inter-process communications by sending and receiving messages through the processors. These messages can, like TCP/IP packets, be received in any order. Each processor, even those in SMP systems, talk to each other through means of passing messages. These message-passing programs consist of cooperating processes, each with its own memory.

MPI seeks to standardize message passing by introducing a layer of extensions to Fortran 77 and C. This allows for people to write portable message programs across parallel machines. MPI is a library for writing programs instead of writing in a virtual distributed operating system such as the environment prepared by Scyld Linux or Mosix. Many different implementations of MPI exist, including LAM/MPI and MPICH, with MPICH being the most widely used implementation. MPI includes two different phases, with phase one implementing simple message passing, and the second phase including remote memory, parallel input/output (I/O) and dynamic processes.

Programming using environments such as PVM also incorporate libraries across a virtual machine. It includes functions for C and C++, and subroutines for Fortran. PVM includes a framework for a homogenous framework to run across heterogeneous computers that are running concurrent or parallel jobs. PVM subsystems also rely on message passing routines between CPUs to communicate.

Although MPI and PVM are similar in that they both provide libraries for parallel computing, they're not interchangeable. PVM was, until the standardization of MPI, the de facto means for message passing; however, it's largely been superseded by MPI. This isn't to say that PVM isn't still in use, but that you might not choose PVM over MPI when programming a parallel cluster.

MPI

The goal of MPI is to develop a standard for message passing across heterogeneous platforms. The goal when developing the interface was to take a best practice approach to message passing. It's designed to take the best of all the message-passing libraries and merge them into its own structure for parallel programming and applications.

You can get MPI for just about any platform that runs parallel code. There's also as many different implementations of MPI as there are distributions of Linux. There's MPICH, a winmpich for Windows NT, and an Illinois High Performance Virtual Machine that's based on MPICH. Local-area mobility-MPI (LAM-MPI) is also popular. There's an MPI for the IBM SP, and the OS/390, MPI for SGI and Digital machines. There's even rumor of MPI for the Palm Pilot.

Getting and Installing MPI

You can download the MPICH implementation of MPI from `http://www-unix.mcs.anl.gov/mpi/index.html`. MPICH is fully compliant with the 1.2 MPI standard, and aims for 2.0 compliance.

Download the program, uncompress it, and install it with `./configure`, `make`, `make install`. If you want others to use the program, install it in another directory, with the `-prefix` option set to configure, such as the following:

```
configure -prefix=/usr/local/mpich
```

Typing ./**configure** -**usage** gives you all the needed command-line options you need to configure MPICH. The make install command is optional, but it enables you to make mpich public.

Next, set your path to run programs from the mpi/bin directory:

```
$ export PATH=$PATH:/usr/local/mpi/bin
```

Examples of MPI programs to run are in /usr/local/mpi/examples/.

Following is an example of a basic Hello World program that is using MPI:

```
#include <stdio.h>
#include "mpi.h"

int main( argc, argv )
int   argc;
char **argv;
{
    int rank, size;
    MPI Init( &argc, &argv );
    MPI Comm size( MPI COMM WORLD, &size );
    MPI Comm rank( MPI_COMM_WORLD, &rank );
    printf( "Hello world from process %d of %d\n", rank, size );
    MPI Finalize();
    return 0;
}
```

Following are a few things to note about the program:

- MPI init initializes the MPI execution environment. argc is a pointer to the number of arguments, and argv is a pointer to the argument vector.

- MPI Comm size determines the size of the group associated with a communicator.

- MPI Comm rank determines the rank of the calling process in the communicator.

- MPI Finalize terminates the MPI environment.

After you finish writing your Hello World program, you can link it with the MPI compilers, just as you use a normal compiler, such as gcc. The first example is for C, the second is for Fortran 77:

```
$ mpicc -o helloworld hello.c
```

```
$ mpif77 -o helloworld hello.f
```

Executing the programs can be done with mpirun. Typically, you'll use

```
$ mpirun -np 2 helloworld
```

where the number 2 can be replaced by any number of processors. Type **mpirun** -**help** for a list of options.

So now you're saying, "That's all fine and good, but this isn't really a clustered application, is it?" No, it's not. Not yet. For that, you've got to use either rhosts or ssh to transmit messages over. Enter the list of workstations to be added to /usr/local/mpi/share/machines.<arch>. Just the hostname should be placed in there.

Make sure that the master node (the node with mpi placed on it) has .rhosts rights to run programs on the nodes in the cluster. You can test the mpi connectivity with /usr/local/mpi/sbin/tstmachines <architecture>. This ensures connectivity and makes sure that the mpi programs can run across all nodes in the cluster. The tstmachines attempt to run rsh across nodes. If it can't access rsh, the test fails. You can substitute Secure Shell instead of rsh by setting the P4_RSHCOMMAND environment variable to ssh in your .profile:

```
export P4_RSHCOMMAND=ssh
```

To set up rsh, you need to create a /etc/hosts.equiv file that's got both your local host, your hostname, and the master node on all the machines in the cluster, or you can't connect.

The ssh command is more involved to set up than .rhosts, but hey, it's secure. You can install it from the instructions given in Chapter 2, "Preparing Your Linux Cluster," however, be sure to configure it with -rsh=ssh so that MPI uses that instead of rsh. Although .rhosts tends to be insecure, ssh puts a little more load on the CPU because of the fact that it's got to encrypt the messages across the network. The rsh command doesn't have those limitations, but then again, it's insecure. However, you might not need to secure your transmissions across an already private network.

Other libraries and programs that use MPI are being built all the time. Numerical libraries for the parallel solution of sparse liner systems and nonlinear equations can be found, as well as Graphics libraries, multi-dimensional algebraic libraries, and thermal fluid simulations.

Summary

Message passing libraries (MPLs), such as PVM and MPI, allow programmers a standardized interface to write portable code across heterogeneous machines. Such code is designed to enable the programmer to access all the nodes in the cluster to solve large computational problems.

With a solid knowledge of C or Fortran, the programming extensions aren't much different from the single processor, single machine environments. For a decent environment, you can either choose to use a dedicated system, such as Scyld Linux, to run your clustered environment, or set up a set of .rsh or ssh to run off your distribution and include a message-passing interface.

10

Cluster Management

CLUSTERS NEED CARE AND FEEDING, just like humans. Of course, you won't find most clusters chowing down at Burger King, but they do need attention nonetheless. Clusters require maintenance and a watchful eye for them to run at optimal efficiency.

All clusters need some sort of monitoring software to keep tabs on what's going on. It's better to find out what might potentially cause problems in the future than to be called by a user wanting to know why they're unable to access certain resources. And it's a good thing to have safeguards in place that can notify you when processes or servers aren't able to function. With the right tools and configurations, you can know something has gone wrong before your supervisor, so that you can be already working on the problem. Surprises aren't a good thing in this game.

Larger clusters need a team of dedicated administrators on them at all times to ensure that the infrastructure is running. They also need consistent monitoring software to maintain hundreds of servers at once. Have you ever tried to log on to each of your large servers and diagnose each and every one? It's just not feasible, and that's why people invent tools to monitor the health of multiple servers at one time.

Learn to Use the Right Tools

Believe it or not, one of the best tools possible for maintaining the health of your servers is plain old pen and paper. Even though most of us like documenting procedures as much as we enjoy stabbing ourselves with a spork, it's a great way to keep up with changes to our environment and servers. Keeping a binder with up-to-the-minute data on equipment is a great way to forecast possible events and to keep a record of things. It's also a handy, one-stop shop that can disseminate information about the history, applications, and maintenance contracts associated with each server.

Although at first glance, the idea of a paperless office is appealing, you might want to stay away from publishing your documentation on the web. On one hand, keeping documentation online makes it easily accessible to anyone that needs access to the web page. However, keeping documentation online also makes it accessible to potentially undesirable individuals. Insecure web pages can get broken into if security isn't up to snuff. Anyone that has access to the web page can extract information about each node, and possibly exploit potential weaknesses. Also, if your documentation server goes down, you lose all hope of pulling up information about other servers.

What's good to include in documentation about your servers? Basically anything that can potentially help you to recover from a crash or potential problem. It's also a great place to house information about serial numbers, maintenance contracts, and application information. Following is a list of things that you might want to keep track of in your binder:

- Server type
- Number of processors
- Amount of RAM
- Maximum amount of RAM
- Bios information
- Hard drive/Partitioning information
- Serial numbers
- Change management information
- Maintenance contracts; support numbers
- Installed applications
- Application owners
- Service level agreements (SLAs)
- List of phone numbers to call should anything happen, with escalation procedures

- Instructions on how to bring the server and applications back up to production mode from a cold power off
- Instructions on how to bring the server down to power off
- Backup schedule and offsite rotation; offsite numbers for tape retrieval
- Emergency restore procedures (Kickstart, SystemImager, CD, and so on)

It's a good idea to grab the binder of information each time that there's a problem with a server. Not only does this keep all the information about each server at your fingertips, but it also makes it convenient to enter any new information.

Change management can't be stressed enough. Although recommended for each node in the cluster, it's essential for systems that potentially are touched by numerous people. When several people work on one system or cluster, there is the possibility of overlapping work or making changes that aren't documented, which can result in an administrator not knowing what changes have been made. It's also a good idea to have meetings about changes; it's often difficult to know what ramifications certain changes can have on the rest of the cluster, much less to the environment as a whole.

Configuring *syslogd* for Your Cluster

One of the best, yet sometimes overlooked tools for administering Linux servers is the simple syslogd facility. This daemon is potentially your best friend. syslogd is responsible for taking all possible information about your machine and putting it into neat little perusable log files that you can manipulate at your disposal. syslogd is great for capturing and displaying information. syslogd notifies you of login events, most importantly, failed login events, File Transfer Protocol (FTP) logins, daemon information, sendmail information, and so on.

One of the best features of syslogd is that it can write information about the events that it receives to a remote host. That means that you can get information about each node in your cluster sent to one main event server. This logging is essential for every type of cluster that you maintain, with the possible exception of distributed clusters. You might not want to get information on 300,000 users' syslogd events.

syslogd is event driven. In each event, it includes a severity and parses the information depending on how you want it to be transmitted. You can send the information to the console, to certain log files, or even email yourself with certain events through scripting.

syslogd's configuration file is typically shipped as /etc/syslog.conf, and is usually started at boot in /etc/init.d/syslog, or some other link. syslogd is started with several options, usually with the -m or -r switch. Starting syslogd with the -m switch tells syslogd to log each event of a certain time period whether or not there was an event that took place. Using syslogd with the -r switch allows syslogd to accept logging information from different hosts. The -d switch turns on debugging information, which logs all debugging information to the current tty.

The main format of the syslog.conf file is facility.level action, as in the following example:

```
mail.debug /var/log/mail
```

This sends all debug information (level) that is generated by mail (facility) and logged to /var/log/mail (action). You can also specify the asterisk wildcard with syslogd, as follows:

```
cron.* /var/log/cron
```

This logs all levels of cron facility information to /var/log/cron.

You can enable remote logging to a log host by appending the @<hostname>, instead of the action attribute, to direct the logging information to the remote log host instead of a local file. It's a good idea to place an entry for the remote log host in /etc/hosts. Be sure that the log host is running with the -r switch.

You can add services from your /etc/inetd.conf to be logged with syslogd by adding the -l switch to enable logging to that service. To add incoming connections from FTP, you change the FTP service to read the following:

```
ftp     stream tcp    nowait root    /usr/sbin/tcpd  in.ftpd -l
```

You can basically add anything to syslogd, if it's listed in /etc/services.

Creating *syslog.conf* Entries

It is fairly simple to enable logging when creating entries in inetd.conf. The trick is in finding out what logs to where and how often. For example, you don't typically want your FTP server to send you messages about email problems. The goal is to maintain as light a load as possible without sacrificing vital logs. You don't want to spend half your day pouring through log messages.

Following is a listing of various levels of importance for syslogd from the man page. You can assign your own levels of importance based on which criteria best suits your operation:

```
EMERG       system is unusable
ALERT       action must be taken immediately
CRIT        critical conditions
```

```
ERR              error conditions
WARNING          warning conditions
NOTICE           normal, but significant, condition
INFO             information messages
DEBUG            debug-level messages
```

Following is a listing of facility arguments for built-in subsystems:

```
AUTHPRIV                security/authorization messages
CRON                    clock daemon (cron and at)
DAEMON                  other system daemons
KERN                    kernel messages
LOCAL0 through LOCAL7   reserved for local use
LPR                     line printer subsystem
MAIL                    mail subsystem
NEWS                    USENET news subsystem
SYSLOG                  messages generated internally by syslog
USER                    generic user-level messages
UUCP                    UUCP subsystem
```

Remember that you can use combinations of these arguments, including the asterisk wildcard. If you want to send all line printer (lpr) messages to /var/log/lpr, you can do that with the following code:

```
lpr.*  /var/log/lpr
```

You can also mail all error conditions to users' root, and news about all news error conditions by entering the following:

```
news.err  root,news
```

You can even send messages to a tty by specifying /dev/ttyS3 for the action:

```
news.err  /dev/ttyS3
```

You can specify different levels of facilty.level by separating them with a ; and the ! expression to denote not. The following example logs all cron entries to /var/log/cronlog, except for informational messages about cron:

```
cron.*;cron.!=info  /var/log/cronlog
```

Following is a sample configuration file that is shipped with Red Hat.

```
# Log all kernel messages to the console.
# Logging much else clutters up the screen.
kern.*               /dev/console

# Log anything (except mail) of level info or higher.
# Don't log private authentication messages!
*.info;mail.none;authpriv.none;cron.none        /var/log/messages

# The authpriv file has restricted access.
authpriv.*                               /var/log/secure
```

```
# Log all the mail messages in one place.
mail.*                                           /var/log/maillog

# Log cron stuff
cron.*                                           /var/log/cron

# Everybody gets emergency messages
*.emerg                                                    *

# Save news errors of level crit and higher in a special file.
uucp,news.crit                                   /var/log/spooler

# Save boot messages also to boot.log
local7.*                                         /var/log/boot.log
```

You can also use the `logger` command to test and place entries in your `syslogd` messages. It provides a shell interface to the `syslogd` module.

The basic format is `logger -p <facility> -t <tag> -f <file>`. The -p switch determines the priority to log at, while the -t switch places a user-defined entry in -f, which is the specified file. You can manually use the `syslogd` facility by entering the following:

```
# logger -p user.notice -t PRINT_NOTICE "Printer queue successfully flushed."
-f /var/log/printlog
```

This enters in `/var/log/printlog` a message of `PRINT_NOTICE`: `Printer queue suc-cessfully flushed`.

You can even try out logger's capabilities simply by entering the following:

```
# logger This is a test, boyo.
```

Check out your `/var/log/messages` after the test message. You see something similar to the following:

```
Nov 14 16:04:22 matrix root: This is a test, boyo.
```

General-Purpose Reporting with *mon*

Although parsing system messages that are logged by `syslogd` can be indicative of problems that are fast approaching, it takes a lot of time to parse messages on a daily basis. Because of time restraints, it's helpful to be able to glance at icons to determine the status of your cluster, or your entire environment.

`mon` takes service monitoring a few steps beyond `syslogd` reporting. It is designed to monitor applications and respond to them based on events. `mon` is written completely in Perl 5, and is designed to monitor network and server availability. Because `mon` is written in Perl, you need the following modules installed before you install it:

- `Time::Period`
- `Time::Hires`
- `Convert::BER`
- `mon::*`

You can grab these all from www.cpan.org. Actually, most of the scripts that `mon` uses are built around these modules. Bookmark www.cpan.org if you haven't already.

`mon` comes packaged with several monitoring services that you can add to your configuration, but it doesn't include the modules for them. You need to grab these from cpan if you're going to include more services, depending on what you're implementing.

Configuring the *mon* Client

The `mon` client is distributed separately from the server. You can get it from `ftp://ftp.kernel.org/pub/software/admin/mon`. Uncompress the software, which is in the `clients` subdirectory. The `mon` client is a series of Perl scripts that query the `mon` server. You need to install the current version of the `mon` `perl` module, which is currently available at Mon-0.11.tar.gz from www.perl.com/CPAN.

Installing the module is done by uncompressing the file, and entering the following lines:

```
# perl Makefile.PL
# make
# make test
# make install
```

Implementing the *mon* Server

Now that you've installed the required Perl modules, you need to grab the latest `mon` source from `ftp://ftp.kernel.org/pub/software/admin/mon/`. Uncompress the file, edit either the `example.cf` or the m4-based `example.m4`, and save it as either `mon.cf` or `mon.m4`. These files are in the `<MonRoot>/etc` directory. Make sure that it best reflects your environment.

The resulting `mon.cf` file can reflect any number of configurations. Following is a sample `mon.cf` file:

```
#
# Example "mon.cf" configuration for "mon".
#
# $Id: example.cf 1.1 Sat, 26 Aug 2000 15:22:34 -0400 trockij $
#
```

```
# global options
#
cfbasedir   = /root/mon/etc
alertdir    = /root/mon/alert.d
mondir      = /root/mon/mon.d
maxprocs    = 20
histlength = 100
randstart = 60s
#
# authentication types:
#   getpwnam     standard Unix passwd, NOT for shadow passwords
#   shadow       Unix shadow passwords (not implemented)
#   userfile     "mon" user file
#
authtype = getpwnam


#
# NB:  hostgroup and watch entries are terminated with a blank line (or
# end of file).  Don't forget the blank lines between them or you lose.
#


#
# group definitions (hostnames or IP addresses)
#
hostgroup serversbd1 matrix neo dumass


#
# For the servers in building 1, monitor ping and telnet
# BOFH is on weekend call :)
#
watch serversbd1
    service ping
        description ping servers in bd1
        interval 5m
        monitor fping.monitor
        period wd {Mon-Fri} hr {7am-10pm}
            alert mail.alert postmaster@domain.com
            alert page.alert oisr-pagers@domain.com
            alertevery 1h
        period NOALERTEVERY: wd {Mon-Fri} hr {7am-10pm}
            alert mail.alert postmaster@domain.com
            alert page.alert oisr-pagers@domain.com
        period wd {Sat-Sun}
            alert mail.alert postmaster@domain.com
            alert page.alert postmaster@domain.com
    service telnet
        description telnet to servers in bd1
        interval 10m
        monitor telnet.monitor
        depend serversbd1:ping
        period wd {Mon-Fri} hr {7am-10pm}
```

```
       alertevery 1h
       alertafter 2 30m
       alert mail.alert postmaster@domain.com
       alert page.alert oisr-pagers@domain.com

monitor telnet.monitor
depend routers:ping serversbd2:ping
period wd {Mon-Fri} hr {7am-10pm}
       alertevery 1h
       alertafter 2 30m
       alert mail.alert postmaster@domain.com
       alert page.alert oisr-pagers@domain.com
```

You don't need to place mon in any special directory to run, but make sure that the mon configuration file reflects where you put it.

Next, edit the auth.cf file. This file authenticates which users can perform which command.

Add the following to /etc/services of your machines so that mon can run as a service:

```
mon            2583/tcp                    # MON
mon            2583/udp                    # MON traps
```

You also want to add a cname of monhost to alias your mon server in your Domain Name System (DNS) server. mon does a lookup of monhost through DNS, so make sure that this is set. If you're not running DNS, place an entry in /etc/hosts. Also, add an environment variable to be this host, such as the following:

```
# export MONHOST="host.domain.com"
```

Next, try starting mon from the distribution directory. You can start the mon.cf version with the following:

```
# ./mon -f -c mon.cf -b `pwd`
```

You can start the mon.m4 version with the following:

```
# ./mon -f -M -c mon.m4 -b `pwd`
# ./clients/moncmd -s localhost list pids
```

This tests if mon is running correctly on your local machine.

Big Brother Is Watching

Although mon is a great, lightweight reporting tool, it's not designed to give the administrator or operators a quick glance view at the environment. Thankfully, there's graphical monitoring tools that can be implemented to react to user-defined events that not only give the administrator an overall picture of the environment, but react in certain ways, similar to `syslogd`. Tivoli and OpenView do a great job of monitoring and reacting to events, although they might be cost prohibitive for smaller organizations.

Enter Big Brother, which is free for non-commercial use, with their "better-than-free" license scheme. This means that you get to try out the software if you're a commercial organization, or simply use it if you're not making any money with your large parallel cluster, trying to solve the mysteries of the universe.

Big Brother shows data about several user-defined processes by displaying through a web page, or through Wireless Markup Language (WML)-enabled wireless application protocol (WAP) devices. Six different icons that represent severity levels about any number of processes are displayed, which allows an administrator to know at a glance how any number of nodes is behaving. Big Brother not only offers these status icons, but also displays the background screen in red, yellow, or green, so that you know just how your environment is doing.

You can get Big Brother server and clients for Linux, other UNIX variants and Windows NT/2000, and clients for Netware, Mac OS 9, VMS, and AS/400. Big Brother also supports extensible plugins, with several already available for download. You can get plugins to monitor toner in a laser printer, NetApp filers, Oracle table space monitoring, and even stock price fluctuations.

Installing and Configuring Big Brother

The first thing you must remember is that Big Brother needs a working web server because it's displayed in web page format. Apache works well for this because it's included in many Linux distributions by default. Big Brother needs to implement its scripts in your `cgi-bin` to work correctly.

You can get Big Brother at `http://bb4.com/download.html`. You can download the server and clients from there after you accept the license agreements.

To install it, you create a separate user that Big Brother can run under. Call the user whatever you want, but be sure that this user owns the resulting directories and files. It's recommended that you install the files initially by `root` and then `chmod` and `chown` to the Big Brother user afterwards. You log in to the `bb` account after creating it, uncompress all the files to the `root` directory, and change to superuser to install the files.

Change to the `bb<version>/install` directory and run `bbconfig <OS-NAME>`. In this case, you probably choose Linux; however, the Big Brother installation is distro-specific. You can choose from Red Hat, Debian, Caldera, Mandrake, or Linux. For example, the following starts an install of Big Brother on Caldera Linux:

```
# ./bbconfig caldera
```

This starts the install script, which asks you a series of questions. It's helpful to prepare a checklist first, or to have a good memory of where files are installed on your system. The configure script displays a copy of the license. If you agree to the license, hit Enter to continue and install the program. The installation script goes through its installation routine, and suggests options as you go. Remember that it's not a great idea to run Big Brother as `root`.

After running the configure script, change back into the `src` directory (`cd ../src`), type `make`, and then `make install`.

After that's done, enter into the `etc` directory (`cd ../etc`) and edit `bb-hosts`. You also edit `bbwarnsetup.cfg` to tell Big Brother how to contact someone if something goes wrong. The `install/README` has more information on this. Read the documentation and edit as necessary.

Run `./bbchkcfg.sh` and then `./bbchkhosts.sh`. These check your configuration files for errors.

Make a symbolic link from your `bb<version>` directory to `bb`. This makes things easier in the future, and allows you to use the preconfigured scripts without modifying everything. For example, make a link that is similar to the following:

```
# ln -s /home/bb/bb18c1 /home/bb/bb
```

Go into the `bb` directory by using the link that you just created and `chown` everything to the Big Brother user that you created:

```
# chown -R <bbuser> .
# cd ..; chown -R <bbuser> bbvar
```

Make a symbolic link from the full path to the `bb/www` directory to the `bb` directory in the web server's `document root` directory. Make sure that that this directory has the proper permissions. You might need to specify a different `document root` directory in your server configuration. For Apache, the default configuration file is `httpd.conf`:

```
# ln -s /home/bb/bb/www /usr/local/apache/htdocs/bb
```

Enter in your `bb` directory (`/home/bb/bb`) and type `./runbb.sh start`.

Adding More Clients to Big Brother

Now that your server is installed, you also need to install the bb monitoring service on each of the clients that you wish to monitor. Because this is potentially a time consuming operation, you might be better of writing a script to do this on each client, and share both the script and the executables over the Network File System (NFS). Either that, or you can make a golden client with SystemImager and install Big Brother from there (see Chapter 3, "Installing and Streamlining the Cluster").

To install the client on each machine, copy the distribution to each client and uncompress the distribution there. The installation is mostly the same; however, you only point the Big Brother host to the master server in your bb-hosts file, and then run ./runbb.sh to start. Big Brother service runs as a daemon, which is polled by the master server, so you only need a web server that is running on the master.

Using Big Brother

Using the Big Brother monitor is self-explanatory. The default web screen shows either a green, yellow, or red background on a black web interface. Each server shows the status of its services on the main screen with any one of six different status markers. Contained in these status markers are the following:

- ok—Everything is fine. No problems noted here. If everything is green, you see a green and black background.
- attention—These reflect warning messages in the message logs.
- trouble—These reports reflect a loss of functionality in the desired service(s). A report of this nature turns the background red.
- no report—This reflects a loss of connectivity with that service for over a half-hour. This turns the screen purple. This might also potentially be the result of a severely overloaded system. Further investigation is warranted.
- Unavailable—This results in a clear icon, and no background is changed.
- Offline—This appears when monitoring for this service is disabled.

Each status icon can be clicked to give a more accurate report of the error code. Big Brother also gives a history of the status by clicking the History button. Adding more hosts and services can be done by editing the bb-hosts file and restarting Big Brother.

Summary

Configuring clusters, nodes, and servers is only half the battle. As the environment grows, it becomes difficult to keep tabs on each system. As the administrator tends to go from a proactive stance to fire fighter, more tools are needed at everyone's disposal to keep systems operational and in line.

Some of the best tools at the system administrator's disposal include monitoring tools that keep a watchful eye on their entire servers and critical systems. There's nothing like being able to have processes watch other processes so that you don't have to. Thankfully, there are enough monitoring tools out there so that you don't have to write your own. Between being able to configure `syslogd` messages to your hearts content, and free (including free for non-commercial usage) monitoring software, an administrator is able to keep a tight reign on their clusters. You might want to also look at other freeware monitoring tools such as `netsaint`, `netview`, `nocol`, and `mrtg`. These monitors all work well enough that you won't need to spend tons of money on commercially available software.

11

Recovering When Disaster Strikes

HAVE YOU EVER NOTICED THAT THE SYSTEM administrator's job seems to have two states applied to it? That they're either ignored or hated? When everything is running smoothly, a system administrator is unnoticed by the end users. After all, if a system isn't broken, why fix it? The problem comes in when things aren't working all that well; namely, the users don't have access to their applications. That's when everyone notices the system administrator, who becomes the object of voodoo charms and curses.

To alleviate this love and hate relationship for the system administrator, he or she often has to play the role of psychiatrist, listening to the problems of the end user in a kind and sympathetic manner while trying to diagnose what happened with the application. The system administrator obviously has to wear many hats to get the job done. Not only do they have to play psychiatrist, but also first-level help desk, damage control, security consultant, application support, and so on.

Diagnosing applications, hardware, and network issues can be made easier by applying a mixture of common sense and patience to most problems. Having a well thought out strategy to fix issues when they come up allows the administrator to familiarize themselves with the environment enough to thwart common problems and to predict possible solutions.

There's always more than one way to diagnose problems with a failed server or cluster. One approach is to go for the quick fix first. If you can remember how you fixed the problem last time, it's a good idea to try that first. If that doesn't work, a more complete method of troubleshooting is needed, including documenting what you've done and the steps you took to try to diagnose the issues. There are times when a quick fix, such as a server reboot or a hang up on sendmail, solves the problem because of something as innocuous as the universe being out of alignment. The problem might never manifest itself again.

If a reboot of the system doesn't solve the problem, more drastic measures are needed, and it's for this reason that it's essential to have good documentation on hand for problems such as this. If you look through the documentation regarding the server in question, you should be able to piece together what issues you're having, if this scenario has happened before. That's assuming that you do have documentation in the first place.

The documentation should be able to tell you what has changed recently on the system, which is a good indication of what happened recently to affect something that now doesn't work. Change management logs usually point you in the right direction. If the system you're setting up is brand new, documentation and change management aren't going to help you much, so you have to rely on common sense troubleshooting methods to eliminate the problem.

Troubleshooting Through Layers

Most often, when your cluster has problems, you know why the application or hardware failed. It's not that hard to diagnose hardware failures, for instance. If you're getting input/output (I/O) disk errors, that's a good indication that something is wrong with a disk drive, and it needs to be replaced. If your application doesn't work for some reason, it's a good idea to check to see if it's even running. Nothing is more embarrassing than calling for support on a failed application and then finding out that it's not running in the first place.

Sometimes, it's not that easy to see what's going wrong. Applications, although installed correctly, simply refuse to work to the befuddlement of everyone involved. There are times when even the application vendors are stumped, their vendors are stumped, and there's nothing you can do besides shrug your shoulders and say that it doesn't work. If you're unlucky enough that the cluster involves more than one department, you can expect a lot of finger pointing. "It's the network," one exclaims. The network guys invariably answer, "No, QA did something to mess it up."

By using the seven-layer approach to networking, one can effectively troubleshoot problem clusters and get a better idea of where the problem lies. Although not a sure fire cure for every problem, you can use this approach to diagnose issues with your cluster or any other problem you're having.

Remember that the seven-layer network (discussed in Chapter 1, "Clustering Fundamentals") is an abstraction of each aspect of interaction between computer to computer and also computer to human. The layers are application, presentation, session, transport, network, data link, and the physical layer. By going through each level step by step, you can troubleshoot the problems that you're having in the cluster and work through the issues.

For example, let's say you're having a problem with a web server that connects to a remote database. You tried everything you can think of, and it still doesn't work. The vendor can't get it to work. There's no sense in contacting QA, because frankly, they're never there. So you decide to take some time and apply the seven-layer approach. Which end you start from is entirely up to you, although it's suggested that you start at the bottom and work your way up.

The Physical Layer

Linux has a variety of tools at its disposal to diagnose issues at the network level. You can diagnose problems at the physical layer with a straight ping to test connectivity. First, ping the relevant machines in your cluster. If your machine needs outside access, ping outside your wide-area network (WAN) or local subnet. This alerts you if your default route is set up or not. Remember, to have any kind of network connectivity, you need three things: an IP address, a subnet mask, and a gateway. If the machines on the subnet aren't using a gateway for their connectivity, the gateways are pointing to their own internal IP.

You also want to make sure that all cables are connected, and that each interface is up and has a link light. This is difficult when you've got a huge cluster, but it's something to think about anyway. One notorious culprit is the cross-over cable, when a straight cable should be in its place. Anyway, make sure the links are up, and the switches are all configured nicely. Make sure the cabling is not loose, and that your computer operator has not chewed through them in frustration. To do so, it's handy to have the right tools for the job to diagnose your network. A decent hand crimper to fix Ethernet cabling is always helpful, as is a cable tester to ensure that everything is up to snuff.

It's also a good idea to have the cable professionally strung from the beginning because of potential problems. Cable has to conform to local wiring laws, and it's easier to diagnose or repair systems when you don't have to inspect yards of cable buried under the server room floor, or overhead in the rafters.

A laptop configured with the right networking tools is a great resource because you can drag it around to different parts of the environment and the cluster, and insert it on the fly. With the notebook configured for the proper subnet, you can easily use tools such as ping and traceroute to diagnose network issues. If it's got the right software installed for your type of cluster, you can easily add it as another node.

The Data-Link Layer

There's not much you can do at the data-link layer. It's difficult to see that the protocols are working well; however, you can run an arp request to test connectivity. Using /sbin/arp <IP> shows you the hardware type of the interface (arcnet, pronet, ax25, netrom), and the Media Access Control (MAC) address of the interface. You can at least test physical connectivity.

The Network Layer

Troubleshooting at the network layer is important for network functionality. It's here where you're going to diagnose most of your network errors. You can see mismatched network masks, misconfigured gateways, and things such as misconfigured hosts tables. The misconfigured gateway always seems to pop up when one least expects it, causing you to lose connectivity outside of your local network. You can check the default gateway with the route command:

```
# route
Kernel IP routing table
Destination     Gateway         Genmask         Flags Metric Ref    Use Iface
172.16.0.0      *               255.255.255.0   U     0      0        0 eth0
127.0.0.0       *               255.0.0.0       U     0      0        0 lo
default         172.16.0.1      0.0.0.0         UG    0      0        0 eth0
```

In this case, the default route at the bottom with the gateway in it states that each packet not headed for the local subnet is going to that address to be relayed.

Linux provides tools such as netstat to diagnose various network issues. Using netstat gives you a good idea of the environment so that you can trace connections. Using /sbin/route is also good for troubleshooting connections, as it gives you an idea of where your packets are headed. The route command shows the kernel's routing tables after being manipulated by the ifconfig command.

```
# netstat
Proto Recv-Q Send-Q Local Address          Foreign Address         State
tcp        0      0 172.16.0.6:1255        172.16.0.2:x11
ESTABLISHED
tcp        0      0 172.16.0.6:1253        172.16.0.2:x11
ESTABLISHED
tcp        0      0 172.16.0.6:1250        172.16.0.2:x11
ESTABLISHED
tcp        0      0 172.16.0.6:1259        172.16.0.2:x11
ESTABLISHED
tcp        0      0 172.16.0.6:1245        172.16.0.2:x11
ESTABLISHED
tcp        0     40 172.16.0.6:1338        172.16.0.2:x11
ESTABLISHED
tcp        0      0 172.16.0.6:1337        172.16.0.2:x11
ESTABLISHED
tcp        1      0 172.16.0.6:1257        209.151.248.200:http
CLOSE_WAIT
tcp        1      0 172.16.0.6:1260        209.151.248.200:http
CLOSE_WAIT
```

Pulling up `netstat` shows active connections on the server that it's being run from. If run from the master node on a cluster, you can see which connections are being made from where, which protocols are in use, and the state that the port is in.

Remember that there might be barriers to your network probes. Firewalls often block `ping`, `traceroute`, and other Internet Control Message Protocol (ICMP) traffic.

The Transport and Session Layers

The transport layer consists of mechanisms for session establishment, which incorporate `tcp` and `udp` traffic. The session layer manages sessions between different presentation entities. Applications that use this layer include the X window system, Network File System (NFS), and Structured Query Language (SQL), among others.

"Okay," you say. "That's all well and good, but how does this apply to diagnosing the cluster?" One way of doing this is by sniffing the traffic on the network. By hooking up a sniffing device or program, you can see whether or not the packets for your particular program are being sent across the wire, and what the network is doing with them. Some great tools exist for Linux that are indispensable for the administrator who's looking to diagnose network issues, and they happen to be freely available under the GNU general license. Among them are `tcpdump`, `ethereal`, and `sniffit`, which are described in more detail in the next section.

The Presentation Layer

The presentation layer is responsible for presenting data to the application layer. It's responsible for translating data and providing coding and conversion. This layer provides services for the application layer. There's not a whole lot of necessary diagnosing that can go on at this level.

The Application Layer

Troubleshooting problems at the application layer depend on the applications themselves, and are different for each type of cluster. Various tools can monitor the health of your applications, not including the applications themselves.

Third party applications such as mon, Big Brother, and NetSaint perform a limited service in maintaining services on the application layer. They can tell you if a particular service is up and running and even take action regarding certain events, as in Simple Network Management Protocol (SNMP). Although it's a great place to test applications on a single machine, it's not a great place to test connectivity.

For true application support, you have to bear down and read the documentation first of all. Secondly, knowing where to get answers for your application is the key to being a good system administrator. Mailing lists, books, search engines, and other administrators are all great resources for learning where to diagnose your application. Of course, sometimes the best place to go is paid application support from the vendors themselves, even though that's not possible all the time.

Diagnosing Applications with Top

Top is a similar program to ps, which is designed to display the top CPU processes and memory hogs in order. Top was inspired by a command, which listed the top five processes, including their use. This achieves a similar goal but is more attuned to ps. It's a great program to display memory hogs and zombie processes. Although the experienced system administrator already has knowledge of Top, it's always good to keep this program in mind for when the need arises. Following is a sample output of the top command. Top refreshes itself naturally every five seconds, but you can easily change that with the d or s commands.

```
1:15pm  up 6 days, 34 min,  3 users,  load average: 0.00, 0.00, 0.00
74 processes: 73 sleeping, 1 running, 0 zombie, 0 stopped
CPU0 states:  0.4% user,  3.0% system,  0.0% nice, 96.0% idle
CPU1 states:  0.0% user,  0.1% system,  0.0% nice, 99.4% idle
```

```
Mem:    158524K av,  155416K used,    3108K free,      0K shrd,   12364K buff
Swap:   415760K av,   27900K used,  387860K free                 114668K
cached
```

```
  PID USER      PRI  NI  SIZE  RSS SHARE STAT %CPU %MEM   TIME COMMAND
29480 edstorm    19   0  5616 5616  5308 S     1.9  3.5   0:24 kdeinit
29769 stomith    14   0  1056 1056   840 R     1.3  0.6   0:00 top
29432 root       11   0  2016 1984  1384 S     0.3  1.2   1:00 sshd
26907 root       10   0   516  276   260 S     0.1  0.1   0:08 sshd
    1 root        9   0   124   72    72 S     0.0  0.0   0:15 init
    2 root        9   0     0    0     0 SW    0.0  0.0   0:00 keventd
    3 root        9   0     0    0     0 SW    0.0  0.0   0:37 kswapd
    4 root        9   0     0    0     0 SW    0.0  0.0   0:00 kreclaimd
    5 root        9   0     0    0     0 SW    0.0  0.0   0:00 bdflush
    6 root        9   0     0    0     0 SW    0.0  0.0   0:20 kupdated
    7 root        9   0     0    0     0 SW    0.0  0.0   0:00 scsi_eh_0
    8 root        9   0     0    0     0 SW    0.0  0.0   0:00 khubd
  268 root        9   0   192    4     4 S     0.0  0.0   0:00 safe_mysqld
  332 root        9   0  5876 1472  1384 S     0.0  0.9   0:00 mysqld
  401 root        9   0  5876 1472  1384 S     0.0  0.9   0:09 mysqld
```

Top displays the processes that take up the most CPU time, down to the ones that take the least. The first column shows the process identification number of the offending process, then the owner, the tasks priority, and the nice value. Remember that the lower the nice value, the higher priority the job. The size column refers to the task's code, plus data stack space in kilobytes. The RSS column displays the total amount of physical memory that the task uses in kilobytes, and the share column displays the amount of shared memory.

The stat column actually means *state* of the task. The letter S refers to a sleeping task, D is uninterruptible sleep, R is running, and Z is for Zombie. A process with a W means that the process is swapped out. The time column represents the total CPU time that the task has used since it started.

Your Linux distribution should come with top installed, as it's extremely helpful. If it's not, you can always find it at ftp.groupsys.com.

Real Administrators Don't Need a Mail Client

If your application is listening on specific ports, you might try to use Telnet to test connectivity. Telnet opens a connection that allows you to see exactly what's going on, regardless of confusing interfaces. Depending on the application, you can arm yourself with the specific Request For Comments (RFC) and manually work the service without a pesky program such as a newsreader or mail client.

For example, take the classic example of mail transmittal and receiving. It's easy to send and receive mail without even using a mail client. Receiving mail through Post Office Protocol (POP) is also extremely easy, although trying to manually get your mail through Internet Message Access Protocol (IMAP) is incredibly hard and won't even be mentioned here. Check out the RFC if you've got the time.

Checking to see if your Simple Mail Transfer Protocol (SMTP) server is up is done through a simple Telnet to port 25 on the remote machine. Just like you're attaching directly to the port which SMTP runs, you can Telnet to 110, the port which POP3 runs on. By receiving a banner after you Telnet to the port, you can know that your application is running. Following is an example:

```
# telnet localhost 25
Trying 127.0.0.1...
Connected to localhost.
Escape character is '^]'.
220 localhost.localdomain ESMTP Sendmail 8.11.6/8.11.6; Thu, 3 Jan 2002
00:43:52 -0800
```

Do you see that banner there with the 220 leering at you? That's sendmail, which is waiting for the next prompt. Mail clients also see that, they just don't display the output for you. This tells you that sendmail is up. Taking it a step further, if you type **help**, you understand that sendmail isn't meant to be run in the background without user intervention.

```
214-2.0.0 This is sendmail version 8.11.6
214-2.0.0 Topics:
214-2.0.0        HELO    EHLO    MAIL    RCPT    DATA
214-2.0.0        RSET    NOOP    QUIT    HELP    VRFY
214-2.0.0        EXPN    VERB    ETRN    DSN     AUTH
214-2.0.0        STARTTLS
214-2.0.0 For more info use "HELP <topic>".
214-2.0.0 To report bugs in the implementation send email to
214-2.0.0        sendmail-bugs@sendmail.org.
214-2.0.0 For local information send email to Postmaster at your site.
214 2.0.0 End of HELP info
```

Programs such as sendmail and POP3, and Network News Transfer Protocol (NNTP) servers, all display help functions at the Telnet level, in case you want to test or even use the application as designed. Following is a manual sendmail session in action:

```
# telnet localhost 25
Trying 127.0.0.1...
Connected to localhost.
Escape character is '^]'.
220 localhost.localdomain ESMTP Sendmail 8.11.6/8.11.6; Thu, 3 Jan 2002
00:43:52 -0800
HELO matrix.etopian.net
250 localhost.localdomain Hello matrix [127.0.0.1], pleased to meet you
Mail From: bob@bob.com
250 2.1.0 bob@bob.com... Sender ok
```

```
RCPT To: stomith@stomith.com
250 2.1.5 stomith@stomith.com... Recipient ok
DATA
354 Enter mail, end with "." on a line by itself
This is a test. This is a test of the email system. This is only a test.
.
250 2.0.0 g03AGFB23641 Message accepted for delivery
quit
221 2.0.0 localhost.localdomain closing connection
Connection closed by foreign host.
```

In this example, there is huge potential for abuse. After connecting to the server itself, it's easy to type in the wrong Mail From attribute, which might make your email come from someone else, such as your boss.

Checking email manually through POP is also a great way to test connectivity, and the protocol is simple enough that you don't have to worry about reading miles of documentation. A POP server only handles six basic commands, user, pass, stat, list, retr, and dele. Following is an example session:

```
$ telnet localhost 110
Trying 127.0.0.1...
Connected to localhost.
Escape character is '^]'.
+OK Qpopper (version 4.0.3) at tiger starting.
user cbookman
+OK Password required for cbookman.
pass p@ssw0rd
+OK cbookman has 1 visible message (0 hidden) in 2166 octets.
list
+OK 1 visible messages (2166 octets)
1 2166
.
retr 1
+OK 2166 octets
Received: from mailhost.uop.edu (IDENT:root@mailhost.uop.edu [138.9.1.1])
Received: (from mail@localhost)
        by proda201.uu.commissioner.com (8.9.3/8.9.3) id LAA26684;
        Tue, 23 Oct 2001 11:10:10 -0400
Message-Id: <sbd5269c.037@mailserv.uop.edu>
Date: Tue, 23 Oct 2001 08:12:53 -0700
From: "Jonathan" <jon@uop.edu>
To: <uopff@football.fantasy.sportsline.com>
Subject: We have a winner!
Mime-Version: 1.0
Content-Disposition: inline
Content-Transfer-Encoding: 8bit
Content-Type: text/plain; charset=US-ASCII
REMEMBER that we have another Thursday thriller!  Colts and Chiefs!  That
game starts at 5:30.  All picks for the week must be in by 4:30 on Thursday!!
Good luck!  J
```

```
.
dele 1
+OK Message 1 has been deleted.
quit
+OK Pop server at tiger signing off.
Connection closed by foreign host.
```

Helpful Tools to Diagnose Your Cluster

Sometimes, a straight ping or top doesn't diagnose an application or service. To fully understand what's happening with your cluster, you have to look behind the scenes and see how the individual machines talk to one another.

Packet Capture provides a great deal of information for diagnosing traffic on the network, which includes telling you the locations of potential bottlenecks and problems. Capturing and viewing all traffic on your network comes with a small price, however. A certain amount of finesse is required to use it effectively, and to protect the security and privacy of your users. You must make sure that you're not breaking any laws, and that the viewing packets abide by the guidelines of your organization.

Capturing and viewing traffic entails monitoring the data that travels across your network and analyzing it for certain patterns. Perhaps you might be looking for certain protocols to be transported over certain areas, or to look for certain handshaking between applications. You can use numerous tools to analyze traffic over your network, which either analyze or interpret the results for you.

Can You View the Data?

The first question you have to ask yourself is if you can actually view the data in question. To view the data, you must get on the network that the data is being transferred over. If you're using your public network to view traffic, it's going to be difficult to view packets transmitted over your private parallel cluster. One way to make this easier is to use remote computers on the network with the proper tools on them, and then hit those various computers remotely. Another way is through creative use of virtual local-area network (VLAN) technology, if your network supports it. By putting a local computer on the same VLAN as your remote network, you can become a part of that network.

If all your data is transmitted over hubs, the data is effectively shared, and viewing the packets doesn't present a problem. The problem comes in when the network isn't composed of hubs. With the advent of cheaper and more reliable switching technology, hubs are becoming a thing of the past. More organizations aren't even considering hubs because of the increased security that switches provide. That's not saying that all is lost, however. If you have physical access to the network in question, you might be able to temporarily replace the switch with a hub, if that section of the network can take a temporary hit in performance. If you can't do that, consider placing a hub on the switch, and only put those network connections on the hub which you want to view.

Packet sniffing works by putting a network interface in promiscuous mode. This forces the interface to grab all packets on the network, rather than accept packets destined for that address specifically. Linux needs the interface to be put into promiscuous mode with the ifconfig command. You need to be root to toggle the interface, which you can do with the following:

```
# ifconfig <device> -promisc
```

Capturing Data with *tcpdump*

Discussion of data capture programs begins with tcpdump, which is one of the most basic programs for capture. The program was written at the Lawrence Berkeley Laboratory at the University of California at Berkeley. The tcpdump program uses libpcap, which is a high-level library that is designed specifically for packet capture.

Using tcpdump allows you to see exactly what's going on with your network. The program isn't a great analysis tool, but that's not what it's designed to do. It's designed to take a snapshot of the network. You can optionally add filters to collect information about a certain part of a network or cluster, which is probably exactly what you want when diagnosing different aspects of your environment.

If tcpdump isn't already installed on your system, you can get it at www.tcp-dump.org. You also need to download and install libpcap. First, install libpcap, and then tcpdump. Both use the standard configure, make, and as root, make install.

Running tcpdump without any options causes the program to start spewing out every bit of possible information about the network and the data that it sees. You can save this information to a file with the redirect > option, or run it in the background with & or nohup.

Using *tcpdump* to Troubleshoot Connections

The best thing you can do with `tcpdump` is use it to collect data for use in other applications, such as Ethereal. By using the -w switch, you enable `tcpdump` to write in raw mode. This switch tells `tcpdump` to directly dump raw binary data onto a text file. The syntax is as follows:

```
# tcpdump -w <textfile>
```

Now that you've got raw data about your network, you can use it in other ways. The -r switch, tcpdump can reread its binary file and display it in human readable format. You can then redirect that human readable format into a text file, such as the following:

```
# tcpdump -r <textfile> > <outputfile>
```

The -c switch tells `tcpdump` to exit after so many packets. The -I switch tells `tcpdump` which interface to listen on. This is a necessary tool if you're using your Linux machine on multiple networks, or as a router.

Filtering *tcpdump* Output

If you don't want to capture the entire network's worth of data, use filters that only capture specific information. The filtering language is also used by other programs, such as Ethereal, so at least a cursory examination of the language is warranted.

Filters can be applied by either appending them to the end of the command line, or by a file. The file is read by using the -F switch with the name of the file. You typically use files for complex filters that are run repeatedly, rather than typing the filter on a constant basis during each command line argument.

The most basic filter is to sort based on type, by using the `host`, `net`, or `port` keywords. With these filters, you can display only the traffic that's related to those services. For example:

```
# tcpdump net 172.16
```

shows you all the traffic on the Class B subnet. Using

```
# tcpdump port 80
```

displays all web traffic on the same network. You can also specify traffic going in a specific direction, with the `src` command, which denotes the source and `dst` for destination.

You can also specify the `proto` keyword to denote the protocol that you want to dump. Possible protocols include `ether`, `fddi`, `tr`, `ip`, `ip6`, `arp`, `rarp`, `decent`, `tcp` and `udp`. You can use these in combination with other filter attributes such as `dst` and `host`.

The `tcpdump` program can even look into the packet headers themselves and match such characteristics as packet length or packet contents. Using

```
# tcpdump greater 150
```

shows all packets with a size greater than 150 bytes.

You can also use compound filters with tcpdump to achieve more granulated results. You can use logical operators such as `and`, `or`, and `not`, otherwise known as `&&`, `||`, and `!` respectively, without taking the highest precedence. If you want to display just IP information from a certain host, you can use the following:

```
# tcpdump host 172.16.100.10 and ip
```

Although these examples of `tcpdump` generate raw data for other programs and advanced network administrators, you most likely need other programs to massage and analyze the data. Some programs that you might want to look into are `tcpslice`, `tcpshow`, `tcp-reduce`, and `tcp trace`. This is just a brief overview of `tcpdump` and what it can do for your cluster troubleshooting. It's recommended that you use it for a while and play around with different filters and filter files. As always, be sure to check the man pages for more specific information; that's always the best place to start.

Analyzing Packets with Ethereal

Ethereal is a free network packet analyzer for both Linux and Windows systems that allows you to capture data from the local network, and to analyze the data captured from other programs such as `tcpdump`. Ethereal also uses the same filter and capture syntax as `tcpdump`, so you can use it from the command line and from a primarily graphical interface.

You can get Ethereal from `www.ethereal.com`. Ethereal needs at least GTK+ 1.2.0 or better to run because of graphic requirements. You also need the familiar `libpcap` installed from `www.tcpdump.org`. Binaries are available for most distributions of Linux, or you can start with the old, `configure`, `make`, `make install` of the source code. Using `make install-man` installs the man pages, which have to be done separately.

Ethereal supports a huge variety of protocols, and the list is constantly growing as more and more people submit protocol dissectors. This program is extremely useful for diagnosing network issues (see Figure 11.1). It tells you more about how the network works, and it shows you communication between clusters on the network.

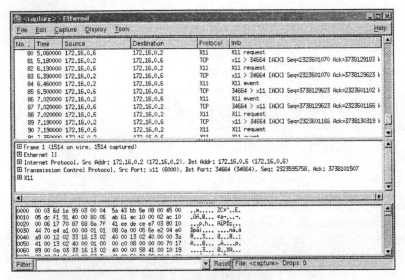

Figure 11.1   Diagnosing network traffic with Ethereal.

You start ethereal by running Ethereal from the command line. This brings up a blank graphical interface.

You can either use Ethereal to capture data itself, or by loading the raw data saved with `tcpdump` and the `-w` switch. Click File, Open, and the name of the `tcpdump-ed` file to analyze the data, or you can use a previously saved Ethereal file.

Using Ethereal to Capture Data

If you want to use Ethereal to capture data, simply select Capture, Start. This brings up another dialog box that you can use to massage the data you want to capture.

The graphical interface lets you choose the network interface that you want to capture data from, and the number of packets. The third field selects the file size limit, as an unlimited sized capture can easily fill up a partition full of raw data. The duration selects the number of packets to capture. The filter dialog box, if you remember correctly, follows the same syntax as `tcpdump`. The File option defines the file that you want to save the capture under when you hit Save As in the main file menu. Capture length here refers to the maximum length of the packet. The maximum length possible is 65,535. Make sure that it's at least as large as your maximum transmission unit (MTU).

Clicking OK starts the capture process, and depending upon the options you've just selected, displays the captured packets in real time.

The resulting dialog box, shown in Figure 11.2, displays all the information that the capture has shown. After you're done capturing data, you can return to the screen to analyze the data. The top pane shows the captured packets by number and time, where they came from, where they're going, and the protocol they're following.

Clicking any packet in the upper frame changes the lower two frames, and shows more data about the specific packet that was selected. The lower pane actually shows the packet collected in both hex and ASCII format, and the middle frame tells you more about what you've selected. One option is to right click the packet and then open it up in its own window for further observation.

Try selecting a portion in the middle frame, such as the Source or Destination address. The resulting hex information in the lower frame is displayed, which shows you the actual data. If you highlight a particular aspect of the frame in this way, and then right click, and select Match Selected, Ethereal updates its own filter for you and displays the relevant data depending on the resulting filter.

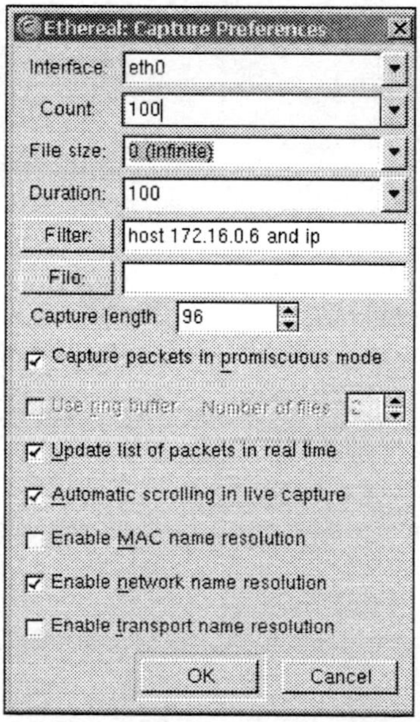

Figure 11.2   Capturing data with Ethereal.

For example, to select all data going to a specific destination, expand the Ethernet II option, highlight the Source field, and right-click in that frame and select Match Selected. To clear the filter and return to the unfiltered data, click the Reset button on the bottom of the frame.

You can also view individual packets and select Follow tcp Stream. This collects all data from the tcp packets and displays it as one stream, which allows you to view information that has been transmitted, including possibly sensitive password information. The main reason to sniff packets isn't for malicious password sniffing, however, but to diagnose the interactivity between applications.

Filtering the Display

One of the most powerful aspects of ethereal is its ability to display data in a variety of formats. Ethereal's interface lets you colorize by protocol and type of packet. You can colorize all Domain Name System (DNS) requests, and any hundred or so protocols. Ethereal also makes its own filters based on your selections.

You also can highlight certain parts of the captured packet, right click in the display, and select Match as Selected. This matches other packet characteristics as necessary, and applies other filters to them, such as highlighting them with color for the display.

Using these, you can quickly see what kind of traffic is taking up the network, and therefore, what kind of information your cluster is passing to and from the other nodes. The documentation for ethereal is well written and worth more than a cursory glance. You can find them constantly updated and housed at www.ethereal.com/docs/user-guide.

When Worse Comes to Worst

If all else fails, and you can't seem to diagnose the application, you might be better off rolling back to a previously known configuration, or installing from scratch because of the time it takes to diagnose what's failed. If you think that diagnosing the application or OS problem will take longer than reinstalling the data, you can probably save time by rolling back to either the last time it worked or from a clean install.

When you're thinking about rolling back to a previous state, remember what media you have to roll back from. This is why a roll back plan needs to be incorporated in each cluster design. You have to ask yourself a few questions before rolling back (reinstalling the OS from scratch). For example, will rolling back and starting from scratch actually solve the problem? Rolling back won't save critical data.

Starting over might be the preferred method for solving any major problem with several nodes, as from a parallel computing or dedicated distributed cluster. These systems don't actually hold any data for the most part, as they're just nodes. Reinstalling from scratch only takes 45 minutes at the most, on a decent 100bt network. It's even faster if you're not doing a complete install or if you have finely tuned your image.

With a decent backup strategy in place, you might only need to roll back to the last incremental or differential backup, if you know where the last good working configuration was. This is preferable to reinstalling from scratch, if you know of a change that was made so that you can at least roll back to before the change.

If your budget can afford it, a standby machine might be an optimal solution. It's much easier to throw in a spare node than to try to diagnose a failed application on a production machine. A hot standby with automatic failover is optimal. You can then repair the failed node or application when it's not critical.

Reimaging from Kickstart

The key here is preparedness. You must have a decent plan to recover at the image level. The trick isn't in installing the OS again, that's easy. A more detailed explanation is found in Chapter 3, "Installing and Streamlining the Cluster." The real issue is adding the necessary applications into the Kickstart routine so that they are available upon startup. The end goal is to use it so that you have a minimum of downtime.

If planned out well, you can use scripts to mount other directories on the network and run install routines so that you don't have to worry about installing packages when installing each time. By using a script similar to this one, you can envision what kinds of things can be done at the install level to automate an entire install. If you prepare your environment and your scripts ahead of time, it's easy to go from bare metal to production in under an hour, not counting potential data.

```
#!/bin/bash
#
# Script to setup services for the correct vlan
#
##############################################################
# Installing name services
cat > /etc/resolv.conf << EOD
domain stomith.com
nameserver 192.168.0.1
nameserver 192.168.1.1
EOD
##############################################################
```

```
# Script creates /etc/rc2.d/S99tempscript to install packages
# off of server daemon and yogsothoth; will remove itself when done.
# install_big_brother, install_mon, install_mosix are pre-built scripts
# off of daemon which install programs onto a machine called with this
# kickstart script.
#
cat > /etc/rc3.d/S99tempscript << EOD
mkdir /root
mkdir -p /import/src
mount 192.168.0.100:/usr/local/src /import/src
cd /import/src
/import/src/install_big_brother
PATH=$PATH:/usr/local/bin;export PATH
/import/src/install_mon
/import/src/install_mosix
rm /etc/rc2.d/S99tempscript
umount /import/src
#
# This portion of the script should install the latest version of SSH.
# Not the free openssh, but the non-commercial version, mind you.
mount 192.168.0.101:/kickstart
cp /mnt/Packages/ssh-3.0.1.tar.gz /root
cd /root
gunzip -c ssh-3.0.1.tar.gz ¦ tar xf -
cd ssh-3.0.1
./configure
make
make install
cd startup/linux/redhat
if [ -f sshd2 ]; then
    cp sshd2 /etc/init.d/
    chmod +x /etc/init.d/sshd2
    ln -s /etc/init.d/sshd2 /etc/rc3.d/S96sshd2
    ln -s /etc/init.d/sshd2 /etc/rc0.d/K86sshd2
else
    :
fi
reboot
EOD
# "Temporary Startup Script Install Complete."
####################################################################
# Make tempscript executable; end script
#
chmod +x /a/etc/rc3.d/S99tempscript
```

This program is called after the Kickstart script starts the post installation. This script installs itself in /etc/rc3.d so that it is called upon at reboot. After the system is rebooted, the script is called and starts running install software from a third server. After the script is done, it removes itself from /etc/rc3.d so that it doesn't get called for an install each time.

In the previous script, the `install_ssh` can also be placed standalone along with the other install scripts. This allows you to call your own scripts from there, or include them in the main install script, whichever works better. Disaster Recovery becomes much easier when you've got a plan.

Ghost Images

As with Kickstart images, it might be easier to reinstall the entire operating system rather than diagnosing errors. You have to keep a golden image on a backup server or tape for this approach. It's a good idea to make an image of the server right before you put it into production; this way, you can roll back to it whenever things get hairy.

It's also a good idea also to make ghost images periodically, although it's difficult at times to bring down production systems to do so. If you can manage to schedule downtime, you can have different images to pick from.

A restore plan at the OS and application level also saves on tapes. There's no need to back up an OS if you have a ghost image or Kickstart method to fall back on. The only restores that you have to make are ones containing the actual changed data.

This Too Shall Pass

Learning how to deal with frustrating users and even more frustrating management is a skill that becomes more honed over time as you learn to adjust to your user base. The more you work with your cluster, the more you find out who uses it. You also find what needs they have, and which applications they have problems with or tend to accidentally delete occasionally. Learning to deal with the human element of the cluster is just as important or more so than all the hardware and software put together.

A good system administrator needs to remain calm at all times. It's understandably hard to keep one's cool when the bastard operator from hell thinks they're doing you a favor by troubleshooting applications or hardware, and then calls you up to say that they couldn't fix it but they absolutely know what the problem is and would you kindly fix it at your convenience (right now). Unless you're building a cluster in a home hobby environment, you will have users for whom you're responsible. Management has to be kept happy, and users have to actually use the cluster if you're using a parallel or distributed environment. The thing to remember is that if you're the one who maintains the cluster, you're the one who has to keep everyone happy.

A good rule of thumb is to keep the appearance of calm at all times. This isn't always easy, especially when you've been frantically trying to fix the disk array to the master node of the web server's load balancer. It always happen that you get a call directly from an end user "just letting you know that the web site is down." It's a good idea to take a Zen-like approach, in that this, too, shall pass. It's likely that the user doesn't know that your mirror replicated the deleted operating system files across both drives and that your backup operator can't restore the data.

If someone calls you screaming because the job that they've been working on for two days is lost somewhere, you can easily calm them down by using a nice, even tone of voice. Your natural instinct might be to yell back at them, but if you keep an even-tempered, calm voice, nine times out of ten you'll find that you've just diffused a potential hazard. It's almost impossible to continue shouting at a calm person.

A common technique in counseling is the idea of "matching behavior." The trick here is to start out matching the behavior of a client. The client might call you on the phone, or even worse, jump into your cube yelling and screaming. If you're the hot-headed type, then by all means, yell and scream back. Naturally, this can only escalate into something you both don't want. The idea here is to start out upset, but gradually ease the conversation down to a nice, even, mellow tone within a short amount of time. The other person will gradually match your behavior, and you've just diffused a potentially harmful situation. Of course, this doesn't happen often, but it's good to arm yourself with knowledge for server room use.

Summary

Troubleshooting a failed cluster can be done if you know why the problem flaked out in the first place. Otherwise, you can use the network layered approach to diagnose failed clusters and their applications.

You can use common knowledge and tools to diagnose what's going on with your network. Sniffing packets and displaying what's going on in the midst of the network gives you a good idea of what's actually happening.

It might be easier to simply recreate the cluster from an image rather than diagnose a failed application. If there's a hardware problem, it might actually be easier to swap out an entire machine than fix it because of the time and cost of repair and maintenance contracts.

If all else fails, get yourself an Emergency System Administrator Kit. This item, not sold in stores, is a large red box with a single pane of glass that you hang on your wall in case of an emergency. If for some reason you can't possibly fix the cluster, or because it's messed up beyond belief, take the arm on the side of it, and break the glass. Within the emergency repair kit, you'll find a copy of your resume. Make copies and distribute liberally.

IV

Appendixes

Cluster Resources

THE POPULARITY AND MODULAR NATURE of open-source operating systems allows for a great many projects and solutions. As you saw in previous chapters, plenty of information is available about Linux clustering, and there are projects for just about every aspect of clustering. There are parallel clusters, high availability clusters, and soon, you'll be able to put together two refrigerators running Linux for redundancy!

The following web sites are included as a further guide in selecting the right information for clustering your systems. They are current as of the publication of this book.

Designing a Cluster

You can find other handy tidbits here on how to build large numbers of clusters from scratch, and how to keep them secure:

- `www.ibiblio.org/mdw/HOWTO/Hardware-HOWTO`—The Linux Hardware Compatibility List.

- `www.informatik.uni-koeln.de/fai`—Fully Automated Installation (FAI). Kickstart for Debian GNU/Linux.

- `www.ferzkopp.net/Software/CloneIt/CloneIt.html`—CloneIt is an image-creation system for large numbers of identical PCs.

- `http://oss.software.ibm.com/developerworks/projects/lui`—Lui is IBM's open-source cluster installation tool. It reports to be entirely configurable based on client demand of resources.
- `www.tripwire.org`—The open-sourced version of the security tool. This auditing tool is a must-have for all essential systems.
- `www.securityfocus.com/bugtraq/archive`—Search for exploits and security issues.
- `www.bastille-linux.org`—A script to harden Red Hat- and Mandrake-based distributions. This is one of the best scripts to secure your systems, but remember that it's easy to secure your system beyond what you intended.
- `www.division17.net` (Telecommunications Division 17 Initiative)—`www.csinet.org/`. Home of the Construction Specifications Institute. This is helpful for datacenter planning and construction.
- `www.myricom.com`—Myricom Corporation. Founders of Myrinet, which is a networking technology similar to Gigabit Ethernet.
- `www.webtechniques.com/archives/1999/08/newton`—Offers technical considerations for planning your computer room.
- `www.isc.org` (Internet Software Consortium)—Makers of software such as BIND, INN, and an open DHCP implementation.

Linux File Systems

Linux, being an open-source operating system, can easily handle different file systems and the standard ext2 file system. You want to look into alternative file systems if you're hosting mission critical applications, just for the journaling, if nothing else:

- `http://parlweb.parl.clemson.edu/pvfs/`—The Parallel Virtual File System. This virtual file system is stored on many nodes throughout a cluster and is accessible through each node.
- `http://oss.sgi.com/projects/xfs/index.html`—XFS, SGI's open-source journaling file system.
- `www.coda.cs.cmu.edu/index.html`—Coda distributed file system.
- `http://oss.software.ibm.com/developerworks/opensource/jfs/?dwzone=open-source` (JFS)—Open-source journaling software for Linux from IBM.
- `www.jetico.com/index.htm#/linux.html`—BestCrypt for Linux supports encrypted file systems as a regular file system on a normal mount point.

- www.gnu.org/software/parted/parted.html—GNU Parted is a program for modifying Linux partitions. Parted can modify existing partitions, copy data between hard disks, and image them.

Monitors

Now that you have your cluster up and running, you need to maintain the cluster. If you're not using a cluster operating system, you might find these programs and scripts helpful to maintaining your cluster's health:

- www.netlib.org/utk/icl/xpvm/xpvm.html—XPVM is a GUI interface and monitor for PVM.

- www.abo.fi/~mats/CMS (Cluster Management System)—A front-end interface for a cluster of machines, which executes the Message Passing Interface (MPI). This keeps up-to-date information such as CPU load, processes, and memory utilization across the cluster.

- http://smile.cpe.ku.ac.th/research/scms1.2.2—The Smile Cluster Management System is another graphical interface that allows for monitoring large clusters and job submission.

- www.alphaworks.ibm.com/tech/clusterstarterkit?open&t=gr,p=Clusters4Linux—The cluster start kit for Linux. Designed by IBM, this allows for the creation and monitoring of up to six nodes from a master node.

- www.netlib.org/benchmark/hpl—A portable implementation of the high-performance Linpack Benchmark for distributed-memory computers.

High Availability Clusters

- www.linux-ha.org (High Availability Linux Project)—Your one-stop shop for all things highly available.

- Linux-HA Mailing list archive:

  - Send a message to linux-ha-subscribe@muc.de to subscribe to the list.

  - Send a message to linux-ha-unsubscribe@muc.de to unsubscribe.

- http://oss.missioncriticallinux.com—Mission Critical Linux.

- www.sgi.com/software/failsafe/—SGI's open-source high availability project.

- www.linuxjournal.com/article.php?sid=4344—High availability cluster checklist.

Parallel Clusters

- www.top500.org—The top 500 supercomputer sites.
- www-unix.mcs.anl.gov/mpi/index.html—MPI Standard.
- www.erc.msstate.edu/misc/mpi/mpi-faq.html— MPI FAQ.
- www.lam-mpi.org—An implementation of the MPI programming environment.
- www.cs.sandia.gov/cplant/—The computational plant at Sandia National Laboratories. Cplant is a software distribution for Linux parallel clusters.
- www.beowulf.org/mailman/listinfo/Beowulf—Beowulf mailing list. Discussion of topics related to Beowulf clusters.
- www.openmp.org—A multiplatform shared-memory programming interface for C, C++, and Fortran.
- http://plogic.com/bcs—Basic cluster scripts for Beowulf systems.
- http://frank.harvard.edu/~coldwell/diskless/—Charles Coldwell's technique on booting diskless clusters.

Load Balanced Clusters

- www.backhand.org/mod_backhand—An Apache module that allows for the seamless redirection of HTTP requests from one server to another.
- www.supersparrow.org—As part of the Vanessa project, Super Sparrow allows users to load balance across diverse geographic points by using BGP routing information.

Distributed Clusters

- http://gnutella.wego.com/—Home of the ever popular Gnutella distributed file-sharing protocol.
- www.sun.com/gridware—Sun's Grid Engine, an open-source implementation of a distributed clustering environment that is ported to Linux.
- http://setiathome.ssl.berkeley.edu/—SETI@home.
- www.mithral.com/products/cs-sdk/—Mithral Software Development Kit is designed to build distributed cluster applications.
- www.stanford.edu/group/pandegroup/Cosm/—Folding at home, a project dedicated to finding out how proteins self-assemble.

B

Kickstart Options

ANY DECENT CLUSTER INSTALLATION OF ANY size can be done automatically to save time and effort. With just a few guidelines, you can make a kickstart install of your Red Hat Linux box to populate any number of machines quickly and easily. The good thing is that with minimal pre-planning, you can install all your Red Hat servers from a floppy. Install the floppy, turn on the box, come back about an hour later, and you've got a fully installed server ready to put into production. And it's not an image, but a freshly installed machine. If you plan it right, you can even keep your installs up to date with the proper patches.

In fact, with a little planning, a kickstart plan can be a decent part of your disaster recovery solution, as long as you've got a kickstart server lying around. A kickstart server with a decent network can jump quite a few boxes at once.

These guidelines have been reprinted, and modified for this printing, from `www.redhat.com/docs/manuals/linux/RHL-7.2-Manual/custom-guide/s1-kickstart2-options.html` for quick reference.

autostep (Optional)

autostep is similar to interactive except that it goes to the next screen for you. You use autostep mostly for debugging.

Authentication

- auth or authconfig (required)—Sets up the authentication options for the system. It's similar to the authconfig command, which can be run after the install. By default, passwords are normally encrypted and are not shadowed.
- --enablemd5—Uses md5 encryption for user passwords.
- --enablenis—Turns on Network Information Service (NIS) support. By default, --enablenis uses whatever domain it finds on the network. A domain is almost always set by hand (through --nisdomain).
- --nisdomain—NIS domain name to use for NIS services.
- --nisserver—Server to use for NIS services (broadcasts by default).
- --useshadow or --enableshadow—Uses shadow passwords.
- --enableldap—Turns on Lightweight Directory Access Protocol (LDAP) support in /etc/nsswitch.conf, which allows your system to retrieve information about users (unique user identifiers (UIDs), home directories, shells, and so on) from an LDAP directory. To use this option, you must have the nss_ldap package installed. You must also specify a server and a base distinguished name (DN).
- --enableldapauth—Uses LDAP as an authentication method. This enables the pam_ldap module for authentication and changing passwords by using an LDAP directory. To use this option, you must have the nss_ldap package installed. You must also specify a server and a base DN.
- --ldapserver=—If you specified either --enableldap or --enableldapauth, as the name of the LDAP server to use. This option is set in the /etc/ldap.conf file.
- --ldapbasedn=—The DN in your LDAP directory tree under which user information is stored. This option is set in the /etc/ldap.conf file.
- --enableldaptls—Uses Transport Layer Security (TLS) lookups. This option allows LDAP to send encrypted usernames and passwords to an LDAP server before authentication.

- --enablekrb5—Uses Kerberos 5 for authenticating users. Kerberos itself does not know about home directories, UIDs, or shells. If you enable Kerberos you need to make users' accounts known to this workstation by enabling LDAP, NIS, or Hesiod, or by using the /usr/sbin/useradd command. If you use this option, you must have the pam_krb5 package installed.

- --krb5realm—The Kerberos 5 realm to which your workstation belongs.

- --krb5kdc—The key distribution center (KDC or KDCs) that serve requests for the realm. If you have multiple KDCs in your realm, separate their names with commas (,).

- --krb5adminserver—The KDC in your realm that is also running kadmind. This server handles password changing and other administrative requests. This server must be run on the master KDC if you have more than one KDC.

- --enablehesiod—Enables Hesiod support for looking up user home directories, UIDs, and shells. More information on setting up and using Hesiod on your network is in /usr/share/doc/glibc-2.x.x/README.hesiod, which is included in the glibc package. Hesiod is an extension of the Domain Name System (DNS) that uses DNS records to store information about users, groups, and various other items.

- --hesiodlhs—The Hesiod LHS (left-hand side) option, set in /etc/hesiod.conf. The Hesiod library uses this option to determine the name to search DNS for when looking up information, similar to LDAP's use of a base DN.

- --hesiodrhs—The Hesiod RHS (right-hand side) option, set in /etc/hesiod.conf. The Hesiod library uses this option to determine the name to search the DNS for when looking up information, similar to LDAP's use of a base DN.

- --enablesmbauth—Enables authentication of users against a Server Message Block (SMB) server (typically a Samba or Windows server). SMB authentication support does not know about home directories, UIDs, or shells. If you enable it you need to make users' accounts known to the workstation by enabling LDAP, NIS, or Hesiod, or by using the /usr/sbin/useradd command. To use this option, you must have the pam_smb package installed.

- --smbservers=—The name of the server(s) to use for SMB authentication. To specify more than one server, separate the names with commas (,).
- --smbworkgroup=—The name of the workgroup for the SMB servers.
- --enablecache—Enables the name service cache daemon (NSCD) service. The NSCD service caches information about users, groups, and various other types of information. Caching is especially helpful if you choose to distribute information about users and groups over your network using NIS, LDAP, or hesiod.

bootloader

- bootloader (required)—Specifies how the boot loader is installed and whether the bootloader is the Linux Loader (LILO) or Grand Unified Bootloader (GRUB).
- --append—Specifies kernel parameters.
- --location=—Specifies where the boot record is written. Valid values are the following: mbr (the default), partition (installs the bootloader on the first sector of the partition containing the kernel), or none (does not install the boot loader).
- --password=*mypassword*—If using GRUB, sets the GRUB bootloader password to *mypassword*. You use this to restrict access to the GRUB shell where arbitrary kernel options can be passed.
- --md5pass=*mypassword*—If using GRUB, similar to --password except that *mypassword* is the password already encrypted.
- --useLilo—Uses LILO instead of GRUB as the bootloader.
- --linear—If using LILO, uses the linear LILO option; this is only for backwards compatibility (linear is now the default).
- --nolinear—If using LILO, uses the nolinear LILO option (linear is now the default).
- --lba32—If using LILO, forces use of lba32 mode instead of autodetecting.

clearpart: **Removing Partitions Based on Partition Type**

- `clearpart` (optional)—Removes partitions from the system prior to the creation of new partitions. By default, no partitions are removed.
- `--linux`—Erases all Linux partitions.
- `--all`—Erases all partitions from the system.
- `--drives`—Specifies which drives to clear partitions from.
- `--initlabel`—Initializes the disk label to the default for your architecture (msdos for x86 and gpt for Itanium). The installation program does not ask if it should initialize the disk label if installing to a brand new hard drive.

device

- `device` (optional)—On most PCI systems, the installation program properly autoprobes for Ethernet and SCSI cards. On older systems and some PCI systems, kickstart needs a hint to find the proper devices. The device command, which tells Anaconda to install extra modules, is in the following format:

  `device <type> <moduleName> --opts <options>`

  `<type>` is either "scsi" or "eth", and `<moduleName>` is the name of the kernel module that is to be installed.
- `--opts`—Options to pass to the kernel module. Multiple options can be passed if they are put in quotes, as in the following example:

  `--opts "aic152x=0x340 io=11"`

deviceprobe

- `deviceprobe` (optional)—Forces a probe of the PCI bus and loads modules for the devices found, if a module is available.

driverdisk

- `driverdisk` (optional)—Driver disks can be used during kickstart installations. You need to copy the driver disk's contents to the root directory of a partition on the system's hard drive. Then you need to use the `driverdisk` command to tell the installation program where to look for the driver disk.

  `driverdisk <partition> [--type <fstype>]`

  `<partition>` is the partition that contains the driver disk.

  `--type` Filesystem type (for example, vfat, ext2, or ext3).

firewall

- `firewall` (optional)—Firewall options can be configured in kickstart. This configuration corresponds to the Firewall Configuration screen in the installation program:

  `firewall [--high | --medium | --disabled] [--trust <device>] [--dhcp]`
  `    [--ssh] [--telnet] [--smtp] [--http] [--ftp] [--port <portspec>]`

Levels of Security

Choose one of the following levels of security:

- `--high`
- `--medium`
- `--disabled`
- `--trust <device>`

Listing a device here, such as eth0, allows all traffic coming from that device to go through the firewall. To list more than one device, use `--trust eth0 --trust eth1`. Do not use a comma-separated format such as `--trust eth0, eth1`.

- `Allow incoming`—Enabling these options allows the specified services to pass through the firewall:
- `--dhcp`
- `--ssh`
- `--telnet`
- `--smtp`
- `--http`

- `--ftp`
- `--port <portspec>`

You can specify that ports be allowed through the firewall by using the `port:protocol` format. For example, if you want to allow IMAP access through your firewall, you can specify `imap:tcp`. You can also specify numeric ports explicitly; for example, to allow UDP packets on port 1234 through, specify `1234:udp`. To specify multiple ports, separate them by commas.

install

- `install` (optional)—Tells the system to install a fresh system rather than upgrade an existing system. This is the default mode.

Installation Methods

You must use one of these commands to specify what type of kickstart installation is being performed:

- `nfs`—Installs from the Network File System (NFS) server specified.
- `--server <server>`—Server from which to install (hostname or IP).
- `--dir <dir>`—Directory that contains the Red Hat installation tree.

For example:

```
nfs --server <server> --dir <dir>
```

cdrom

- `cdrom`—Installs from the first CD-ROM drive on the system.

For example:

```
cdrom
```

harddrive

- `harddrive`—Installs from a Red Hat installation tree on a local drive, which must be either `vfat` or `ext2`.
- `--partition <partition>`—Partition to install from (such as `sdb2`).
- `--dir <dir>`—Directory containing the Red Hat installation tree.

For example:

```
harddrive --partition <partition> --dir <dir>
```

url

- url—Installs from a Red Hat installation tree on a remote server through File Transfer Protocol (FTP) or Hypertext Transfer Protocol (HTTP).

For example:
```
url --url http://<server>/<dir>
url --url ftp://<username>:<password>@<server>/<dir>
```

interactive

This optional command uses the information provided in the kickstart file during the installation, but allows for inspection and modification of the values given. You are presented with each screen of the installation program with the values from the kickstart file. You either accept the values by clicking Next or change the values and click Next to continue. See also the *autostep* section.

keyboard

- keyboard (required)—Sets the system keyboard type. The list of available keyboards on i386 and Alpha machines is as follows:

ANSI-dvorak, azerty, be-latin1, be2-latin1, bg, br-abnt2, cf, croat, cz, cz-lat2, cz-lat2-prog, cz-us-qwertz, de, de-latin1, de-latin1-nodeadkeys, defkeymap, defkeymap_V1.0, dk, dk-latin1, dvorak, dvorak-l, dvorak-r, emacs, emacs2, es, es-cp850, et, et-nodeadkeys, fi, fi-latin1, fr, fr-latin0, fr-latin1, fr-pc, fr_CH, fr_CH-latin1, gr, gr-pc, hebrew, hu, hu101, is-latin1, it, it-ibm, it2, jp106, la-latin1, lt, lt.l4, lv-latin4, lv-latin7,mk, nl, nl-latin1, nl-latin1-nodeadkeys, no, no-latin1, pc-dvorak-latin1, pc110, pl, pl1, pt-latin1, pt-old, ro, ru, ru-cp1251, ru-ms, ru-yawerty, ru1, ru2, ru3, ru4, ru_win, se-latin1, sg, sg-latin1, sg-latin1-lk450, sk-prog, sk-prog-qwerty, sk-prog-qwerty, sk-qwerty, sk-qwertz, slovene, sr, sr, tr_f-latin5, tr_q-latin5, tralt, trf, trq, ua, ua-utf, ua-utf-ws, ua-ws, uaw, uaw_uni, uk, us, us-latin1, wangbe

The list for SPARC machines is as follows:
sun-pl-altgraph, sun-pl, sundvorak, sunkeymap, sunt4-es,
sunt4-no-latin1, sunt5-cz-us, sunt5-de-latin1, sunt5-es,
sunt5-fi-latin1, sunt5-fr-latin1, sunt5-ru, sunt5-uk, sunt5-us-cz

lang

- lang (required)—Sets the language to use during installation. For example, to set the language to English, the kickstart file must contain the following line:

- lang en_US—Valid language codes are the following (please note that these are subject to change at any time):

  cs_CZ, da_DK, en_US, fr_FR, de_DE, hu_HU, is_IS, it_IT, ja_JP.eucJP, no_NO, ro_RO, sk_SK, sl_SI, sr_YU, es_ES, ru_RU.KOI8 R, uk_UA KOI8-U, sv_SE, tr_TR

langsupport

- langsupport (required)—Sets the language(s) to install on the system. The same language codes that you use with lang can be used with langsupport.

- --default—Sets the default language to use for any language-specific aspect of the installed system.

The following example installs English and French and uses English as the default language:

```
langsupport --default en_US fr_FR
```

lilo

- lilo (replaced by bootloader)—This option has been replaced by bootloader and is only available for backwards compatibility. Refer to the *bootloader* section.

Specifies how the bootloader is to be installed on the system. By default, LILO installs on the MBR of the first disk, and installs a dual-boot system if a DOS partition is found (the DOS/Windows system boots if the user types **dos** at the LILO: prompt).

- --append *<params>*—Specifies kernel parameters.
- --linear—Uses the linear LILO option; this is only for backwards compatibility (linear is the default).
- --nolinear—Uses the nolinear LILO option (linear is now the default).
- --location—Specifies where the LILO boot record is written. Valid values are the following: mbr (the default) or partition (installs the boot loader on the first sector of the partition that contains the kernel). If no location is specified, LILO is not installed.
- --lba32—Forces the use of lba32 mode instead of autodetecting.

lilocheck (Optional)

If lilocheck is present, the installation program checks for LILO on the MBR of the first hard drive, and reboots the system if it is found. In this case, no installation is performed. This can prevent kickstart from reinstalling an already installed system.

mouse

- mouse (required)—Configures the mouse for the system, both in GUI and text modes.
- --device *<dev>*—Device the mouse is on (such as --device ttyS0).
- --emulthree—If present, simultaneous clicks of the left and right mouse buttons are recognized as the middle mouse button by the X Window System. You use this option if you have a two-button mouse.

After options, the mouse type can be specified as one of the following:
   alpsps/2, ascii, asciips/2, atibm, generic, generic3
   genericps/2, generic3ps/2, genericusb, generic3usb
   geniusnm, geniusnmps/2, geniusprops/2, geniusscrollps/2
   thinking, thinkingps/2, logitech, logitechcc, logibm
   logimman, logimmanps/2, logimman+, logimman+ps/2
   logimmusb, microsoft, msnew, msintelli, msintellips/2
   msintelliusb, msbm, mousesystems, mmseries, mmhittab
   sun, none

If the mouse command is given without any arguments, or it is omitted, the installation program attempts to autodetect the mouse. This procedure works for most modern mice.

network

- network (optional)—Configures network information for the system. If the kickstart installation does not require networking (if it is not installed over NFS, HTTP, or FTP), networking is not configured for the system. If the installation does require networking and network information is not provided in the kickstart file, the Red Hat Linux installation program assumes that the installation is to be done over eth0 through a dynamic IP address (Bootstrap Protocol/Dyamic Host Configuration Protocol (BOOTP/DHCP)), and configures the final, installed system to determine its IP address dynamically. The network option configures networking information for kickstart installations through a network and for the installed system.
- --bootproto—One of dhcp, bootp, or static (defaults to DHCP, and dhcp and bootp are treated the same). Must be static to use static IP information.
- --device <device>—Selects a specific Ethernet device for installation. Using --device <device> is not effective unless the kickstart file is a local file (such as ks=floppy) because the installation program configures the network to find the kickstart file.

For example:

```
network --bootproto dhcp --device eth0
```

- --ip—IP address for the machine to be installed.
- --gateway—Default gateway as an IP address.
- --nameserver—Primary nameserver, as an IP address.
- --netmask—Netmask for the installed system.
- --hostname—Hostname for the installed system.

There are three different methods of network configuration:

- DHCP
- BOOTP
- Static

The DHCP method uses a DHCP server system to obtain its networking configuration. The BOOTP method is similar, requiring a BOOTP server to supply the networking configuration.

The static method requires that you enter all the required networking information in the kickstart file. As the name implies, this information is static, and you use it during and after the installation.

To direct a system to use DHCP to obtain its networking configuration, use the following line:

```
network --bootproto dhcp
```

To direct a machine to use BOOTP to obtain its networking configuration, use the following line in the kickstart file:

```
network --bootproto bootp
```

The line for static networking is more complex because you must include all the network configuration information on one line. You need to specify the following:

- IP address
- Netmask
- Gateway IP address
- Nameserver IP address

Following is an example of a static line:

```
network --bootproto static --ip 10.0.2.15 --netmask 255.255.255.0
    --gateway 10.0.2.254 --nameserver 10.0.2.1
```

If you use the static method, be aware of the following two restrictions:

- All static networking configuration information must be specified on one line; you cannot wrap lines using a backslash.
- You can only specify one nameserver. However, you can use the kickstart file's %post section (see the section, "%post: Post-Installation Configuration Section") to add more name servers, if needed.

part

- part or partition (required for installs, ignored for upgrades)—Creates a partition on the system.
- *<mntpoint>* —Where the partition is mounted, and must be in this form:
    /<mntpoint>

For example:

```
, /, /usr, /home
```

- `swap`—The partition is used as swap space.

- `raid.<id>`—The partition is used for software RAID (see the *raid* section).

- `--size <size>`—The minimum partition size in megabytes. Specify an integer value such as 500. Do not append the number with MB.

- `--grow`—Tells the partition to grow to fill the available space (if any), or up to the maximum size setting.

- `--maxsize <size>`—The maximum partition size in megabytes when the partition is set to grow. Specify an integer value. Do not append the number with MB.

- `--noformat`—Tells the installation program not to format the partition, for use with the `--onpart` command.

- `--onpart <part>` or `--usepart <part>`—Tells the installation program to put the partition on the *already existing* device `<part>`. For example, `partition /home --onpart hda1` puts `/home` on `/dev/hda1`, which must already exist.

- `--ondisk <disk>` or `--ondrive <drive>`—Forces the partition to be created on a particular disk. For example, `--ondisk sdb` puts the partition on the second disk on the system.

- `--asprimary`—Forces automatic allocation of the partition as a primary partition or the partitioning fails.

- `--bytes-per-inode=<N>`—`<N>` represents the number of bytes per inode on the filesystem when it is created. It must be given in decimal format. This option is useful for applications where you want to increase the number of inodes on the filesystem.

- `--type=<X>` (replaced by `fstype`)—This option is no longer available. Use `fstype`.

- `--fstype`—Sets the filesystem type for the partition. Valid values are `ext2`, `ext3`, `swap`, `vfat`.

- `--start`—Specifies the starting cylinder for the partition. It requires that a drive be specified with `--ondisk` or `ondrive`. It also requires that the ending cylinder be specified with `--end` or the partition size be specified with `--size`.

- --end—Specifies the ending cylinder for the partition. It requires that the starting cylinder be specified with --start.
- --badblocks—Specifies that the partition should be checked for bad sectors.

All partitions created are formatted as part of the installation process unless you use --noformat and --onpart.

If you use --clearpart in the ks.cfg file, you cannot use --onpart on a logical partition. If partitioning fails for any reason, diagnostic messages appear on virtual console 3.

raid

- raid (optional)—Assembles a software RAID device. This command has the following form:

```
raid <mntpoint> --level <level> --device <mddevice><partitions*>
```

The *<mntpoint>* is the location where the RAID filesystem is mounted. If it is /, the RAID level must be 1 unless a boot partition (/boot) is present. If a boot partition is present, the /boot partition must be level 1 and the root (/) partition can be any of the available types. The *<partitions*>* (which denotes that multiple partitions can be listed) lists the RAID identifiers to add to the RAID array.

- --level *<level>*—RAID level to use (0, 1, or 5).
- --device *<mddevice>*—Name of the RAID device to use (such as md0 or md1). RAID devices range from md0 to md7, and each can only be used once.
- --spares=*N*—Specifies that there should be *N* spare drives allocated for the RAID array. Spare drives rebuild the array in case of drive failure.
- --fstype—Sets the filesystem type for the RAID array. Valid values are ext2, ext3, swap, and vfat.
- --noformat—Does not format the RAID array.

The following example shows how to create a RAID level 1 partition for /, and a RAID level 5 for /usr, assuming that there are three SCSI disks on the system. It also creates three swap partitions, one on each drive:

```
part raid.01 --size 60 --ondisk sda
part raid.02 --size 60 --ondisk sdb
part raid.03 --size 60 --ondisk sdc
part swap --size 128 --ondisk sda
```

```
part swap --size 128 --ondisk sdb
part swap --size 128 --ondisk sdc
part raid.11 --size 1 --grow --ondisk sda
part raid.12 --size 1 --grow --ondisk sdb
part raid.13 --size 1 --grow --ondisk sdc
raid / --level 1 --device md0 raid.01 raid.02 raid.03
raid /usr --level 5 --device md1 raid.11 raid.12 raid.13
```

reboot (Optional)

reboot reboots after the installation is complete (no arguments). Normally, kickstart displays a message and waits for the user to press a key before rebooting.

rootpw (Required)

- rootpw [--iscrypted] <password>—Sets the system's root password to the <password> argument.

- --iscrypted—If this is present, the password argument is assumed to already be encrypted.

skipx (Optional)

If skipx is present, X is not configured on the installed system.

text (Optional)

text performs the kickstart installation in text mode. Kickstart installations are performed in graphical mode by default.

timezone (Required)

- timezone [--utc] <timezone>—Sets the system time zone to <timezone>, which can be any of the time zones listed by timeconfig.

- --utc—If present, the system assumes that the hardware clock is set to UTC (Greenwich Mean) time.

upgrade (Optional)

upgrade tells the system to upgrade an existing system rather than install a fresh system.

xconfig

- xconfig (optional)—Configures the X Window System. If this option is not given, the user needs to configure X manually during the installation, if X was installed; this option is not used if X is not installed on the final system.

- --noprobe—Does not probe the monitor.

- --card <card>—Uses card <card>; this card name is from the list of cards in Xconfigurator. If this argument is not provided, Anaconda probes the PCI bus for the card. Because AGP is part of the PCI bus, AGP cards are detected, if supported. The probe order is determined by the PCI scan order of the motherboard.

- --videoram <vram>—Specifies the amount of video RAM the video card has.

- --monitor <mon>—Uses monitor <mon>; this monitor name is from the list of monitors in Xconfigurator. This is ignored if --hsync or --vsync is provided. If no monitor information is provided, the installation program tries to probe for it automatically.

- --hsync <sync>—Specifies the horizontal sync frequency of the monitor.

- --vsync <sync>—Specifies the vertical sync frequency of the monitor.

- --defaultdesktop=GNOME or --defaultdesktop=KDE—Sets the default desktop to either GNOME or KDE (and assumes that GNOME or KDE has been installed through %packages).

- --startxonboot—Uses a graphical login on the installed system.

- --resolution <res>—Specifies the default resolution for the X Window System on the installed system. Valid values are 640×480, 800×600, 1024×768, 1152×864, 1280×1024, 1400×1050, and 1600×1200. Be sure to specify a resolution that is compatible with the video card and monitor.

- --depth <cdepth>—Specifies the default color depth for the X Window System on the installed system. Valid values are 8, 16, 24, and 32. Be sure to specify a color depth that is compatible with the video card and monitor.

zerombr: Partition Table Initialization

- zerombr (optional)—If zerombr is specified, and yes is its sole argument, any invalid partition tables found on disks are initialized. This destroys all the contents of disks with invalid partition tables.
- zerombr yes—No other format is effective.

%packages: Package Selection

Use the %packages command to begin a kickstart file section that lists the packages you'd like to install (this is for installations only, as package selection during upgrades is not supported).

Packages can be specified by component or by individual package name. The installation program defines several components that group together related packages. See the RedHat/base/comps file on any Red Hat Linux CD-ROM for a list of components. The components are defined by the lines that begin with a number, followed by a space and the component name. Each package in that component is then listed, line-by-line. Individual packages lack the leading number found in front of component lines.

Additionally, three other types of lines are in the comps file:

```
Architecture specific (i386:, ia64:, alpha:, and sparc64:)
```

If a package name begins with an architecture type, you only need to type in the package name, not the architecture name. For example: For i386: apmd, you only need to use the apmd part for that specific package to be installed.

- Lines beginning with ?—Lines that begin with a ? are used by the installation program and must not be altered.
- Lines beginning with --hide—If a package name begins with --hide, you only need to type in the package name, without the --hide. For --hide Network Server, you only need to use the Network Server part for that specific package to be installed.

In most cases, it's only necessary to list the desired components and not individual packages. The base component is always selected by default, so it's not necessary to specify it in the %packages section.

The following is an example of a %packages section:

```
%packages
@ Network Managed Workstation
@ Development
@ Web Server
@ X Window System
xgammon
```

As you can see, components are specified, one to a line, starting with an @ symbol, a space, and the full component name (as given in the `comps` file). Specify individual packages with no additional characters (the `xgammon` line in the preceding example is an individual package).

You can also direct the kickstart installation to install the default packages for a workstation (`KDE` or `GNOME`) or server installation (or choose an everything installation to install all packages). To do this, simply add one of the following lines to the `%packages` section:

- @ GNOME

- @ KDE

- @ Server

- @ Everything

%pre: Pre-Installation Configuration Section

You can add commands to run on the system immediately after the `ks.cfg` has been parsed. This section must be at the end of the kickstart file (after the commands) and must start with the `%pre` command. You can access the network in the `%pre` section; however, *name service* has not been configured at this point, so only IP addresses work. The following is an example of a `%pre` section:

```
%pre
# add comment to /etc/motd
echo "Kickstart-installed Red Hat Linux `/bin/date`" > /etc/motd
# add another nameserver
echo "nameserver 10.10.0.2" >> /etc/resolv.conf
```

This section creates a message-of-the-day file that contains the date the kickstart installation took place. It also gets around the network command's limitation of only one name server by adding another nameserver to `/etc/resolv.conf`.

> **Note**
> The pre-install script is not run in the change root environment.

%post: Post-Installation Configuration Section

You have the option of adding commands to run on the system once the installation is complete. This section must be at the end of the kickstart file and must start with the `%post` command.

If you configured the network with static IP information, including a nameserver, you can access the network and resolve IP addresses in the `%post` section. If you configured the network for DHCP, the `/etc/resolv.conf` file has not been completed when the installation executes the `%post` section. You can access the network, but you cannot resolve IP addresses. Thus, if you are using DHCP, you must specify IP addresses in the `%post` section.

Following is an example of a `%post` section that creates a message-of-the-day file that contains the date that the kickstart installation took place, and gets around the network command's limitation of one nameserver only by adding another nameserver to `/etc/resolv.conf`:

```
%post
# add comment to /etc/motd
echo "Kickstart-installed Red Hat Linux `/bin/date`" > /etc/motd
# add another nameserver
echo "nameserver 10.10.0.2" >> /etc/resolv.conf
```

The post-install script is run in a `chroot` environment; therefore, performing tasks, such as copying scripts or RPMs from the installation media, does not work.

- `--nochroot`—Allows you to specify commands that you might like to run outside of the `chroot` environment.

The following example copies the file `/etc/resolv.conf` to the file system that was just installed:

```
%post --nochroot
cp /etc/resolv.conf /mnt/sysimage/etc/resolv.conf
```

- `--interpreter /usr/bin/perl`—Allows you to specify a different scripting language, such as Perl. (Replace `/usr/bin/perl` with the scripting language of your choice.)

The following example uses a Perl script to replace `/etc/HOSTNAME`:

```
%post --interpreter /usr/bin/perl
# replace /etc/HOSTNAME
open(HN, ">HOSTNAME");
print HN "1.2.3.4 an.ip.address\n";
```

These Kickstart options are republished under the Open Publication License (www.opencontent.org/openpub). All material referring to Kickstart is under copyright by Red Hat, Inc. Original authors: Red Hat, Inc. and Tammy Fox. Original Publisher: Red Hat Inc.

C

DHCP Options

THE DYNAMIC HOST CONFIGURATION PROTOCOL (DHCP) is an essential resource when configuring a large amount of machines in a cluster. Using DHCP frees you from configuring each machine's network settings individually. A DHCP server allows you to maintain network settings out of a centralized database to reduce the amount of overhead required in maintaining a cluster.

These options are designed to be placed in the dhcpd.conf file. Obviously, you won't need to select each attribute here for your configuration file; only the needed attributes are used.

Here's a list of the options from the dhcp-options man page, alphabetized for easy reference. These are taken from the Internet Software Consortium's (ISC) version of DHCP. These options enable you to fully customize your network parameters at boot time. The most common parameters suitable for clustering are included:

- option all-subnets-local flag;—Specifies whether the client can assume that all subnets of the IP network to which the client is connected use the same maximum transmission unit (MTU) as the subnet of that network to which the client is directly connected.

A value of 1 indicates that all subnets share the same MTU. A value of 0 means the client assumes that some subnets of the directly connected network might have smaller MTUs.

- `option arp-cache-timeout uint32;`—Specifies the timeout, in seconds, for ARP cache entries.
- `option bootfile-name string;`—Identifies a bootstrap file. If supported by the client, it has the same effect as the filename declaration. BOOTP clients are unlikely to support this option. Some DHCP clients support it, and others actually require it.
- `option broadcast-address ip-address;`—Specifies the broadcast address in use on the client's subnet. Legal values for broadcast addresses are specified in section 3.2.1.3 of STD 3 (RFC1122).
- `option default-ip-ttl uint8;`—Specifies the default time to live (TTL) that the client uses on outgoing datagrams.
- `option default-tcp-ttl uint8;`—Specifies the default TTL that the client uses when sending TCP segments. The minimum value is 1.
- `option domain-name-servers ip-address(s);`—Specifies a list of Domain Name System (DNS)(STD 13, RFC 1035) name servers available to the client. Servers are listed in order of preference.
- `option domain-name string;`—Specifies the domain name that the client uses when resolving hostnames through the DNS.
- `option host-name string;`—Specifies the name of the client. The name might or might not be qualified with the local domain name. (It is preferable to use the `domain-name` option to specify the domain name.) See RFC 1035 for character set restrictions.
- `option interface-mtu uint16;`—Specifies the MTU to use on this interface. The minimum legal value for the MTU is 68.
- `option log-servers ip-address(s);`—Specifies a list of MIT-LCS User Datagram Protocol (UDP) log servers available to the client. Servers should be listed in order of preference.
- `option lpr-servers ip-address(s);`—Specifies a list of RFC 1179 line printer servers available to the client. Servers should be listed in order of preference.
- `option max-dgram-reassembly uint16;`—Specifies the maximum size datagram that the client is prepared to reassemble. The minimum value legal value is 576.

- option merit-dump string;—Specifies the pathname of a file to which the client's core image is dumped in the event that the client crashes. The path is formatted as a character string consisting of characters from the Network Virtual Terminal (NVT) ASCII character set. (The ASCII set is a standard using 7-bit codes for characters.)

- option nis-domain string;—Specifies the name of the client's Sun Network Information Services (NIS) domain. The domain is formatted as a character string that consists of characters from the NVT ASCII character set.

- option nis-servers ip-address(s);—Specifies a list of IP addresses that indicates NIS servers available to the client. Servers should be listed in order of preference.

- option nisplus-domain string;—Specifies the name of the client's NIS+ domain. The domain is formatted as a character string that consists of characters from the NVT ASCII character set.

- option nisplus-servers ip-address(s);—Specifies a list of IP addresses that indicates NIS+ servers available to the client. Servers should be listed in order of preference.

- option ntp-servers ip-address(s);—Specifies a list of IP addresses that indicates NTP (RFC 1035) servers available to the client. Servers should be listed in order of preference.

- option path-mtu-aging-timeout uint32;—Specifies the timeout, in seconds, to use when aging Path MTU values discovered by the mechanism as defined in RFC 1191.

- option path-mtu-plateau-table uint16(s);—Specifies a table of MTU sizes to use when performing Path MTU Discovery as defined in RFC 1191. The table is formatted as a list of 16-bit unsigned integers, ordered from smallest to largest. The minimum MTU value cannot be smaller than 68.

- option routers ip-address(s);—Specifies a list of IP addresses for routers on the client's subnet. Routers are listed in order of preference.

- option smtp-server ip-address(s);—Specifies a list of SMTP servers available to the client. Servers should be listed in order of preference.

- option static-routes ip-address ip-address(s);—Specifies a list of static routes that the client installs in the routing cache. If multiple routes to the same destination are specified, they are listed in descending order of priority.

The routes consist of a list of IP address pairs. The first address is the destination address, and the second address is the router for the destination.

The default route (0.0.0.0) is an illegal destination for a static route. To specify the default route, use the `routers` option.

- `option subnet-mask ip-address;`—Specifies the subnet mask for the client. If one isn't declared, the DHCPD server uses the subnet from the current subnet.

- `option tcp-keepalive-interval uint32;`—Specifies the interval, in seconds, that the client TCP waits before sending a keepalive message on a TCP connection. The time is specified as a 32-bit unsigned integer. A value of zero indicates that the client is generating keepalive messages on connections unless specifically requested by an application.

- `option tftp-server-name string;`—Identifies a TFTP server and, if supported by the client, has the same effect as the server-name declaration. BOOTP clients are unlikely to support this option. Some DHCP clients support it, and others actually require it.

- `option time-offset int32;`—Specifies the offset of the client's subnet in seconds from Coordinated Universal Time (UTC).

- `option time-servers ip-address(s);`—Specifies a list of RFC 868 time servers available to the client. Servers should be listed in order of preference.

- `option x-display-manager ip-address(s);`—Specifies a list of systems that are running the X Window System Display Manager and are available to the client. Addresses should be listed in order of preference.

D

Condor ClassAd Machine Attributes

THE FOLLOWING ATTRIBUTES ARE LISTED as a quick reference for Condor's matchmaking-like attributes. These attributes match jobs to specific machines. Condor client machines advertise their attributes so that each job submitted, which uses these attributes, matches the client advertising these specific resources.

For example, a client can advertise architecture, operating system (OS), RAM, disk space, and so on. You can display each machine in the cluster with the condor_status command. Using these attributes allows you to match the job with the resource. You can find information about Condor at www.cs.wisc.edu/condor. These class attributes, and more configurations, can be found at www.cs.wisc.edu/condor/manual/ v6.2/3_6Configuring_Startd.html.

- Activity—A string that describes Condor job activity on the machine, which can have one of the following values:
  - Idle: There is no job activity.
  - Busy: A job is busy running.
  - Suspended: A job is currently suspended.

- Vacating: A job is currently check pointing.
- Killing: A job is currently being killed.
- Benchmarking: The startd is running benchmarks.

- Arch—A string with the architecture of the machine, which is typically one of the following:
  - INTEL: Intel x86 CPU (Pentium, Xeon, and so on).
  - ALPHA: Digital Alpha CPU.
  - SGI: Silicon Graphics MIPS CPU.
  - SUN4u: Sun UltraSparc CPU.
  - SUN4x: A Sun Sparc CPU other than an UltraSparc, such as the sun4m or sun4c CPU found in older Sparc workstations such as the Sparc 10, Sparc 20, IPC, IPX, and so on.
  - HPPA1: Hewlett Packard PA-RISC 1.x CPU-based workstation (such as the PA-RISC 7000 series CPU).
  - HPPA2: Hewlett Packard PA-RISC 2.x CPU-based workstation (such as the PA-RISC 8000 series CPU).

- ClockDay—The day of the week, where 0 = Sunday, 1 = Monday, 6 = Saturday.
- ClockMin—The number of minutes passed since midnight.
- CondorLoadAvg—The portion of the load average generated by Condor (either from remote jobs or running benchmarks).
- ConsoleIdle—The number of seconds since activity on the system console keyboard or console mouse was last detected.
- Cpus—The number of CPUs in this machine, such as 1 = single CPU machine, 2 = dual CPUs, and so on.
- CurrentRank—A float that represents this machine owner's affinity for running the Condor job which it is currently hosting. If not currently hosting a Condor job, CurrentRank is -1.0.
- Disk—The amount of disk space on this machine available for the job in kbytes (such as 23,000 = 23 megabytes). Specifically, this is the amount of disk space available in the directory that is specified in the Condor configuration files by the EXECUTE macro, minus any space reserved with the RESERVED_DISK macro.

- EnteredCurrentActivity—The time at which the machine entered the current Activity (refer to the Activity entry). On all platforms (including NT), this is measured in the number of seconds since the UNIX epoch (00:00:00 UTC, Jan 1, 1970).

- FileSystemDomain—A domain name configured by the Condor administrator that describes a cluster of machines which all access the same, uniformly mounted, networked file systems, usually through NFS or AFS. This is useful for Vanilla universe jobs that require remote file access.

- KeyboardIdle—The number of seconds since activity on any keyboard or mouse associated with this machine has last been detected. Unlike ConsoleIdle, KeyboardIdle takes activity on pseudo-terminals into account (such as virtual "keyboard" activity from telnet and rlogin sessions). KeyboardIdle is always equal to or less than ConsoleIdle.

- Kflops—The relative floating point performance as determined by a Linpack benchmark.

- LastHeardFrom—The time when the Condor central manager last received a status update from this machine; expressed as seconds since the epoch (integer value). The central manager only inserts this attribute after it receives the ClassAd. It is not present in the condor_startd copy of the ClassAd. Therefore, you cannot use this attribute in defining condor_startd expressions.

- LoadAvg—A floating point number with the machine's current load average.

- Machine—A string with the machine's fully qualified hostname.

- Memory—The amount of RAM in megabytes.

- Mips—The relative integer performance as determined by a Dhrystone benchmark.

- MyType—The ClassAd type; always set to the literal string "Machine".

- Name—The name of this resource; typically the same value as the Machine attribute, but it can be customized by the site administrator. On SMP machines, condor_startd divides the CPUs into separate virtual machines, each with a unique name. These names are in the form "vm#@full.hostname"; for example, "vm1@vulture.cs.wisc.edu" signifies virtual machine 1 from vulture.cs.wisc.edu.

- OpSys—A string that describes the OS that is running on this machine. For Condor Version 6.3.1, it is typically one of the following:
  - HPUX10: For HPUX 10.20.
  - IRIX6: For IRIX 6.2, 6.3, or 6.4.
  - IRIX65: For IRIX 6.5.
  - LINUX: For Linux 2.0.x or Linux 2.2.x kernel systems.
  - OSF1: For Digital UNIX 4.x.
  - SOLARIS251
  - SOLARIS26
  - SOLARIS27
  - SOLARIS28
  - WINNT40: For Windows NT 4.0.
- Requirements—A boolean that, when evaluated within the context of the machine ClassAd and the job ClassAd, must evaluate to TRUE before Condor allows the job to use this machine.
- StartdIpAddr—A string with the IP and port address of the *condor_startd* daemon, which is publishing this machine ClassAd.
- State—A string that publishes the machine's Condor state. The string can be any of the following:
  - Owner: The machine owner is using the machine, and it is unavailable to Condor.
  - Unclaimed: The machine is available to run Condor jobs, but a good match is either not available or not yet found.
  - Matched: The Condor central manager has found a good match for this resource, but a Condor scheduler has not yet claimed it.
  - Claimed: The machine is claimed by a remote *condor_schedd* and is probably running a job.
  - Preempting: A Condor job is preempted (possibly through check pointing) to clear the machine for either a higher priority job or because the machine owner wants the machine back.
- TargetType—This describes what type of ClassAd to match with. Always set to the string literal "Job" because machine ClassAds want to be matched with jobs, and vice versa.

- UidDomain—A domain name configured by the Condor administrator that describes a cluster of machines that all have the same passwd file entries; therefore, they all have the same logins.

- VirtualMemory—The amount of currently available virtual memory (swap space) expressed in kbytes.

Index

HOW TO CONTACT US

VOICES THAT MATTER

VISIT OUR WEB SITE

WWW.NEWRIDERS.COM

On our web site, you'll find information about our other books, authors, tables of contents, and book errata. You will also find information about book registration and how to purchase our books, both domestically and internationally.

EMAIL US

Contact us at: **nrfeedback@newriders.com**

- If you have comments or questions about this book
- To report errors that you have found in this book
- If you have a book proposal to submit or are interested in writing for New Riders
- If you are an expert in a computer topic or technology and are interested in being a technical editor who reviews manuscripts for technical accuracy

Contact us at: **nreducation@newriders.com**

- If you are an instructor from an educational institution who wants to preview New Riders books for classroom use. Email should include your name, title, school, department, address, phone number, office days/hours, text in use, and enrollment, along with your request for desk/examination copies and/or additional information.

Contact us at: **nrmedia@newriders.com**

- If you are a member of the media who is interested in reviewing copies of New Riders books. Send your name, mailing address, and email address, along with the name of the publication or web site you work for.

BULK PURCHASES/CORPORATE SALES

The publisher offers discounts on this book when ordered in quantity for bulk purchases and special sales. For sales within the U.S., please contact: Corporate and Government Sales (800) 382-3419 or **corpsales@pearsontechgroup.com**. Outside of the U.S., please contact: International Sales (317) 581-3793 or **international@pearsontechgroup.com**.

WRITE TO US

New Riders Publishing
201 W. 103rd St.
Indianapolis, IN 46290-1097

CALL/FAX US

Toll-free (800) 571-5840
If outside U.S. (317) 581-3500
Ask for New Riders
FAX: (317) 581-4663

New Riders

WWW.NEWRIDERS.COM

olutions from experts you know and trust.

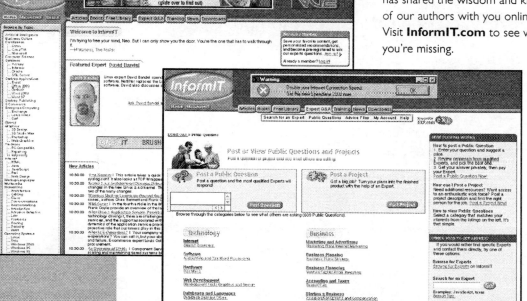

VIEW CART

search

› Registration already a member? Log in. › Book Registration

Publishing the Voices that Matter

OUR AUTHORS

PRESS ROOM

| web development | design | photoshop | new media | 3-D | server technologies |

EDUCATORS

ABOUT US

CONTACT US

You already know that New Riders brings you the **Voices that Matter**.

But what does that mean? It means that New Riders brings you the

Voices that challenge your assumptions, take your talents to the next

level, or simply help you better understand the complex technical world

we're all navigating.

Visit **www.newriders.com** to find:

- ▸ *Discounts* on specific book purchases
- ▸ Never before published chapters
- ▸ Sample chapters and excerpts
- ▸ Author bios and interviews
- ▸ Contests and enter-to-wins
- ▸ Up-to-date industry event information
- ▸ Book reviews
- ▸ Special offers from our friends and partners
- ▸ Info on how to join our User Group program
- ▸ Ways to have your Voice heard

New Riders

WWW.NEWRIDERS.COM

Colophon

Pictured on the cover is a photograph by Ken Usami of a beautiful, misty waterfall as it cascades over the rocks.

"Contemplate the workings of this world, listen to the words of the wise, and take all that is good as your own. With this as your base, open your own door to truth. Do not overlook the truth that is right before you. Study how water flows in a valley stream, smoothly and freely between the rocks… Everything—even mountains, rivers, plants and trees—should be your teacher."

—Morihei Ueshiba, founder of Aikido

This book was written and edited in Microsoft Word, and laid out in QuarkXPress. The font used for the body text is Bembo and MCPdigital. It was printed on 50# Husky Offset Smooth paper at Von Hoffman Graphics Inc. in Owensville, MO. Prepress consisted of PostScript computer-to-plate technology (filmless process). The cover was printed at Moore Langen Printing in Terre Haute, Indiana, on 12pt, coated on one side.